寿险资金
支持实体经济研究

国务院发展研究中心金融研究所 著

中国发展出版社
CHINA DEVELOPMENT PRESS

图书在版编目（CIP）数据

寿险资金支持实体经济研究 / 国务院发展研究中心金融研究所著.
—北京：中国发展出版社，2018.12

ISBN 978-7-5177-0947-3

Ⅰ.①寿… Ⅱ.①国… Ⅲ.①人寿保险—资金管理—研究—中国
②中国经济—经济发展—研究 Ⅳ.①F842.62 ②F124

中国版本图书馆CIP数据核字（2018）第 299847号

书　　　名：寿险资金支持实体经济研究
著作责任者：国务院发展研究中心金融研究所
出 版 发 行：中国发展出版社
　　　　　　（北京市西城区百万庄大街16号8层　100037）
标 准 书 号：ISBN 978-7-5177-0947-3
经 销 者：各地新华书店
印 刷 者：河北鑫兆源印刷有限公司
开　　　本：787mm×1092mm　1/16
印　　　张：21.75
字　　　数：207千字
版　　　次：2019年4月第1版
印　　　次：2019年4月第1次印刷
定　　　价：79.00元

联 系 电 话：（010）68990630　68990692
购 书 热 线：（010）68990682　68990686
网 络 订 购：http://zgfzcbs.tmall.com//
网 购 电 话：（010）88333349　68990639
本 社 网 址：http://www.develpress.com.cn
电 子 邮 件：370118561@qq.com

课 题 组

国务院发展研究中心金融研究所方面

课题顾问：张承惠　吴振宇

课题负责人：陈道富

课题协调人：朱俊生

主要参与人：张丽平　田　辉　朱俊生　刘　煊

　　　　　　王　刚　朱鸿鸣　王　洋　薄　岩

英国保诚集团方面

Steve Bickell, Paul Lynch, Johnny Chang,

Angela Yin, Stephan Van Vliet, Nadir Maruf

序　一

　　随着我国社会主义市场经济不断发展完善，金融体系在资金配置中的地位和作用日益深化。保险业作为现代金融体系的重要组成部分，吸收和运用的资金量快速增加。2107年，保险资金运用余额高达149206亿元人民币，当年新增资金15295亿元，约占社会融资规模的7.8%,有力支持了实体经济的发展。寿险资金是保险资金的主体，具有规模大、期限长、资金来源稳定等特征,在支持实体经济方面有天然的优势。随着我国人口老龄化程度不断提高，居民健康养老等保险保障和财富管理需求不断增加，长期寿险资金将快速增长，从而在支持实体经济发展中发挥越来越重要的作用。研究寿险资金支持实体经济存在的问题与政策障碍，提出相关政策建议，对于拓宽寿险资金支持实体经济的渠道，促进保险业持续向服务实体经济发力、聚力，具有重要的理论价值与积极的现实意义。

　　为了拓展理论视野、吸收国际先进经验，国务院发展研究中心金融研究所与英国保诚集团相关部门于2017年下半年到2018年上半年共同开展了"寿险资金支持实体经济研究"。本书在课题研究报告基础上修改而成。全书结构如下：第一章，中国寿险业服务实体经济的内涵与实践。在界定寿险业服务实体经济内涵的基础上，评估了中国寿险业服务实体经济情况，并提出寿险资金支持实体经济的意义和方向；第二章，寿险资金支持实体经济的现状。考察了寿险资金支持实体经济发展的政策环境、主要方式，尤其是基础设施建设等另类投资在寿险资金对接实体经济中的重要性以及寿险资金服务实体经济取得的积极成效。第三章，寿险资金支持实体经济的挑战、风险与政策障碍。结合调研中市场主体以及政策监管部门的反馈，考察了寿险资金支持实体经济面临的主要挑战、存在的主要风险和政策障碍。第四章，寿险资金支持实体经济的国际经验、教训和发展动向。结合国际上寿险资金支持实体经济的最新发展动态，考察了主要的国际经验、教训、发展动向及其对中国的启示。第五章，促进寿险资金支持实体经济的政策建议。结合我国寿险资金支持实体经济存在的问题以及国际经验，提出促进中国寿险资金支持实体经济的政策建议。

当前，金融工作的核心任务是支持实体经济发展，促进融资便利化，降低实体经济成本，提高资源配置效率。国务院发展研究中心金融研究所一直致力于研究金融改革与发展中重要的理论和政策问题。我希望《寿险资金支持实体经济研究》通过总结寿险资金支持实体经济中的新情况、新探索和新问题，能够为保险机构创新支持实体经济机制、金融监管部门调整监管政策以及政策制定部门完善相关政策提供一定的启示与借鉴，从而有助于推进我国金融改革和发展。

吴振宇

国务院发展研究中心金融研究所所长

2018年10月

序 二

英国保诚集团与中国中信集团成立的合资公司于2000年起开始在中国开展业务。18年来，中国经历了巨大的社会经济变革，数百万人摆脱贫困，一个庞大的中产阶级正在快速形成。但巨大的社会经济挑战依然存在，中国正在积极探索跨越"中等收入陷阱"之途径。在中国当前的五年计划中，发展更具社会包容性和可持续性的经济是重中之重。我们坚信寿险资金在支持政府完成2021年之前全面建成小康社会和2049年之前成为完全发达国家的宏伟目标方面将发挥重要作用。我们很荣幸能与中国国务院发展研究中心金融研究所携手，开展"寿险资金支持实体经济研究"的课题研究。

实体经济需要具有特点各异的融资选择。银行专注于相对短期的借贷，其特点是风险预期更高且具有流动性需求。寿险资金需要长期资产来匹配其在储蓄和保障方面对客户所做的长期承诺。这种长期融资是培育可持续增长和维护金融稳定的重要工具。缺失这种工具会严重阻碍经济增长。迄今为止，虽然寿险和养老金各有特点，但它们在新兴市场中一直都不是实体经济重要的融资来源。然而，这一切即将改变。

寿险保费的累积和运用潜力强大，保险客户的资金可以转化为支持强劲经济增长的生产性长期资金。长期资金，以政府或城市的长期债券或投资级公司债的形式导入经济体。时机适宜，寿险资金也会成为股市的重要机构投资者，长远看，可以平衡短期波动性。亚洲各国政府已经认识到要实现可持续增长，需要对基础设施项目进行大规模投资。寿险公司在与政府开展富有成效的合作中，通过债权或股权形式，利用项目融资或资本市场融资，为战略性长期项目提供资金，例如那些"一带一路"倡议下的项目。

寿险行业之所以重要，不仅因为其是实体经济发展的融资来源，它也是职业发展和人才开发的贡献者。寿险对财富保护，鼓励创业和个人消费以及投资有着积极的影响。英国智库牛津分析公司一项由保诚集团资助的研究发现：就业、个人消费和投资的乘数效应意味着寿险保费上每花费的一美元都会带来将近三美元的GDP增长。[①]

一套完善和运转正常的监管框架可以强化和协助实现寿险行业及寿险资金所带来的积极效益。国务院发展研究中心金融研究所与英国保诚集团携手成立课题组，对如何运用适宜的政策惠及实体经济进行了深入研究，提出了支持寿险资金支持实体经济发展的政策建议。我们希望政府与保险行业加深对话，采纳相关政策建议，让寿险资金在支持实体经济发展中发挥更大的作用。

Paul Lynch

英国保诚集团亚太区政府关系总监

2018年11月

[①] 牛津分析公司（Oxford Analytica），《印尼人寿保险行业-经济影响评估报告》（The Indonesian life insurance sector – an economic impact assessment），2013年7月1日

目　录

概　要

　　截至2017年底，我国保险资金运用余额149206.21亿元人民币，有力地支持了实体经济的发展。寿险资金具有规模大、期限长、资金来源稳定等特征，对于支持实体经济具有天然的优势。随着我国人口老龄化程度不断加深，居民健康养老等保险保障和财富管理需求不断增加，长期寿险资金将稳步增长，并在支持实体经济发展中发挥越来越重要的作用。研究寿险资金支持实体经济存在的问题，并提出相关政策建议，对于拓宽寿险资金支持实体经济的渠道，促进保险业持续向服务实体经济发力、聚力，具有重要的理论价值与积极的现实意义。

一、中国寿险业服务实体经济的内涵与实践

（一）寿险业服务实体经济的内涵

　　必须从功能、效率、风险等多角度来理解寿险业服务实体经济的内涵。"寿险业服务实体经济"的内涵包括：寿险业服务实体经济的前提是必须大力推动（而不是抑制）寿险业高质量发展；寿险业服务实体经济应以风险保障功能为核心，以负债业务为根基；寿险业支持实体经济发展的方式多种多样，包括提供经济减震器、增加长期投资者、拓展财富管理和社会保障渠道；寿险业

服务实体经济应能产生积极的正面效果，既有助于促进经济增长，也有助于稳定金融市场；寿险业服务实体经济不能简单套用其他金融部门的标准。既不能由于保险资金借助银行、证券市场等通道进行间接投资，就断定保险业"脱实向虚"，也不能将保险资金通过债权计划、股权计划等方式直接为企业发展提供资金，就简单等同于保险业在为实体经济服务。

（二）中国寿险业服务实体经济情况评估

随着资金实力的不断扩大，中国寿险业在服务实体经济方面发挥着越来越重要的作用，特别是在创造就业、增加税收等方面表现突出。中国寿险业在服务实体经济方面表现出不同于西方发达经济体的特点。最鲜明的特征是，在运营和发展过程中受到更强烈的政府引导。与此同时，中国寿险业的各项功能还未充分发挥，服务实体经济的方式和力度跟国外保险强国相比仍有很大差距。近年来中国寿险业出现了一些"脱实向虚"现象，具有典型的初级阶段发展特征，是中国寿险市场尚不够成熟的体现。

（三）中国寿险资金支持实体经济的意义和方向

当前，积极推动寿险资金服务实体经济具有特别重大的意义。主要原因在于：我国未来经济发展需要大量长期资金支持，然而，现有的资金供给并不能满足需求。尽管从总量上看，我国的资金并不短缺，资金供给十分充足，但从结构上看，在银行为主的金融体系下，短期、债权性资金可能过剩，但长期、权益类资金明显不足，而这正是寿险资金的强项。寿险资金具有独特的优势，包括：规模大、来源稳定、期限长、要求的回报率相对不高，是理想的长期资金来源。在这种背景下，寿险资金的独特优势与中国经济发展所亟须的资金特点相契合，有助于弥补资金需求不足，从而使寿险公司作为资金提供方具有不可替代性。

有鉴于此，中国寿险投资应主要围绕实体经济的有效需求发力，重点包括：助力国家战略的推进，包括"一带一路"、京津冀一体化、长江经济带等；助力供给侧结构改革，包括国有企业改革、经济结构向绿色、创新等转型；助力切实增强人民的获得感、幸福感、安全感，包括财富管理、社会保障等；助力打好"防范化解重大风险、精准脱贫、污染防治"三大攻坚战。

二、中国寿险资金支持实体经济的现状

（一）保险监管部门引导寿险资金支持实体经济发展

第一，加大政策引导。2006年开始，保监会先后印发一系列政策文件，不断拓展保险资金投资范围和领域，促进与实体经济的对接。2017年以来，保监会先后印发《关于保险业支持实体经济发展的指导意见》等系列文件以及修订《保险资金运用管理办法》，致力于提升保险服务实体经济的效率和水平。

第二，丰富投资工具。产品形态更加多元，交易结构更加灵活，满足实体经济的各类融资需求。

第三，强化监管和防范风险。一是建立了集中、专业和规范的运作机制；二是实行大类资产比例监管；三是强化偿付能力监管；四是实施投资能力牌照化管理；五是推进资产负债匹配监管；六是运用内部控制、信息披露、资产五级分类等方式，强化事中事后监管。

（二）寿险资金主要通过三种方式支持实体经济

寿险资金支持实体经济主要有以下三种方式：第一，通过银行存款转化为银行贷款对实体经济融资。截至2017年底，保险机构在银行存款19274.07亿元，占比12.92%，其中多为长期协议存款和定期存款，成为商业银行中长期贷款的重要资金来源。第二，通过投资债券、股票等资本市场工具对实体经济提供融资。截至2017年底，保险资金投资债券51612.89亿元，占比34.59%；证券投资基金7524.77亿元，占比5.04%；股票10828.94亿元，占比7.26%；各类债券、基金和股票合计超过6.9万亿元。第三，通过发行或投资股权计划、债权计划、资管计划等方式对实体经济提供项目融资。截至2017年底，保险资金买入返售金融资产、长期股权投资、投资性房地产、保险资产管理公司产品、金融衍生工具、贷款、拆借资金以及其他投资59965.53亿元，占比40.19%。其中，保险资金通过债权投资计划、股权投资计划、资产支持计划、产业基金、信托计划、私募基金等方式投资实体经济超过4.6万亿元，投资领域涉及交通、能源、市政、环保、水务、棚改、物流仓储、经适房、工业园区等领域。

（三）另类投资在寿险资金对接实体经济中的重要性日益增强

近年来，越来越多地寿险资金通过另类投资的方式支持实体经济项目融资。从运作模式看，寿险资金的另类投资主要有六种模式，即综合运用债权投资计划、股权投资计划、项目资产支持计划、信托计划、私募基金、直接股权投资等方式为实体经济提供融资。其中，占比最大的是债权计划与股权计划，尤其债权计划是目前寿险资金支持实体经济发展的最重要方式。

保险资金其他投资从2013年的1.3万亿元，增加到2017年的超过5.9万亿，占保险资金运用额的比例也从2013年的16.90%提高到2017年的40.19%。其他投资的快速增长，很大程度上是由于保险资产管理机构发起设立各类债权、股权和项目资产支持计划不断增加。截至2017年12月底，累计发起设立债权投资计划和股权投资计划843项，合计备案（注册）规模20754.14亿元。

另类投资较快增长有四方向的原因。一是为提高投资收益。近年来，金融市场竞争激烈，寿险业负债端成本逐步上升，这迫使保险机构寻找新的投资领域。二是替代贷款渠道的管制。保险资金不能开展贷款业务，从而转向投资信托、资产支持计划、基础设施投资计划等具有贷款性质的金融产品。三是体现长期资金的价值。四是保险资金投资政策不断放开。2012年下半年以来，保监会发布了20多项资金运用方面的新政策，拓宽了投资渠道，从制度和机制方面促进了另类投资的增长，更好地支持了实体经济发展。

（四）基础设施是保险另类投资的重要领域

通过债权和股权计划投资于基础设施是包括寿险资金在内的保险资金支持实体经济发展的重要渠道。截至2016年底，险资累计投资基础设施项目437个，投资额累计12850亿元，平均每个项目规模约30亿元。

基础设施领域另类投资呈现如下基本特征：第一，投资领域集中于交通、能源等重点领域，项目数量和投资额都约占2/3。第二，投资区域初期主要集中于东部地区，近年来逐步向中西部转移。中西部投资占比由2013年的36%提高到2016年的57%，同期东部投资占比则由60%下降到30%。第三，以债权计划为主。截至2016年底，累计债权投资417个项目，投资金额合计为11098亿元，分别占投资项目和投资额的95.4%和86.4%。第四，债权计划以A类和B类增信（分别指银行和企业提供担保）为主，近年来企业担保成为最重要的增信方式，免增信项目呈上升趋势。C类增信（抵质押担保）则由于"门槛"标准较高，比例相对较小。第五，融资主体主要是政府融资平台和国有企业及其子公司，企业类融资主体占比不断提升。截至2016年底，在债权投资项目中，偿债主体为政府部门、政府融资平台、国有企业及其子公司、民营企业的占比分别为4.1%、60.2%、35.3%和0.5%。地方投融资平台作为偿债主体的项目所占比例，由2014年的72.5%下降到2016年底的58.1%，企业类融资主体的项目则由2014年的27.5%提高到2016年的41.9%。第六，投资主体多元，且市场集中度较高。截至2016年底，共有26家保险资管主体投资基础设施。居前八位的累计投资349个项目共10243亿元，项目数和投资额均占约80%。第七，单体投资规模较大。截至

2016年底，累计投资项目单体平均投资29.4亿元。第八，投资期限较长，收益率相对较高。截至2016年底，债权投资项目投资期限平均为7.3年，平均收益率为6.48%。

（五）寿险资金有望成为"一带一路"基础设施建设资金的重要提供者

基础设施互联互通是"一带一路"建设优先领域。许多"一带一路"沿线国家与地区的物质性与社会性基础设施的建设滞后于发展的需要，不同程度面临融资的困难，迫切需要金融的支持。寿险资金期限较长，有望成为"一带一路"基础设施建设资金的重要提供者。近年来，保险资金积极参与长周期、大规模的"一带一路"基础设施项目。截至2017年底，保险资金以债权、股权计划形式，支持"一带一路"建设投资规模达8568.26亿元人民币。中国的实践表明，保险资金，特别是寿险资金是支持"一带一路"沿线新兴市场基础设施投资的重要主体。

（六）寿险资金不断拓展支持实体经济新领域

近年来，寿险资金不断拓展支持实体经济的新兴领域，如参与不良资产处置。保险机构作为重要的长期资金提供方，在有效防范风险的前提下审慎参与不良资产市场化处置，既可以缓解长期保险资金的配置压力，又可以促进保险资金更好地服务实体经济。

（七）寿险资金服务实体经济取得积极成效

我国寿险资金通过投资国家重大项目、支持地方经济发展和助力民生工程建设等方式支持实体经济发展，取得了积极的成效：一是主动服务国家供给侧结构性改革；二是积极支持"一带一路"倡议；三是积极支持国家区域发展战略；四是积极参与PPP项目和重大工程建设；五是支持军民融合发展和制造业转型升级。

三、中国寿险资金支持实体经济的挑战、风险与政策障碍

（一）寿险资金支持实体经济面临的挑战

寿险资金支持实体经济，面临的重要挑战在于寿险业自身需要推进重大转型。

第一，寿险发展不充分不利于寿险资金支持实体经济。寿险资金是寿险业支持实体经济发展的基础。寿险业发展不充分不利于积聚期限长、稳定性高的资金，从而制约了寿险资金支持实体经济的广度和深度。

第二，寿险发展方式转型不到位不利于寿险资金支持实体经济。寿险投资活动主要基于负债活动展开，寿险转型不到位造成负债结构不合理，不利于寿险资金支持实体经济。

第三，不规范行为弱化了寿险资金支持实体经济的效果。近年来，由于万能险的发展出现异化、资本市场的相关规则有待完善以及金融跨界与联动带来一定的监管空白等原因，寿险资金在支持实体经济中出现了非理性举牌、与一致行动人非友好投资、非理性跨境跨领域大额投资和并购、激进经营和激进投资以及产品多层嵌套和监管套利等问题，一定程度上弱化了对实体经济的支持。

第四，寿险投资的结构性问题不利于转变经济发展方式。例如，寿险资金的另类投资主要投向地方政府与国有企业，对民营企业的支持偏弱；寿险资金以债权型投资为主，股权型投资偏少。这些均不利于中国经济发展方式的转型。

（二）寿险资金支持实体经济存在的主要风险

第一，资产负债不匹配风险。一是负债端成本高企倒逼投资端提升风险偏好。二是期限不匹配。一方面，存在"长钱短配"现象。我国资本市场缺乏长期投资品种，长期寿险资金不得不被动配置短期限资产，不仅降低了投资收益，也增加了短期波动性。另一方面，也存在"短钱长配"现象。一些短期资金投向收益高、流动性低、期限较长的不动产、基础设施、信托等另类资产，"短钱长配"现象凸显。三是流动性风险。负债端的业务结构调整或满期给付引发流动性风险，而另类投资作为非标资产，流动性较差，交易不活跃，变现周期较长，加剧了一些公司面临的现金流不足的风险。

第二，信用风险。在经济转型、去杠杆和打破刚性兑付背景下，寿险资金支持实体经济面临的信用风险加大。特别是随着地方政府债务压力的上升，潜在的地方信用风险可能会释放。

第三，跨市场跨领域风险。随着寿险资金参与金融市场和服务实体经济的广度、深度不断提升，寿险资金运用风险已经与经济金融风险深刻交织交融在一起，风险错综复杂。风险跨产品、跨行业、跨监管传染叠加，风险识别应对难度加大。

第四，增加地方政府隐性债务风险。一些股权计划中存在"明股实债"等不规范行为，一定程度上成为新增地方政府债务。

第五，境外投资的风险。以寿险资金参与"一带一路"建设为例，由于沿线国家的发展环境差异大、基础设施投资缺乏可靠稳定的盈利模式、地缘政治风险较大，增加了寿险资金参与"一带一路"建设的投资风险。

第六，拓展新兴领域的风险。以参与不良资产处置为例，保险机构面临的潜在风险包括：一是不良资产处置方式自身可能带来的潜在风险；二是不良资产处置市场存在的问题诱发风险；三是保险机构风险防范与控制能力不足带来的风险。

（三）寿险资金支持实体经济存在的主要政策障碍

第一，保险资金运用政策有待优化。一是基础设施债权计划相关的管理规则有待完善。首先，融资主体免于增信的条件有待完善。目前债权投资计划的增信要求标准高，方式手段要求严。其次，投资计划资金用途有待拓宽。目前基础设施债权投资计划在资金使用用途上的管制，不但限制了债权投资计划产品本身的发展，而且增加了融资主体的成本。二是保险资金投资股权的范围有待进一步放开。首先，间接投资股权的范围有待放开，以适应私募基金的多种投资方式。其次，直接投资股权的范围有待进一步放开。最后，对保险股权投资的审批制有必要适时放宽。

第二，不动产抵押登记的政策有待完善。寿险资金通过债权或股权等方式直接或间接投资于不动产相关项目时，无法通过不动产抵押担保方式保障其债权实现，从而限制了寿险资金服务实体经济手段和空间。

第三，投资养老健康产业的政策有待完善。如养老健康服务产业的进入标准、配套设施和专业服务等均尚未形成完善而统一的行业标准，与之相关的监管制度不健全；对于用地性质以及营利性的优惠政策尚不明确等。

第四，参与PPP项目存在制约因素。相关的平等契约关系、风险保障机制等缺少法律保障，相关的政策环境不太健全，影响保险机构投资积极性。

第五，参与不良资产处置的政策环境有待完善。一是参与不良资产证券化的政策需要进一步完善。需要相关部门放开保险机构参与不良资产证券化的政策，并对不良资产的评级、风险管控等作出明确的规定，完善相关的法律法规。二是参与债转股的政策尚不配套。包括：市场化债转股风险与收益不尽匹配；国有股权交易进场以及评估的相关规则有待完善；存在双重征税，加重了债转股企业的综合成本；上市公司市场化债转股与现有相关规定存在一定的张力，如发行规模和发行股价受再融资新规限制，募集资金用于偿还贷款的监管较严，债权无法纳入发行股份购买资产标的。

四、寿险资金支持实体经济的国际经验、教训和发展动向

（一）国际经验

第一，寿险公司以规模大、期限长等鲜明特点成为实体经济投资领域的重要力量。保险公司，特别是寿险公司往往成为发达国家经济增长的一股重要力量，为各类融资活动提供了规模大和投资期限长的不可替代的资金来源。

第二，寿险投资活动主要基于负债活动展开，以资产负债匹配为根本指导原则。寿险公司从事的是典型的负债驱动资产型投资。在很大程度上，有什么样的保险产品组合，就有什么样的资产配置组合。确保资产负债匹配是寿险资金投资的首要原则。

第三，寿险投资对宏观经济大势和政策走向保持高度敏感，灵活调整投资方向和投资组合配置。不管是出于追求自身回报还是确保投资业务有效支持负债业务考虑，都要求保险投资必须遵循宏观大势，积极响应实体经济提出的各项需求。

第四，寿险投资与资本市场保持密切互动，对资本市场深化做出积极贡献。资本市场和寿险投资是相生相合、相互促进的关系，寿险投资离不开健全的资本市场和丰富的金融产品，同样地，资本市场的深化也需要借助寿险公司这类长期机构投资者的力量。

（二）国际教训

第一，保险资产和负债业务均应稳健经营，切忌过度激进。由于保险特殊的业务性质，稳健经营对个体公司和整个行业而言均十分重要。稳健经营既

包括负债业务，也包括资产业务，如果整个经营模式背离了稳健原则，过度激进，即使资产负债相匹配，也会使公司陷入危险境地，甚至对整个行业乃至金融体系的稳定造成冲击。

第二，寿险投资离不开有效监管，缺乏有效监管很容易出现严重问题。寿险业是需要严格监管的行业，同时也是高度依赖市场创新的行业。如何在控制风险和鼓励创新之间保持平衡，对所有监管机构都是一道难题。在缺乏有效监管，存在大量监管空白和监管套利的情况下，市场竞争很容易偏离正常的轨道，产生大量问题，甚至酿成系统性风险的大爆发。

（三）国际发展动向

第一，寿险公司正以更加积极的态度介入基础设施、新创企业等另类投资领域，另类资产占比显著增加。2008年国际金融危机以来，由于长期的低利率环境以及股票、债券公开市场投资不确定性的加剧，全球范围内寿险投资的一个明显动向是显著增加了在另类资产上的配置比例，以期获取更高回报率，同时提高投资的多样化程度，熨平短期波动，降低风险。

第二，越来越多的寿险公司投资保险科技，以改善风险管理，提高投资组合回报率。保险科技在投资活动中大有可为，主要原因在于，保险投资活动正变得更为复杂。其一，在持续低利率以及资本市场波动率不断上升的背景下，以往传统的投资组合构建方式已经变得日趋过时。其二，另类资产配置比例的提高意味着资产组合构建的方式更为复杂。其三，偿付能力II等新的监管规则对保险公司信息基础设施建设提出了新的要求。由于上述新变化，保险公司需要采用比以往更加动态、更加复杂的方法来进行资产负债匹配，需要更及时、准确的数据以及快速、高效的资产组合构建能力加以支持。新的保险科技的发展有利于帮助保险公司更好地开展投资管理，以适应新形势发展的需要。

第三，保险业与系统性风险的相关性呈现上升趋势，如何防控资产和负债业务风险、维持行业稳定成为巨大挑战。与过去相比，保险业与银行、证券等金融部门的同质性增强，保险投资组合蕴含的风险显著增加，保险业正变得越来越不稳定，与系统性风险的相关性显著提升。

五、促进中国寿险资金支持实体经济的政策建议

（一）推动寿险业转型与高质量发展

第一，促进寿险业转型。一是要实现保费增长模式从趸交推动向续期拉动的转型，以增强保费收入增长的可持续性与业务发展的稳定性。二是产品结构调整。行业和公司要创新产品体系，着力发展为死亡风险提供财务保障人寿保险、为病残风险提供财务保障的健康保险、为长寿风险提供财务保障的养老年金险。三是要提升渠道价值。推动银行和保险公司在业务领域的深度融合，促进银保合作的深化，促进银保模式的升级。提高代理人人均产能与销售效率，规范销售行为，保护消费者利益，实现从数量扩张到质量提升的飞跃。四是防范化解行业转型中的流动性风险。为了平稳推进寿险业转型，要避免短期内保费收入大幅下滑，尽可能使续期保费的增量与趸交保费的减少量相匹配，实现转"大弯"，避免转"急弯"衍生出新的风险。为此，要把握好监管的力度以及行业转型的节奏，给公司留下结构调整的时间与空间。五是防范和化解转型过程中短期行为造成的新的利差损与费差损风险。

第二，推动寿险业高质量发展。为了推动寿险业高质量发展，提升保险资产在金融业总资产中的比重以及寿险业的发展水平，要深化行业的供给侧结构性改革，不断深化保险要素市场化配置改革，提高供给质量，强化科技创新，推动行业优化升级。为此，要推动行业实现质量变革、效率变革、动力变革，不断提高保险业全要素生产率。推动寿险业实现高质量发展，要求充分发挥保

险机制在经济转型过程中的作用，促进寿险业发挥长期稳健风险管理和保障的功能，重塑寿险市场良序运行的制度基础。

（二）促进寿险资金支持实体经济的发展思路

第一，坚持市场化运作。寿险资金收益性和安全性的要求决定其应秉持市场化原则，主要投资有良好发展预期的优质实体经济项目，以实现可持续发展。坚持市场化运作，除了以市场的方式支持国家重大战略发展外，需要积极探索寿险资金支持民营经济发展，使市场在寿险资金运用中起决定性作用，从而促进经济发展方式转型。

第二，秉持寿险资金运用的基本原则。一是稳健审慎，这是寿险资金运用的根基。二是服务主业。寿险资金运用应为发挥保险保障功能提供支撑。三是长期投资、价值投资、多元化投资。四要资产负债匹配管理，这是寿险公司稳健经营的重要基础，是风险管理的核心内容。五是依法合规。

第三，支持寿险资金运用服务实体经济发展。在坚持市场化运作，秉持资金运用的基本原则的基础上，要支持寿险资金服务实体经济发展，充分发挥保险资金在服务实体经济中具有明显优势。

第四，促进负债端保险业务与资产端投资业务的融合。

第五，加强科技在资产管理领域的运用。

（三）防范寿险资金支持实体经济中的风险

第一，要进一步引导寿险业调整负债结构，解决负债端成本高企倒逼投资端提升风险偏好的问题。寿险业要以保障功能为基础，风险管理与财富管理相结合，以养老险和健康险为主导，建立可持续的资产负债管理模式，并成为国家养老和健康保障体系的重要组成部分。

第二，提升保险机构以资产负债管理为核心的风险管理能力。保险公司要实现资产端和负债端的良性互动，建立可持续的资产负债管理模式。一是保险机构不断提升资产负债管理意识和能力，加强组织体系和机制建设，建立资产负债管理的决策体系，建立起公司内部各部门尤其是负债管理部门与资产管理部门之间的横向沟通和协调机制，加强各部门之间的信息交流与反馈。二是优化保险公司团队建设。三是转变保险高管理念。四是全面提升投资资产和负债的流动性。五是优化考核体系，推动资产负债管理的有效实施。

第三，加快构建以防风险为中心的寿险资金运用监管体系。一是加快推进资产负债管理监管，实现资产端和负债端的良性互动。为此，要建立定量评估、定性评估和压力测试等规则，综合评估保险公司资产负债匹配状况和资产配置能力，差别化实施偿付能力政策和资金运用政策。进一步科学划分和调整大类资产种类和比例，校准偿二代风险因子，优化对不同资产品种和投资行为的资本约束。二是推进通过外部审计、资本监管、信息披露、分类监管、内部控制、社会监督等多种方式，全面严格保险资金运用监管。三是推动保险统计信息系统和保险资产管理监管信息系统建设，进一步加强保险资金托管银行系统与监管信息系统对接。四是研究探索保险资金投资黄金及相关金融产品，运用股指期货、国债期货、利率互换等更多金融衍生产品来对冲和管理风险。五是加强保险业务监管、资金运用监管、偿付能力监管的协调联动，形成监管合力。

第四，要加强对关键领域风险的监控与防范。一是加强对保险债权投资计划前后端的管理和风险防控，防范信用风险。二是进行资产配置压力测试，评估资产配置计划对现金流的影响，并做好现金流风险的应急计划，防范资产负债错配风险与流动性风险。三是规范股权投资计划，避免增加地方政府隐性债务。为此，要回归"股权投资"本源，杜绝"明股实债"。同时，要加强主动管理，消除通道业务和多层嵌套，防控金融风险。

第五，要加强金融监管部门之间的协调与配合。银行保险、证券监管部门要加强监管协调和合作，防范监管套利，消除金融跨界所带来的监管空白地带。密切监测货币、财税、外贸、外汇、利率、房地产、股票、社会保障等宏观因素的变化可能给保险业带来的影响，分析评估风险传导机制与传递通道，有效防范跨市场跨领域风险。

第六，以合作改善投资环境。对于寿险资金参与"一带一路"建设，应加强合作，大力改善域内基础设施投资环境。合作的重点包括：一是加强沿线国家多边、双边沟通与协商，构建致力于改善整个区域基础设施投资环境的合作和对话机制。二是在寿险资金与基础设施项目之间搭建起信息互通、风险共担、利益共享的平台，在条件允许的领域率先形成制度化合作机制。三是在域内基础设施投资风险的识别、防范与应对方面加强合作。

第七，提升地方政府的契约精神。

第八，强化行业风险管理。

（四）完善寿险资金支持实体经济的政策环境

第一，深化保险资金运用市场化改革。要拓展投资领域，在合规的前提下把更多选择空间和选择权交给市场主体，将支持实体经济发展作为创新资金运用方式的出发点和落脚点。一是扩大保险资金的投资范围。二是出台保险资管产品业务细则。三是完善相关监管规定。

第二，明确不动产抵押登记政策。建议明确保险机构在资金融出方面享有与银行等金融机构同等的主体地位，推动相关部门出台规范土地抵质押登记的政策，允许保险机构依法办理土地抵质押登记手续。

第三，消除保险机构投资养老健康产业面临的市场准入、土地和财税政策等方面障碍。明确养老健康服务产业的进入标准、配套设施和专业服务等行业标准，明确养老健康服务产业的用地性质以及营利性的养老健康服务行业税收优惠政策等。

第四，完善PPP领域的相关配套政策。进一步完善政府和社会资本合作领域的立法，加大对保险机构参与投资的土地、财税政策等方面的支持；完善对保险资金投资股权金融产品收益的税收政策。

第五，优化寿险资金参与"一带一路"建设的政策环境。建议保险与外汇监管部门在有效监管的基础上支持寿险资金审慎开展境外投资。为此，要适时将更多的"一带一路"沿线国家纳入寿险资金可投资国家或地区的范围。同时，鼓励和支持寿险资金管理机构开发"一带一路"相关投资产品。

第六，完善寿险资金参与不良资产处置的政策环境。首先，适时放开保险机构参与不良资产证券化投资，并对不良资产的评级、风险管控等作出明确的规定，完善相关的法律法规。其次，完善市场化债转股的配套政策。一是将债转股和国有企业混合所有制改革相结合，致力于转变企业经营机制。二是完善国有股权交易进场和评估方面的规则。三是对金融机构通过金融产品实施债转股，取消双重征收所得税。四是探索允许锁价非公开发行，适当放宽非公开发行规模、募集资金用途及发行股份购买资产范围等，以鼓励寿险资金探索上市公司市场化债转股。

第七，探索寿险资金开展贷款业务。

第八，积极培育保险资产管理市场。

第一章　中国寿险业服务实体经济的内涵与实践

一、寿险业服务实体经济的内涵

中国寿险业已成为中国乃至全球金融市场上一支重要力量：以保费规模看，稳居全球第3位，贡献了全球新增寿险保费收入的最大份额；拥有全球最大的寿险公司之一，也是中国资本市场最大的机构投资者之一。考虑到中国寿险业自20世纪80年代初刚刚恢复国内业务，几乎从零开始起步，至今历史尚不足40年，其发展速度之快、累积实力之强，不由得让人惊叹！

中国寿险业在其发展历程中，也不是一帆风顺，而是几经波折。最近一波"挫折"来自对寿险业"脱实向虚"的批评。自2015年以来，社会舆论、政府相关部门以及监管机构，普遍对包括寿险业在内的中国金融体系未能很好地服务实体经济、反而"脱实向虚"展开了深刻反思。在寿险业语境下，"脱实向虚"不仅表现为对"风险保障"这一基本功能的偏离，以至于"保险不姓保"，还体现为随着民营资本大举进入保险业、资产驱动负债模式兴盛、保险公司频繁举牌上市公司、短期高现价万能险产品超常规发展、保险资金开展多层嵌套/通道业务等现象的发酵而伴生的流动性风险、资产负债不匹配风险、声誉风险等不断累积和叠加，最终导致寿险业成为中国不断攀升的金融风险链条上一个极具重要性的环节。在此背景下，不论是从防范化解金融风险考虑，还是从促进行业自身转型出发，如何推动寿险业摆脱"脱实向虚"，回归初心，更好地服务实体经济，就成为一个既迫切而又关键的议题。

那么，如何理解寿险业服务实体经济？事实上，综合考虑国际经验以及中国国情，"寿险业服务实体经济"有其特定含义。

（一）寿险业服务实体经济的前提是必须大力推动（而不是抑制）寿险业高质量发展

近些年来，我国金融业增加值占GDP的比重逐年提高，从2005年的4%迅速攀升至2015年的8.44%，其间个别时点超过9%，2016～2017两年虽略有下滑，但仍处于高位，甚至超过了金融市场高度发达的英美等国家[①]。短时间内金融增加值快速攀升，并且金融业增速显著高于工业增速[②]，意味着当前我国金融市场发展过度，并对实体经济发展产生了挤出或掠夺效应。强调金融业服务实体经济正是在此背景下提出来的，隐含之意在于金融业需要适当收缩规模，以与实体经济发展相匹配。然而，可以说银行业发展过度，却绝不能说保险业发展过度。当前我国保险业占GDP的比重不到1%，远远低于欧美发达国家水平。对银行业的未来发展而言，可能总量已经不再是问题，关键是结构问题，但对于保险业而言，不仅面临结构调整问题，还面临总量发展不足问题。有鉴于此，保险业服务实体经济，隐含的前提之一是必须大力促进保险业的发展，推动业务规模的扩张，而不应当是抑制发展和收缩规模。当然，寿险业的发展必须以高质量为导向，不能像以往那样一味追求规模，只快不好，而应该在追求质量和效益的基础上推动业务总量的继续扩张。

---

① 与美英日等发达国家相比，我国金融业增加值占比于2013年超过美国，于2015年超过英国。2015年，中美日英四国的金融业增加值占比分别为8.4%、7.2%、4.4%、7.2%，中国已超过另外三国。

② 2012～2016年我国金融业增加值的增速为9.4%、10.6%、9.9%、16%和5.7%，而工业增加值的增速为8.1%、7.7%、7%、6%和6%，除2016年外，金融业增速均高于工业增速。

（二）寿险业服务实体经济应以风险保障功能为核心，以负债业务为根基

一般来说，金融业的功能不是单一的[①]，对于不同金融部门而言，功能经常相互交叉、重叠。然而，不同金融部门的核心功能通常具有独特性。例如，清算和支付是银行业的核心功能，但却不是寿险业的核心功能。核心功能的差异既有助于确保实体经济获得金融业全面而综合的服务，同时又增加了整个金融体系多元化的收益，有利于金融稳定的实现。

寿险业的核心功能是对处于不同生命周期的客户提供财务稳定和保护，帮助其管理死亡、疾病、生存、长寿等风险。换句话说，风险保障是寿险业的核心功能，承载保障功能落地的负债业务是寿险业立足的根基。尽管随着寿险业的不断发展，已经衍生出不少其他功能，但都无法越过"风险保障"这一核心功能，否则其存在就失去了意义。相应地，大力推动保险业务扩张，其基础在于大力推动保险保障业务的扩张。

（三）寿险业支持实体经济发展的方式多种多样

从风险保障这一核心功能出发，衍生出了寿险业服务实体经济的多种方式。具体来说主要包括：①经济减震器：通过分摊意外事故损失和提供损失/收入补偿，创造一个不确定性减少的环境，使社会经济生活更加稳健；②长期投资者：寿险公司是具有长期投资视野的重要机构投资者，不仅能为基础设施等长期项目提供资金融通，还能够对金融市场的壮大和深化做出积极贡献；③财

---

①　根据墨顿的概括，金融体系具有如下六项基本功能：①清算和支付功能，即提供便利商品、劳务和资产交易的支付清算手段；②融通资金和股权细化功能，即通过提供各种机制，汇聚资金并导向大规模的物理上无法分割的投资项目；③为在时空上实现经济资源转移提供渠道，即金融体系提供了促使经济资源跨时间、地域和产业转移的方法和机制；④风险管理功能，即提供应付不测和控制风险的手段及途径；⑤信息提供功能，即通过提供价格（利率、收益率和汇率等）信号，帮助协调不同经济部门的非集中化决策；⑥解决激励问题，即帮助解决在金融交易双方拥有不对称信息及委托代理行为中的激励问题。

富管理：寿险合同通常将保障和投资因素有机结合，通过独有的强制储蓄、延税、资产保全等功能，使财富得到有效管理；④社会保障：寿险业是多层次社会保障体系的一个重要组成部分，特别是在退休和医疗领域，商业保险与社会保险的积极配合，能够有效缓解公共财政压力，提高社会保障体系的效率。以上这些方式相互配合，推动寿险业经历漫长的发展历史最终成为一种被全球广泛接受、不可或缺的金融服务。

　　表1不仅对寿险服务实体经济的各类方式进行了解析，还将之与其他金融部门进行了比较，从中不难看出寿险功能的独特性。例如，面对意外事故发生后的人身伤害或收入损失风险，保险和银行贷款都能够介入，但保险的优势不仅在于是事前机制，而且在于事故发生后，客户就可以获得赔偿，资金无须偿还。又例如，在退休生活的保障方面，尽管银行储蓄也可承担这一功能，但保险仍具有税收递延、强制储蓄、定期给付等独特性。在长期投资、资产保全等方面，寿险的独特优势更是不容置疑。

表1　　　　　　　　寿险业服务实体经济的多种方式解析

方式	内涵	对社会经济的作用	与银行等其他金融部门相比的独特性
经济减震器	保险事故发生后给予经济补偿	减少不确定性，推动消费，培育投资与创新	事前机制，赔偿资金无需偿还
资金动员融通	保险准备金通过资本市场等投资渠道为实体经济提供资金	长期资金提供者，推动了资本市场的发展	在投资的长期性、资金来源的稳定性等方面具有明显优势
财富管理	通过强制储蓄、延税、资产保全等功能使得财富保值增值	帮助经济可持续发展	例如，定期支付保费容易形成一种强制储蓄行为，而银行储蓄则是自愿的，很容易就遗漏
社会保障功能	在政府主导的基本养老、医疗保险之外提供补充保障	提高保障的整体水平和效率	寿险产品具有延税、定期支付等优势

　　此外，从对象来看，寿险业服务的主体范围很广，既包括个人和家庭，也包括企业、公共服务机构以及政府部门。

（四）寿险业服务实体经济应能产生积极的正面效果，既有助于促进经济增长，也有助于稳定金融市场

寿险业作为重要的现代服务业，不仅通过各项功能的发挥为经济增长提供支持，而且通过创造就业、增加税收等方式成为国民经济增长的有机组成部分。

更重要的是，寿险业的相关活动应有助于稳定而非扰乱金融市场、缓解而非放大系统性风险爆发的概率。值得庆幸的是，理论和实践均表明，传统保险活动不是系统性风险的来源，只要确保经营模式不扭曲，确保"保险业姓保"，寿险业就足以担当金融市场"稳定器"角色。

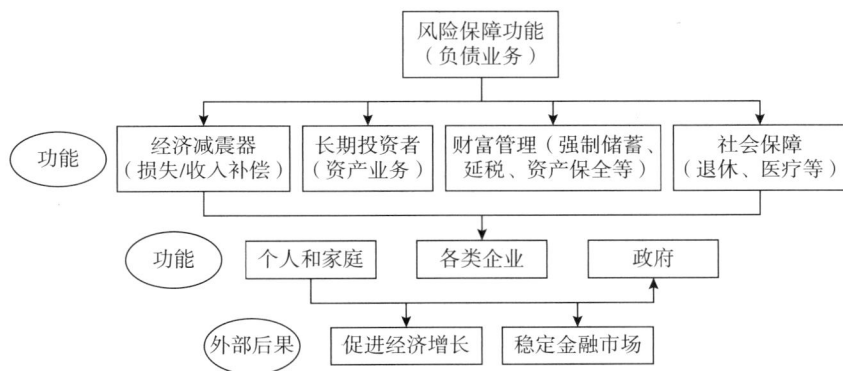

图1　寿险业支持实体经济的方式

（五）寿险业服务实体经济不能简单套用其他金融部门的标准

在"脱实向虚"一词中，"实"是指实体经济，"虚"是主要是指金融部门，简单来说，所谓"脱实向虚"是指金融部门未能充分发挥功能，无法有效支持非金融部门发展。

对于不同的金融部门而言，由于各自的业务性质有所差别，因而服务实体经济的内涵和方式也有所不同。以银行业和寿险业进行对比。当前银行业"脱实向虚"的一个重要表现在于同业资产、同业负债大量增加，导致资金在金融体系内部循环。然而，无法用"资金在金融体系内部循环"这个标准简单套用到寿险业身上，因为国内外实践均表明，保险资金一直是银行存款和证券市场的重要投资者。例如，在德国，保险资金大量投资于银行体系。以市场价值来衡量，截至2014年一季度末，整个保险投资中对银行的投资大约占41%（约为4740亿欧元），而在寿险公司的投资组合中，对银行的投资比例约为42%（刚过3000亿欧元）[①]。显然，不能由于保险资金借助银行、证券市场等通道进行间接投资，就断定保险业"脱实向虚"；更不能将保险资金通过债权计划、股权计划等方式直接为企业发展提供资金，就简单论断为保险业在为实体经济服务。

二、中国寿险业服务实体经济情况评估

（一）随着实力的不断扩大，中国寿险业在服务实体经济方面发挥着越来越重要的作用，特别是在创造就业、增加税收等方面表现突出

自20世纪80年代初恢复业务算起，国内寿险业只有短短40年的发展历史，但行业实力不断壮大，意味着服务实体经济有了日益强健的根基，扮演着日益重要的角色。下表显示了1997~2016年间中国寿险业的实力变化，可以发现，不论是从保费收入规模还是保险业总资产看，中国寿险业在20年间均有了长足的进步。

[①] 数据来源：Deutsche Bundesbank，"Analyses of the importance of the insuranceindustry for financial stability"，Monthly Report，July 2014。

表2	过去20年中国寿险业实力变化	
	1997年	2016年
寿险保费收入（亿美元）	75.6	2626.2
寿险规模全球排名（位）	15	3
寿险保费全球份额（%）	0.61	10.03
人均寿险保费（美元）	6.1	189.9
寿险保费占GDP的比重（%）	0.82	2.3
保险业总资产（亿人民币）*	2604	167500
保险业总资产占GDP的比重（%）*	3.3	20.3

*保险业总资产和保险资产占GDP的比重，历史数据选取的是1999年，而非1997年。

资料来源：Swissre，中国保监会。

寿险业的繁荣发展对中国经济带来了重要影响，最突出表现在创造就业和增加税收两大方面。受限于资料的获取，下面用保险业的数据替代寿险业的数据加以说明。

一是在创造就业方面表现突出。1980年，中国保险从业人员仅有3941人，而截至2015年10月底已经达到近600万人。根据第三次全国经济普查主要数据公报，2013年末，全国共有金融业企业法人单位2.9万个，从业人员513.9万人，其中保险业从业人员112.3万人，占全部金融从业人员的比重为21.9%。

表3	按行业分组的金融业企业法人单位和从业人员	
	企业法人单位（万个）	从业人员（万人）
货币金融服务	1.5	369.5
资本市场服务	0.1	26.2
保险业	1.2	112.3
其他金融业	0.1	6.0
合计	2.9	513.9

资料来源：第三次全国经济普查主要数据公报（http://www.stats.gov.cn/tjsj/zxfb/201412/t20141216_653701.html）。

保监会发布的数据显示，2018年初，保险从业人员已达925万人[1]，在2017年末全国就业人员77640万人中所占的比重达到1.2%。相比2017年末保险业对中

---

① 资料来源：陈文辉副主席在2018年全国保险监管工作会议上的讲话，2018年1月22日。

国GDP的贡献不到1%，保险业对就业的贡献显然更加不容忽视。

二是在增加税收方面表现突出。不少研究表明，中国保险业的实际税负率不仅明显高于银行业、证券业和其他金融业，而且明显高于25%的法定企业所得税率[①]。实际税负率偏高表明保险业对中国税收增长的相对贡献较高。实际上，在"营改增"之前，金融保险业的营业税已经成为一些地方政府税收的重要来源。以福建省为例，2010～2014年福建省金融业地税税收收入保持快速增长，年均增长率比同期地税税收收入增速高3.8个百分点。其中，金融保险业营业税贡献突出，占福建地税金融业税收收入比重保持在六成以上。相应地，金融保险业营业税对福建省地方公共财政收入的贡献率不断提高，从2010年的4.4%上升到2014年的5.9%[②]。

（二）中国寿险业在服务实体经济方面表现出不同于发达经济体的特色

最鲜明的特征是，在运营和发展过程中受到更强烈的政府引导。

毋庸置疑，在中国，政府的影响力显著强于许多发达经济体，相应地，保险业服务实体经济的方式和力度也受到宏观调控政策和监管制度的更大影响，负债业务和资产业务均不例外。欧美发达国家寿险公司的投资活动同样受到政府政策的引导，但在中国，这种引导的影响力更为显著。

以资产业务为例。在2014年颁布的《国务院关于加快发展现代保险服务业的若干意见》中，集中体现了政府对保险投资的引导："鼓励保险资金利用债权投资计划、股权投资计划等方式，支持重大基础设施、棚户区改造、城镇化建设等民生工程和国家重大工程。鼓励保险公司通过投资企业股权、债权、基

---

① 例如，有研究以沪深股市68家金融业企业2015年的财务数据为基础，按银行业、证券业、保险业和其他金融业的行业分类，各个行业的税负率分别为：保险业39.08%、银行业31.99%、证券业31.20%、其他金融业31.17%。以2015年保险市场中开业三年以上的123家保险公司为样本计算，财产保险公司和人身保险公司的税负率分别为48.98%和33.38%。http://www.sohu.com/a/128519972_479770。
② 资料来源：福建地税局课题组，"金融保险业"营改增"对地方税收收入的影响及对策建议"，载于《福建金融》，2015年第1期。

金、资产支持计划等多种形式，在合理管控风险的前提下，为科技型企业、小微企业、战略性新兴产业等发展提供资金支持。研究制定保险资金投资创业投资基金相关政策"。在宏观引导下，自2006年开始，中国寿险公司已经开始通过债权计划、股权计划等方式大量参与基础设施投资，为中国的城镇化建设提供长期低成本资金。此外，保险资金还积极支持绿色经济发展。其背景是，自十八届三中全会以来，加快生态文明制度建设、推进绿色发展已成为中国经济社会发展的一项战略任务。这个思路在"十三五"规划中得到了进一步体现。"十三五"规划提出了包括"绿色发展"在内的五大发展理念，作为中国经济未来发展的指导原则。为了响应中国经济绿色转型的需要，保险资金的绿色化倾向表现得也相当明显。根据保险资产管理协会的统计，截至2017年3月底，共有20家专业管理机构注册200项债权投资计划投向清洁交通、清洁能源、资源节约与循环利用、污染防治等多个绿色产业领域，累计注册规模达到5506.25亿元，共占债权投资计划累计注册规模的39.20%。中国保险资金投资基础设施建设和绿色经济发展的规模和比重，明显高于国际同业，成为中国保险业服务实体经济的一大亮点，而这一亮点主要源于遵循政府的宏观引导。

（三）中国寿险业的各项功能还未充分发挥，服务实体经济的方式和力度跟国外保险强国相比仍有很大差距

中国无疑已是保险大国，但还算不上保险强国，一个重要表现是保险普及度很低，无论是以人均保单拥有量还是以保险密度、保险深度来衡量，均远远低于发达国家水平（表4）。例如，根据保监会数据，我国寿险保单持有人只占总人口的8%，人均持有保单数量仅有0.13张。偏低的普及度意味着寿险业的各项功能远未发挥出来。

表4　　　　　　　　　　　　　2016年五国寿险市场实力比较

	美	英	德	日	中
寿险保费收入（百万美元，2016）	558847	199369	94661	354053	262616
寿险保费占全球比重	21.36%	7.62%	3.62%	13.53%	10.03%
寿险保费全球排名	1	4	8	2	3
寿险保费深度（寿险保费收入/GDP）	3.02%	7.58%	2.75%	7.15%	2.34%
寿险保费密度（人均寿险保费，2016，美元）	1724.9	3033.2	1150.6	2803.4	189.9

　　选取几个重点领域进行评估也能得出上述结论。例如，在当前金融的融资功能被过度强调而风险管理功能被大大忽视的背景下，寿险业所提供的风险保障功能十分薄弱；在银行为主导的中国金融体系下，寿险业对推动中国资本市场深化发展作用有限；在第一支柱占据主导的社会保障体系中，通过商业保险提供的退休收入保障整体上微乎其微（表5）。

表5　　　　　　　　　　　　　寿险业各项功能发挥的对比

	中国	欧美发达国家
风险保障功能	中国寿险保单持有人只占总人口的8%，人均持有保单仅有0.13张，远低于发达国家1.5份以上的水平。目前中国寿险业发挥的风险保障作用极低，以死亡保障为例，瑞士再保险2011年发布的研究报告表明，2010年在中国，对于每100美元的保障需求，仅存在12美元的储蓄和保险覆盖，保障缺口高达88美元。从2000-2010年，中国的死亡保障缺口从3.7万亿美元扩大至18.7万亿美元	发达国家也存在一定的保障缺口，但相比中国，缺口要小得多，其寿险普及率远远高于中国
深化资本市场发展	中国的股票市场投资者仍然是以散户为主，近年来机构投资者持股比例快速上升，但加总后的持股比例在20%左右，占到A股流通股市值的三分之一左右，其中保险资金持股占A股总市值比重不到3%。在债券市场，1998年，保险公司作为商业银行和特殊结算会员之外，首个非银行机构投资者进入银行间债券市场，一直到2012年始终保持除上述两者外，债券市场第一大非银行机构投资者、第二大机构投资者的地位；在2012年这一地位被基金超过。换句话说，在债券市场上，保险公司作为机构投资者的相对重要性近年来明显下降	在多数发达国家，保险公司要么是最重要的机构投资者，要么是仅次于养老基金的第二大机构投资者。在公司债券、外国债券、股票等特定领域，美国寿险公司是具有系统重要性的机构投资者。2009年美国寿险公司约持有美国公司债券和外国债券的16.7%，商业按揭的10.3%，公司股票的6.2%。在欧元区，保险公司则是政府债券的最大持有者，2014年欧元区政府债券的40%由保险公司持有

续表

	中国	欧美发达国家
社会保障体系	在中国，三支柱养老保险体系虽然已经建立起来，但发展并不均衡，其中第一支柱——基本养老保险（企业职工养老保险和城乡居民养老保险）覆盖了最广大的人群（2017年参保9.15亿人），占据着绝对主导地位；第二支柱、第三支柱覆盖的人群有限，提供的替代率更是可以忽略不计（例如，2017年末企业年金、职业年金只覆盖了2300多万人）。寿险公司主要通过提供商业养老保险、参与企业年金受托管理等方式介入社保体系建设，中国不均衡的养老保险体系意味着寿险公司在社保体系建设中发挥的作用极其有限	目前在全球多数地区，公共养老金计划在确保老年收入安全方面扮演着重要角色。根据国际劳工组织2014年数据，在OECD国家，65岁及以上的老年人，其家庭收入的59%来自公共养老金收入，17%来自资本收入，其中资本收入主要由私人养老金构成。保险公司是私人养老金体系的重要参与者，在提高退休收入替代率方面扮演着越来越重要的角色
居民财富管理	中国居民的家庭财富以房产为主导，约占60%以上，其他理财方式主要是储蓄，保险占比极低	2012年，欧元区保险公司对保单持有人的合同责任平均占据该地区家庭财富的32%，其中德国保险公司的负债对应着全国家庭金融财富的36%

（四）近年来中国寿险业出现了一些"脱实向虚"现象，具有典型的初级阶段发展特征，是中国寿险市场尚不成熟的体现

生存和赶超的压力及动力、相对狭小的保险业务发展空间叠加初级发展阶段特征，导致近年来我国部分寿险公司，特别是中小和新设寿险公司行为异化，快速推高了行业风险。其中，寿险业出现了不少"脱实向虚"的表现，与当前保险业尚处于初级发展阶段具有密切关系。由于中国保险业经营历史尚不超过40年，仍处于发展的初级阶段，这一阶段特有的不成熟性在中小公司创新进程中被进一步放大，导致了行为的异化。突出表现在以下三方面。

一是股东经营目标的异化。整个社会对保险的认识还很肤浅，可以说正处于学习曲线的初期。不少新进资本也不例外。例如，尽管保险是负债和资产

双轮驱动的行业,负债业务是根基,但新进资本们往往看重资产业务,对负债业务既不了解,也不重视,甚至无视行业运营的一些基本规则,成为保险业的"野蛮人和外行人"。

二是经营模式的异化。不少中小寿险公司高举"资产驱动负债模式"大旗,激进地实施赶超策略。在这一过程中,往往完全抛弃了负债业务这一根基,寿险公司不再是以承接生老病死风险为主的机构,而完全沦为纯粹的资产管理机构。以规模保险/原保费收入的倍数这一指标来衡量保险经营模式的异化程度,倍数越高,表明保险公司更类似于一个"资产管理机构",经营模式更加异化。表6表明,2013~2016年,寿险行业整体的异化程度逐渐提高,其中中小寿险公司的异化程度远高于老七家,而内资中小寿险公司的异化程度又显著高于外资公司。2017年,随着保监会一系列强监管措施的逐步实施,行业异化程度有所减弱。

表6　　　　　　　　2013~2017中国寿险公司规模保费/保费收入变化

年度	老七家	剩余全部中小寿险公司	剩余全部中资中小寿险公司	行业平均
2013	1.15	1.94	2.22	1.31
2014	1.15	1.82	1.97	1.33
2015	1.17	2.2	2.39	1.52
2016	1.26	2.03	2.53	1.59
2017	1.17	1.35	1.38	1.24

资料来源:根据保监会网站数据自行计算。

三是经营环节的异化。在目标和模式异化的背景下,具体经营环节的异化就是自然而然的事情了。例如在产品方面,不少中小寿险公司将高现价短期万能险产品当作推动业务规模快速扩张的主要利器。这类产品期限短、成本高、保障功能极其薄弱,完全颠覆了原本的形象;在投资方面,为了匹配短期高现价产品的特点,不得不大量进行高风险资产配置,短钱长用风险异常突出。

目前不论是机构、市场还是监管都处于"防风险、治乱象、补短板"的进程中，加大对实体经济的服务力度已成共识。

三、中国寿险资金支持实体经济的意义和方向

本报告在寿险业服务实体经济的大框架下，重点讨论寿险资金支持实体经济发展的情况。

相比风险保障功能，投资虽然是寿险业的派生功能，但异常重要：一方面，保险投资属于典型的负债驱动型投资，保险资产业务支持实体经济的情况很大程度上反映出负债业务支持实体经济的情况；另一方面，寿险保障、理财等功能的充分发挥均离不开投资活动的贡献。

当前，积极推动寿险投资服务实体经济具有特别重大的意义。主要原因在于：我国未来经济发展需要大量长期资金支持。中国十九大报告首次提出要建设现代化经济体系，在这一进程中，不管是城镇化、工业化，还是经济发展向绿色、创新的转型，均需要长期资金的支持；杠杆偏高的事实也决定着权益资金更受欢迎。然而，现有的资金供给并不能满足需求。尽管从总量上看，我国的资金并不短缺，资金供给十分充足，但从结构上看，在银行为主的金融体系下，短期、债权性资金可能过剩，但长期、权益类资金明显不足，而这正是寿险资金的强项。寿险资金具有独特的优势，包括：规模大、来源稳定、期限长、要求的回报率相对不高，是理想的长期资金来源。在这种背景下，寿险资金的独特优势与中国经济发展所亟须的资金特点相契合，有助于弥补资金需求不足，从而使寿险公司作为资金提供方具有不可替代性。

有鉴于此，中国寿险投资应主要围绕实体经济的有效需求发力，重点包括：①助力国家战略的推进，包括"一带一路"、京津冀一体化、长江经济带

等；②助力供给侧结构改革，包括国有企业改革、经济结构向绿色、创新等转型；③助力切实增强人民的获得感、幸福感、安全感，包括财富管理、社会保障等；④助力打好"防范化解重大风险、精准脱贫、污染防治"三大攻坚战。

实体经济的上述需求均蕴含着巨大的投资机会，同时也对寿险业带来巨大挑战。中国寿险业必须通过建立更加有效的政府—市场合作关系、灵活运用多种投资方式、强化风险管理能力等方式积极应对。

第二章　中国寿险资金支持实体经济的现状

寿险资金具有规模大、期限长、稳定性高的特点，契合实体经济发展的资金需求，寿险资金支持实体经济具有较为独特的优势。近年来，寿险资金支持实体经济的政策环境不断优化，另类投资成为寿险资金对接实体经济项目融资的主要方式。寿险资金通过另类投资的方式积极参与基础设施项目，并不断拓展支持实体经济新领域。寿险资金支持实体经济取得的成效主要包括：主动服务国家供给侧结构性改革，积极支持"一带一路"倡议，积极支持国家区域发展战略，积极参与PPP项目和重大工程建设，支持军民融合发展和制造业转型升级。

一、寿险资金的特点及其支持实体经济的潜在优势

（一）寿险资金的特点契合实体经济发展的资金需求

截至2017年底，中国保险资金运用余额149206.21亿，其中约85%为寿险资金。寿险公司的负债期限较长，从而使得寿险资金具有规模大、期限长、稳定性高等特点,可以积极参与长周期、大规模的实体经济项目。

随着中国保险监管导向与环境的变化，寿险业转型力度正在不断加大，长期保单所占比例还将继续增加，寿险资金的长期属性将进一步体现。以2017年为例，在新单期交原保险保费收入中，3年期以下154.13亿元，占比2.60%；3至5年期1776.95亿元，占比29.93%；5至10年期918.90亿元，占比15.48%；10年期及以上3087.04亿元，占比52.00%。可见，随着寿险行业的转型，5年期以上，特别是10年期及以上的新单增加迅速。长期负债形成的长期属性的资金需要与长期投资项目对接，与实体经济项目资金需求大、建设周期长、收益稳定的特点非常匹配，可以为实体经济提供长期、稳定的资金。随着人口老龄化程度的不断加深，居民健康养老等保险保障和财富管理需求不断扩大，长期的寿险资金还将稳步增长，能够在支持实体经济中发挥越来越重要的作用。

（二）寿险资金支持实体经济的独特优势

寿险资金支持实体经济的优势体现在以下三个方面。

第一，能跨周期提供长期稳定的资金保障。寿险资金以长期投资为主，秉承长期投资、价值投资、稳健投资的投资理念，可以成为实体经济的重要资金提供方。在资金供应上，寿险业可以提供大量中长期资金，与其他金融部门短期性、流动性资金形成互补；在资金价格上，以固定利率为主，追求资产负债匹配和合理回报，成本相对稳定。

第二，支持重大工程建设成效显著。寿险资金规模大、期限长、来源稳定等属性，使其与实体经济项目的资金需求相契合。

第三，寿险资金支持实体经济的方式和路径非常多样化。寿险资金可以通过债权、股权、股债结合、股权投资计划、资产支持计划和私募基金等方式，直接或间接投资实体经济重大投资项目。另外，寿险公司还可以同时提供资金融通与风险保障等服务，降低项目融资成本和风险管理成本。

二、寿险资金支持实体经济的政策环境不断优化

近年来，保险监管部门主要通过政策制度引导、丰富投资工具以及强化监管与防范风险等，促进寿险资金支持实体经济发展。

（一）加大政策制度引导

2006年开始，保监会先后印发《保险资金间接投资基础设施项目试点管理办法》《基础设施债权投资计划管理暂行规定》等政策制度，允许保险资金通过债权或股权形式投资基础设施项目。2010年以来，印发《保险资金投资股权管理暂行办法》《保险资金投资不动产暂行办法》《关于保险资金投资股权和不动产有关问题的通知》等一系列政策制度，不断拓展保险资金投资股权和不动产的范围和领域，陆续放开开保险资金投资创业板、优先股、创业投资基金、私募股权投资基金、资产支持计划等，基本实现与实体经济的全面对接。

2017年5月，保监会印发《关于保险业支持实体经济发展的指导意见》，有针对性地围绕经济社会发展的重点领域和薄弱环节，创新保险服务，提升保险服务实体经济的效率和水平。随后，陆续印发《关于保险资金投资政府和社会资本合作项目有关事项的通知》《关于债权计划投资重大工程有关事项的通知》等系列配套文件，从技术细节上明确了具体支持政策。

保监会于2018年1月颁布修订后的《保险资金运用管理办法》，于2018年4月1日起实施。《保险资金运用管理办法》将近几年保险资金支持实体经济有益的实践经验和相关规范性文件上升为部门规章，更好提升法律效力。主要包括：明确保险资金可以投资创业投资基金等私募基金和设立不动产、基础设施、养老等专业保险资产管理机构，进一步支持小微企业发展，提高保险资金支持基础设施、养老等重点领域产业的广度和深度，有利于促进保险资金支持实体经济的发展。

（二）丰富投资工具

在产品形态上，除基础设施债权投资计划外，股权投资计划、资产支持计划、组合类资产管理产品、保险私募股权投资基金等正在逐步发展。在交易结构上，已经逐步从债权、股权等较为单一的交易结构，逐步向股债结合、优先股等更为灵活的交易结构发展，满足不同实体经济不同融资需求。2015年，组建中国保险投资基金，初期规模3000亿元。

在产品发行机制上，2013年开始，保监会将基础设施投资计划等保险资管产品发行方式由备案制改为注册制，改变过去逐单备案核准的方式。不断完善注册标准、注册流程等，并授权中国保险资产管理业协会负责具体注册工作。截至2017年末，累计发起设立债权投资计划和股权投资计划843项，合计备案（注册）规模20754.14亿元。

（三）强化监管和防范风险

一是建立了集中、专业和规范的运作机制。推进保险总公司统一集中管理保险资金。保险公司通过专门建立资产管理部、保险资产管理公司进行专业化管理。二是实行大类资产比例监管。设置股权、不动产、金融产品等投资比例上限，并对单一投资品种设置集中度上限，防范系统性风险。三是强化偿付能力监管。四是实施投资能力牌照化管理。落实风险责任人，加强对股票、股权等7类高风险领域的投资能力监管和牌照化管理，要求建立完善有关制度、人员及运作机制等。五是推进资产负债匹配监管。六是运用内部控制、信息披露、资产五级分类等方式，强化事中事后监管。

此外，新修订的《保险资金运用管理办法》强调保险资金运用必须以服务保险业为主要目标；明确保险资金运用应当坚持独立运作，保险公司股东不得违法违规干预保险资金运用工作；强化境外投资监管，明确保险资金从事境外投资应符合保监会、人民银行和国家外管局的相关规定；明确保险资产管理机构开展保险资产管理产品业务，应当在保监会认可的资产登记交易平台进行发行登记和信息披露等业务，构造数据分析和风险预警系统，进一步加强资管产品业务监管；加强委受托管理，要求投资管理人受托管理保险资金，不得将受托资金转委托或为委托机构提供通道服务，加强去嵌套、去杠杆和去通道工作；明确对保险资金运用违法违规行为可采取的行政处罚措施，强调对保险机构和相关责任人的"双罚"机制，并强化内部责任追究；严格保险机构开展证券投资业务的法规约束，进一步明确应当遵守证券行业相关法律法规等。这些新增加的规定将非常有利于推进保险资金运用建立覆盖事前事中事后的风险防范机制，培育审慎稳健的投资文化，推动保险资金更好服务保险主业和实体经济发展。

三、另类投资是寿险资金支持实体经济的重要方式

在监管部门的政策引导下，保险机构不断探索寿险资金支持实体经济的方式与运作模式。

（一）寿险资金主要通过三种方式支持实体经济

在监管部门的引导下，寿险资金服务实体经济主要有以下三种方式。

第一，通过银行存款转化为银行贷款对实体经济间接融资。截至2017年底，保险机构在银行存款银行存款19274.07亿元，占比12.92%，其中多为长期协议存款和定期存款，成为商业银行中长期贷款的重要资金来源。

第二，通过购买债券、股票等金融工具对实体经济直接融资。截至2017年底，保险资金投资债券51612.89亿元，占比34.59%；证券投资基金7524.77亿元，占比5.04%；股票10828.94亿元，占比7.26%；各类债券、基金和股票合计

超过6.9万亿元。

第三，通过股权、债权、基金等方式对实体经济项目融资。截至2017年底，保险资金以买入返售金融资产、长期股权投资、投资性房地产、保险资产管理公司产品、金融衍生工具、贷款、拆借资金以及其他投资59965.53亿元，占比40.19%。这些保险资金通过债权投资计划、股权投资计划、资产支持计划、产业基金、信托计划、私募基金等方式投资实体经济，投资领域涉及交通、能源、市政、环保、水务、棚改、物流仓储、经适房、工业园区等领域。

（二）另类投资在寿险资金对接实体经济中的重要性日益增强

寿险资金对接实体经济项目融资主要是通过另类投资的方式，即除传统的银行信贷和在银行间市场及证券交易所市场交易的债券、股票、基金等标准化金融产品之外的金融产品。另类投资具有非标准化的特征，即资金的利率、期限、担保措施、偿付安排等核心要素和主要条款通常由资金供需双方协商确定。同时，另类投资采取场外交易，流动性较差，收益率通常高于标准化产品。

从产品性质看，另类投资可以分为债权、股权、资产证券化类；从开发机构看，主要包括银行的理财产品、信托公司的集合信托和单一信托计划，保险资产管理机构的债权投资、股权投资、资产支持计划，证券公司的专项资产管理计划以及基金子公司的"类信托"产品等；从运作模式看，目前寿险资金的另类投资主要有六种模式，即综合运用债权投资计划、股权投资计划、项目资产支持计划、信托计划、私募基金、直接股权投资等方式为实体经济提供融资。

1. 债权投资计划

债权投资计划是指保险资产管理公司等专业管理机构作为受托人，根据《保险资金间接投资基础设施项目管理办法》和《基础设施债权投资计划管理暂行规定》，面向委托人发行受益凭证，募集资金以债权方式投资实体经济项目（基础设施项目），按照约定支付预期收益并兑付本金的金融产品。

2. 股权投资计划

股权投资计划是指保险资产管理公司等专业管理机构作为受托人，根据《保险资金间接投资基础设施项目管理办法》，面向委托人发行受益凭证，募集资金以股权方式投资实体经济项目（基础设施项目），为受益人获取股利、股权出售后的资本利得收益等利益的金融产品。同时，股权投资计划作为保险资金间接投资股权的一种方式，还须符合《保险资金投资股权暂行规定》（保监发〔2010〕79号）、《关于保险资金投资股权和不动产有关问题的通知》（保监发〔2012〕59号）等有关规定。按照投资标的，股权投资计划可分为企业型和基金型。其中，企业型指受托人按照委托人意愿，以自己的名义将股权投资计划募集资金作为有关实体经济项目的股权；基金型指受托人按照委托人意愿，以自己的名义将股权投资计划募集资金，投资某个特定的股权投资基金，然后再通过股权投资基金对有关实体经济项目投资。

3. 资产支持计划

资产支持计划是指保险资产管理公司等专业管理机构作为受托人设立支持计划，以基础资产产生的现金流为偿付支持，面向保险机构等合格投资者发行受益凭证的业务活动。根据《资产支持计划业务管理暂行办法》（保监发〔2015〕85号）的规定，基础资产，是指符合法律法规规定，能够直接产生独立、可持续现金流的财产、财产权利或者财产与财产权利构成的资产组合。

4. 信托计划

信托计划是指保险资产管理公司等专业管理机构投资集合资金信托计划。根据《关于保险资金投资有关金融产品的通知》（保监发〔2012〕91

号）以及《关于保险资金投资集合资金信托计划有关事项的通知》（保监发〔2014〕38号）的规定，保险资金投资的集合资金信托计划，基础资产限于融资类资产和风险可控的非上市权益类资产。其中，固定收益类的集合资金信托计划，信用等级不得低于国内信用评级机构评定的A级或者相当于A级的信用级别。不得投资单一信托，不得投资基础资产属于国家明令禁止行业或产业的信托计划。

5. 私募基金

保险资金可以设立私募基金，范围包括成长基金、并购基金、新兴战略产业基金、夹层基金、不动产基金、创业投资基金和以上述基金为主要投资对象的母基金。根据《中国保监会关于设立保险私募基金有关事项的通知》（保监发〔2015〕89号）的规定，保险资金设立私募基金，投资方向应当是国家重点支持的行业和领域，包括但不限于重大基础设施、棚户区改造、新型城镇化建设等民生工程和国家重大工程；科技型企业、小微企业、战略性新兴产业等国家重点支持企业或产业；养老服务、健康医疗服务、保安服务、互联网金融服务等符合保险产业链延伸方向的产业或业态。

6. 直接股权投资

直接投资股权是指保险公司（含保险集团（控股）公司）以出资人名义投资并持有企业股权的行为。直接投资股权须符合《保险资金投资股权暂行规定》（保监发〔2010〕79号）、《关于保险资金投资股权和不动产有关问题的通知》（保监发〔2012〕59号）等有关规定。根据新修订的《保险资金运用管理办法》（保监会令〔2018〕1号）的规定，保险集团（控股）公司、保险公司购置自用不动产、开展上市公司收购或者从事对其他企业实现控股的股权投资，应当使用自有资金。保险集团（控股）公司、保险公司对其他企业实现控股的股权投资，应当满足有关偿付能力监管规定。保险集团（控股）公司的保险子公司不符合中国保监会偿付能力监管要求的，该保险集团（控股）公司不得向非保险类金融企业投资。实现控股的股权投资应当限于下列企业：（一）保险类企业，包括保险公司、保险资产管理机构以及保险专业代理机构、保险经纪机构、保险公估机构；（二）非保险类金融企业；（三）与保险业务相关的企业。

在上述六种模式中，占比最大的是债权计划与股权计划，尤其是债权计划，这是目前寿险资金支持实体经济发展的主导模式，也是报告接下来分析的重点。

四、寿险资金另类投资的发展状况

（一）另类投资的总体发展状况及其原因

1. 另类投资的总体发展状况

截至2017年底，保险资金买入返售金融资产、长期股权投资、投资性房地产、保险资产管理公司产品、金融衍生工具、贷款、拆借资金等其他投资59965.53亿元。其他投资从2013年的1.3万亿元，增加到2017年底的超过5.9万亿，占保险资金运用额的比例也从2013年的16.90%提高到2017年底的40.19%，占比不断提升（参见图1）。其中，保险资金通过债权投资计划、股权投资计划、资产支持计划、产业基金、信托计划、私募基金等方式投资实体经济超过4.6万亿元，投资领域涉及交通、能源、市政、环保、水务、棚改、物流仓储、经适房、工业园区等领域。

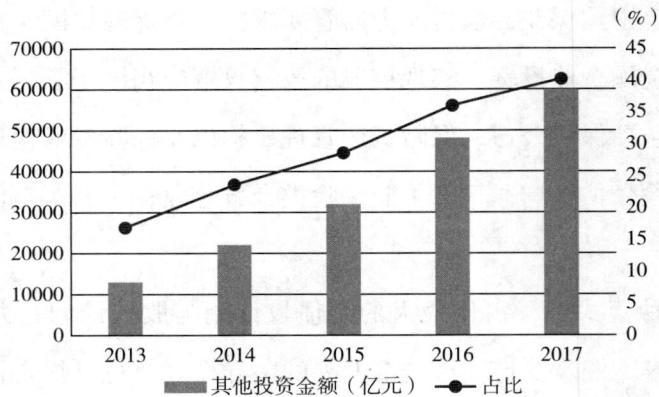

图1　近年来我国保险资金其他投资金额与占比情况

资料来源：中国保监会、中国保险业资产管理协会。

其他投资的快速增长，很大程度上是由于保险资产管理机构发起设立各类债权、股权和项目资产支持计划不断增加。2013年至2017年，分别注册各类资管产品103、175、121、152、216项（参见表1、图2），注册金额分别为3688.27亿、3801.02亿、2706.13亿、3174.39亿和5075.47亿元（参见表1、图3）。截至2017年底，累计发起设立债权投资计划和股权投资计划843项，合计备案（注册）规模20754.14亿元。

表1　各类保险资产管理产品注册项目数与注册规模（2007~2017）

	基础设施债权投资计划		不动产债权投资计划		股权投资计划		项目资产支持计划		注册项目合计（个）	注册规模合计（亿元）
	注册项目（个）	注册规模（亿元）	注册项目（个）	注册规模（亿元）	注册项目（个）	注册规模（亿元）	注册项目（个）	注册规模（亿元）		
2007~2012	—	—	—	—	—	—	—	—	—	2941
2013	—	—	—	—	—	—	—	—	103	3688.27
2014	—	—	—	—	—	—	—	—	175	3801.02
2015	42	1027.45	69	1019.68	5	465	5	194	121	2706.13
2016	57	1477.53	77	1001.86	18	695	0	0	152	3174.39
2017	81	2466.45	123	2113.52	11	488.5	0	0	216	5075.47

资料来源：中国保险业资产管理协会。下同。

注册项目合计（个）

图2 近年来我国各类保险资产管理产品注册项目数

注册规模合计（亿元）

图3 近年来我国各类保险资产管理产品注册规模

在各类保险资产管理产品中，注册项目和规模最大的是基础设施及不动产债权投资计划。基础设施及不动产债权投资计划主要以5年期以上贷款利率作为基准利率，分为固定利率和浮动利率两种。此类计划主要投向市政建设、高速公路、铁路、电力等／公租房、棚户区改造。

2007年至2012年间，保险债权投资计划产品累计注册规模为2,941亿元；2013年新增债权投资计划的注册规模相当于前6年的累计注册规模总量，达到2877.6亿元。2014～2016年，新增债权投资计划的注册规模分别达到3109.6亿元、2047.13亿元和2479.39亿元。2017年，24家保险资产管理公司注册基础设施债权投资计划81项，注册规模2466.45亿元；不动产债权投资计划123项，注册规模2113.52亿元；基础设施及不动产债权计划合计注册4579.97亿元（参见图4）。

基础设施及不动产债权投资计划（亿元）

图4 近年来基础设施及不动产债权投资计划注册规模

股权计划也是保险资产管理产品的重要组成部分。股权类非标产品主要包括基础设施股权投资计划、不动产股权投资计划、股权型项目资产支持计划、未上市企业股权及股权投资基金等，多为"明股实债"的股债结合方式，是债权投资计划的替代产品，很大程度上是对债权投资计划供给的补充。2015、2016、2017年股权投资计划注册规模分别为465亿元、695亿元和495.50亿元。

股权投资计划注册规模（亿元）

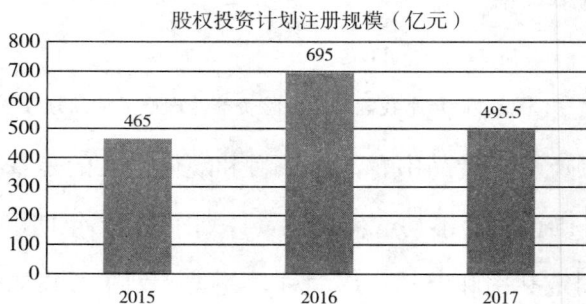

图5 近年来股权投资计划注册规模

保险资产管理产品还包括项目资产支持计划，主要投资于缺乏流动性但具有可预测现金流的资产或资产组合（基础资产），并以该基础资产产生的现金流作为还款支持的金融产品。2015年，保险资产管理机构共注册项目资产支持计划5个，注册规模194亿元。2016、2017年没有注册项目资产支持计划。

2. 另类投资快速发展的原因

我国保险业另类投资较快增长，主要原因有以下几个方面。

一是为提高投资收益。近年来，金融市场竞争激烈，保险负债端成本逐步上升。银行存款、债券等传统投资品种已无法满足保险资产对收益率的需求，这迫使保险机构寻找新的投资领域。

二是替代贷款渠道的管制。经过这几年的市场化改革，我国保险资金配置情况已基本上与国际接轨，但同时也存在一些显著的差别，其中很重要的表现是保险资金不能直接发放贷款。美国、日本、德国等国家的保险资金均可以通过贷款的形式，直接对接实体经济，甚至发放个人住房按揭贷款。而在我国，保险资金不能开展贷款业务，可选择的投资品种不足，实践上形成相当比例的保险资金存放于银行。由于缺少像国外保险机构直接发放贷款投资渠道，保险资金不得不转向投资信托、资产支持计划、基础设施投资计划等具有贷款性质的金融产品。从某种意义上说，有些信托、资产支持计划等投资项目本质上与银行贷款类似。

三是体现长期资金的价值。我国资本市场缺乏长期投资品种，长期资产配置难，保险资金不得不被动配置短期限资产，造成了资产与负债期限的不匹配，既牺牲了投资收益，也增加了短期波动性。

四是保险资金投资政策不断放开。2012年下半年以来，保监会发布了20多项资金运用方面的新政策，拓宽了投资渠道，改进了比例监管政策，其中包括放开对信托等金融产品的投资，开展资产管理产品试点工作。同时，推进基础设施债权计划备案制转为注册制的改革，大大提高发行效率，从制度和机制方面促进了保险业另类投资的增长，更好地支持了实体经济发展。

值得指出的是，由于我国保险业另类投资很大一部分具有贷款的属性，这使得其与国际上的另类投资有所不同。国际上，区分另类投资与传统投资的一个重要标准是定价机制是否公平透明，以及收益是否相对稳定。若定价机制不透明、不公开，并且收益也不确定，就归为另类投资。按照这一标准，我国保险资金投资的一些新的投资品种，比如基础设施债权计划、信托、资产支持计划、组合类资管产品等，它们是具有债券性质的类固定收益产品，本质上不属于国际所指的另类投资。其实，真正算得上另类投资只有直接不动产投资和长期股权投资，真正另类投资的规模并不太大。

（二）基础设施是保险另类投资的重要领域

如上所述，债权和股权计划等另类投资是保险资金服务实体经济的重要的形态，其中通过债权和股权计划投资于基础设施是保险资金支持实体经济发展的重要渠道。

2006年以来，除2015年受宏观环境因素影响外，险资投资基础设施的项目数和投资额总体呈现上升态势。特别是2013和2014年，投资额都分别达到近3000亿元。截至2016年底，险资累计投资基础设施项目437个，投资额累计12850亿元，平均每个项目规模约30亿元（参见图6）。

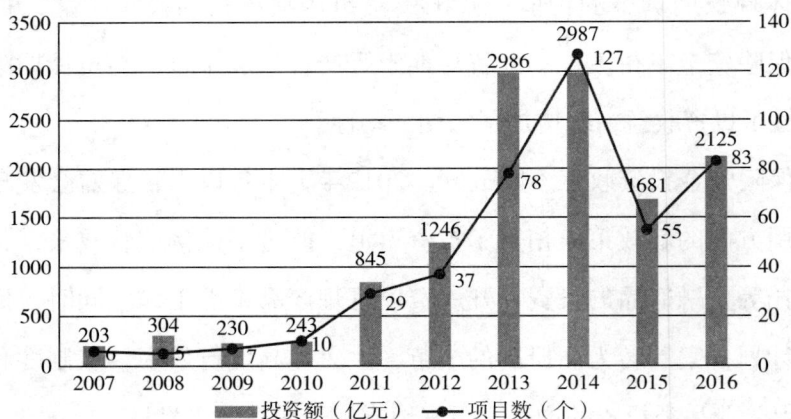

图6 近年来险资投资基础设施的项目数量和投资额

1. 投资领域

交通、能源是险资投资基础设施的重点领域，项目数量和投资额都约占2/3，其余的投资于市政、棚户区改造、土地储备、水利、保障房等民生领域。截至2016年底，累计交通领域基础设施投资5683亿元，占44.22%，能源领域基础设施投资2950亿元，占22.96%，市政领域基础设施投资1204亿元，占9.37%，棚户区改造领域基础设施投资968亿元，占7.53%，土地储备领域投资940亿元，占7.31%，其他（包括水利、保障房、旧城改造、环保、钢铁、养老不动产等）领域的基础设施投资合计1105亿元，占8.6%（参见图7、图8）。

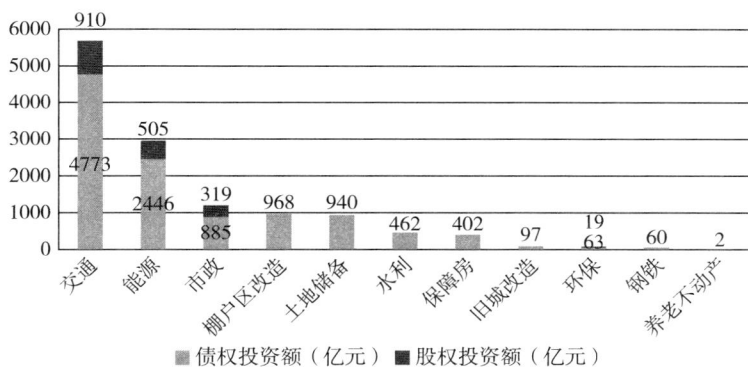

图7　险资基础设施投资领域投资金额分布

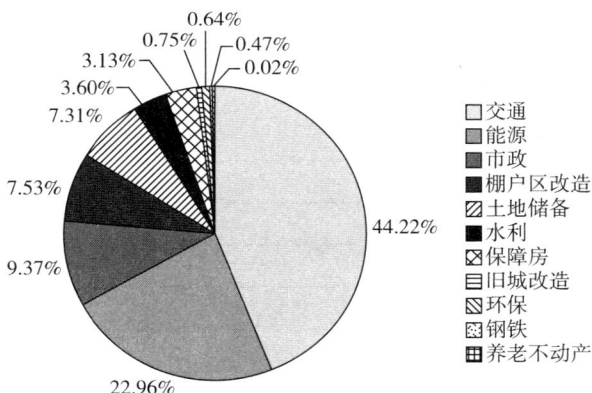

图8　险资基础设施投资领域比例分布

从变化轨迹看，起步阶段主要集中在交通，之后交通投资占比下降，由2009年的74%下降到2011年的20%；2012年起止跌且一直保持上升态势，2016年占56%。能源投资占比2011年达到39%，从2012年起逐步下滑，2016年占14%。2011年开始市政投资，占比温和上升，2016年达到11%。其他投资占比在2013年前波动较大，2014年至今稳定在20%左右。

从投资行业分布看，投资项目数量和投资额最多的是公路、电力、铁路、煤炭、城市轨道交通等交通和能源领域，五个行业合计投资数量249个，投资额6714亿元。截至2016年底，公路累计投资额为2847亿元，占22.2%；电力1500亿元，占11.7%（其中清洁能源发电626亿元，占4.9%）；铁路1012亿元，占7.9%；煤炭838亿元，占6.5%，城市轨道交通517亿元，占4.0%。

2. 投资区域

四大区域中，险资基础设施投资主要集中于东部地区，截至2016年底，在东部地区累计投资183个项目，投资额累计为5505亿元，分别占投资项目和投资额的41.9%和42.8%；在西部地区累计投资124个项目，投资额累计为2716亿元，分别占投资项目和投资额的28.4%和21.1%；在中部地区累计投资87个项目，投资额累计为1939亿元，分别占投资项目和投资额的19.9%和15.1%；在东北地区的投资项目极少，过去10年仅累计投资9个项目，投资额累计仅为169亿元，分别占投资项目和投资额的2.1%和1.3%（参见图9、图10）。

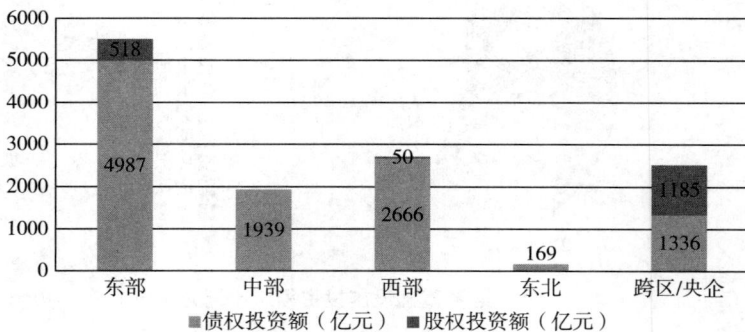

图9 险资基础设施投资额的区域分布

注：对于债权投资计划，跨区包括两种形式：一是单个项目跨地域；二是同一个投资计划内有多个项目且分布在不同区域。对于股权投资计划，先按央企和地方企业划分，然后对地方企业按地域区分。

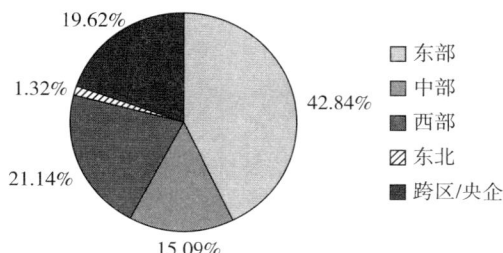

图10　险资投资基础设施的区域分布（按投资额计算）

　　从变化趋势看，2009年后对东部投资呈占比下降趋势，逐步向中西部倾斜。2013年以来这一趋势更显明显，中西部投资占比由2013年的36%提高到2016年的57%，同期东部投资占比则由60%下降到30%。

　　此外，债权投资计划还包括一些跨区域的项目，截至2016年底，累计跨区域债权投资项目共26个，投资金额为1336亿元。而股权投资计划中很大一部分投给了央企，截至2016年底，累计对央企股权投资项目共8个，投资金额为1185亿元。

3. 投资方式

　　险资投资基础设施主要有债权和股权投资两种方式（参见表2和图11）。

表2　　　　　　　　　　险资投资基础设施的方式

年份	债权投资项目数（个）	债权投资额（亿元）	股权投资项目数（个）	股权投资额（亿元）
2007	6	203		
2008	4	144	1	160
2009	7	230		
2010	10	243		
2011	29	845		
2012	37	1246		
2013	77	2626	1	360
2014	120	2583	7	405
2015	53	1272	2	409
2016	74	1706	9	419
合计	417	11098	20	1753

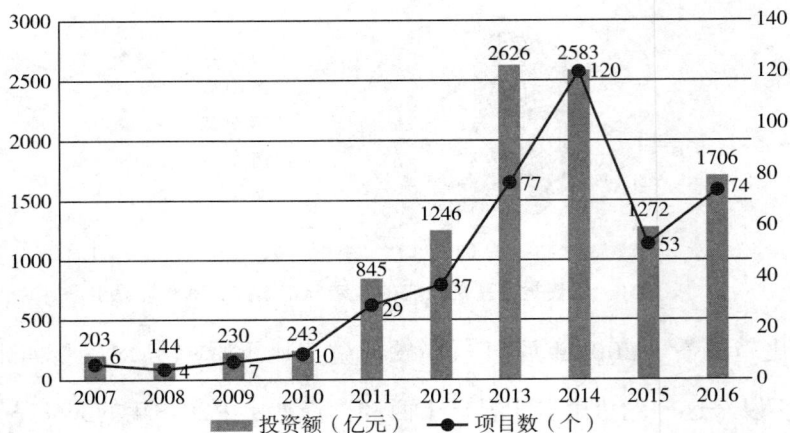

图11　债权投资计划投资基础设施情况

其中，险资投资基础设施以债权计划为主，截至2016年底，累计债权投资417个项目，投资金额合计为11098亿元，分别占投资项目和投资额的95.4%和86.4%（参见图13、图14）。

截至2016年底，累计股权投资20个项目，投资金额合计为1753亿元（参见图12），分别占投资项目和投资额的4.6%和13.6%（参见图13、图14）。其中，绝大多数股权投资为明股实债，真正意义的纯股权投资仅3项①，投资额仅为305亿元，分别仅占投资项目和投资额的0.7%和2.4%。

从时间分布看，2013年之前除京沪高铁外，没有其他的股权投资项目。2013年之后，明股实债开始兴起，2016年达到9项，投资额为419亿元。

股权投资计划的分布结构表现出如下几个特点。

一是以明股实债为主。截至2016年底共17个，累计投资1448亿元，分别占股权投资计划数量和投资额的85%和83%。纯股权投资计划仅3项，合计305亿元，分别仅占股权投资计划数量和投资额的15%和17%。

二是企业型股权投资计划的数量相对较少但单体投资较大，基金型股权投资计划的数量较多但单体投资较小。截至2016年底，企业型股权投资计划共6

---

①　3项纯股权投资分别为：京沪高铁160亿元、人保资产投中石化销售公司94.9亿元以及长江养老投中石化销售公司50亿元。

个，合计1049亿元，分别占股权投资计划数量和投资额的30%和60%，平均每个投资额175亿元。与之相比较，基金型股权投资计划的投资额较低。截至2016年底，基金型股权投资计划共14个，合计704亿元，分别占股权投资计划数量和投资额的70%和40%，平均每个投资额50亿元。

三是股权投资计划主要集中在交通、市政、能源领域。其中，以交通最多，共9项计978亿元，分别占股权投资计划数量和投资额的45%和56%，平均每个投资额109亿元；市政共6项计251亿元，分别占股权投资计划数量和投资额的30%和14%，平均每个投资额42亿元；能源数量不多，但单体投资较大，共3项计505亿元，分别占股权投资计划数量和投资额的15%和29%，平均每个投资额168亿元；环保数量最少且单体投资最少，共2项计19亿元，分别占股权投资计划数量和投资额的10%和1%，平均每个投资额10亿元。

四是投资标的几乎都是央企或北京、上海、广东、江苏等东部发达省市的地方国企和政府主导基金。其中只有贵州铁路发展基金股权投资计划除外。

五是有7家保险资管机构发行过股权投资计划，其中以人保系（其中含人保资产和人保资本）数量最多，共8个计415亿元，分别占股权投资计划数量和投资额的40%和24%；泰康投资额最大，共2个计480亿元，分别占股权投资计划数量和投资额的10%和27%；中保投仅1个，但单体投资额最大，为400亿元。

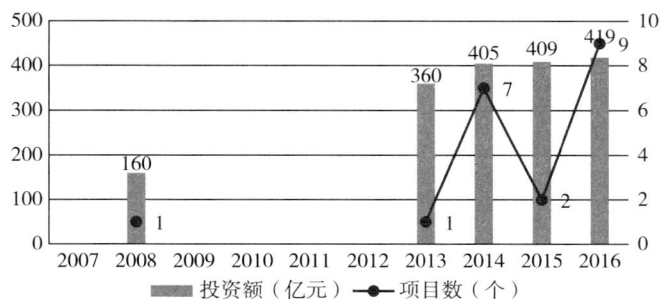

图12　股权投资计划投资基础设施情况

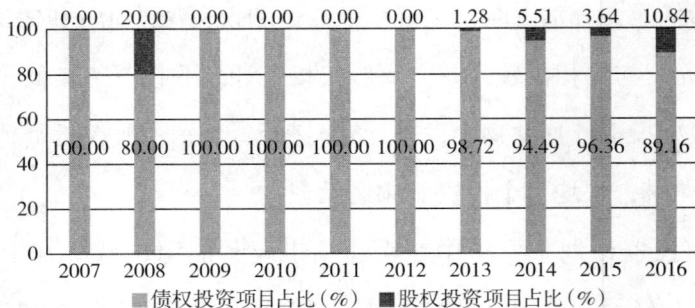

图13　险资投资基础设施不同方式占比（按项目数计算）

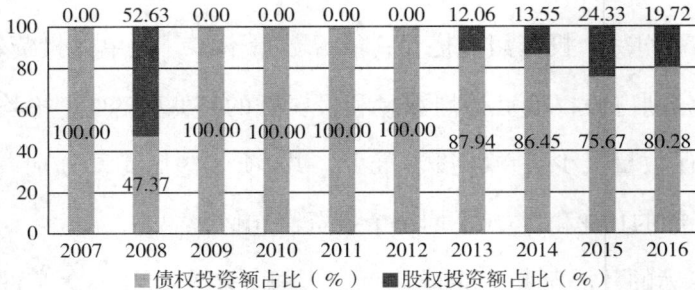

图14　险资投资基础设施不同方式占比（按投资额计算）

4. 债权计划增信状况

根据《基础设施债权投资计划管理暂行规定》（保监发〔2012〕92号），专业管理机构设立债权投资计划，应当确定有效的信用增级，并符合下列要求：（一）信用增级方式与偿债主体还款来源相互独立。（二）信用增级采用以下方式或其组合：第一，A类增级方式：国家专项基金、政策性银行、上一年度信用评级AA级以上（含AA级）的国有商业银行或者股份制商业银行，提供本息全额无条件不可撤销连带责任保证担保。上述银行省级分行担保的，应当提供总行授权担保的法律文件，并说明其担保限额和已提供担保额度。

第二，B类增级方式：在中国境内依法注册成立的企业（公司），提供本息全额无条件不可撤销连带责任保证担保，并满足下列条件：①担保人信用评级不低于偿债主体信用评级；②债权投资计划发行规模不超过20亿元的，担保人上年末净资产不低于60亿元；发行规模大于20亿元且不超过30亿元的，担保人上年末净资产不低于100亿元；发行规模大于30亿元的，担保人上年末净资产不低于150亿元；③同一担保人全部担保金额，占其净资产的比例不超过50%。全部担保金额和净资产，依据担保主体提供担保的资产范围计算确定；④偿债主体母公司或实际控制人提供担保的，担保人净资产不低于偿债主体净资产的1.5倍；⑤担保行为履行全部合法程序。

第三，C类增级方式：以流动性较高、公允价值不低于债务价值2倍，且具有完全处置权的上市公司无限售流通股份提供质押担保，或者以依法可以转让的收费权提供质押担保，或者以依法有权处分且未有任何他项权利附着的、具有增值潜力且易于变现的实物资产提供抵押担保。质押担保应当办理出质登记，抵押担保办理抵押物登记，且抵押权顺位排序第一，抵押物价值不低于债务价值的2倍。抵质押资产的公允价值，应当由具有最高专业资质的评估机构评定，且每年复评不少于一次。抵质押资产价值下降或发生变现风险，影响债权投资计划财产安全的，专业管理机构应当及时采取启动止损机制、增加担保主体或追加合法足值抵质押品等措施，确保担保足额有效。

债权投资计划同时符合下列条件的，可免于信用增级：（一）偿债主体最近两个会计年度净资产不低于300亿元、年营业收入不低于500亿元，且符合《管理办法》和本规定要求；（二）偿债主体最近两年发行过无担保债券，其主体及所发行债券信用评级均为AAA级；（三）发行规模不超过30亿元。

2017年，中国保监会发布《关于债权投资计划投资重大工程有关事项的通知》（保监资金〔2017〕135号），提出为支持保险资金投资关系国计民生的重大工程，进一步服务实体经济，债权投资计划投资经国务院或国务院投资主管部门核准的重大工程，且偿债主体具有AAA级长期信用级别的，可免于信用增级。

可见，除了对国家信用支持的重大工程以及资质要求很高的偿债主体等少数项目外，要求以A、B、C三种方式之一或其组合提供担保。简单地说，A类增信是银行提供担保，B类增信是企业提供担保，C类增信是抵质押担保，各类增信对提供担保的主体或抵押资产都有较高的要求。截至2016年底累计债券投资计划中，免增信项目51个，投资额为2169亿元，分别占项目数量和投资总额的12.38%和20.27%；A类增信项目159个，投资额为3180亿元，分别占项目数量和投资总额的38.59%和29.71%；B类增信项目174个，投资额为4060亿元，分别占项目数量和投资总额的42.23%和37.94%；C类增信项目28个，投资额为1293亿元，分别占项目数量和投资总额的6.80%和12.08%。可见，约80%的项目采用A类和B类增信，投资额约占70%（参见图15、图16、图17）。

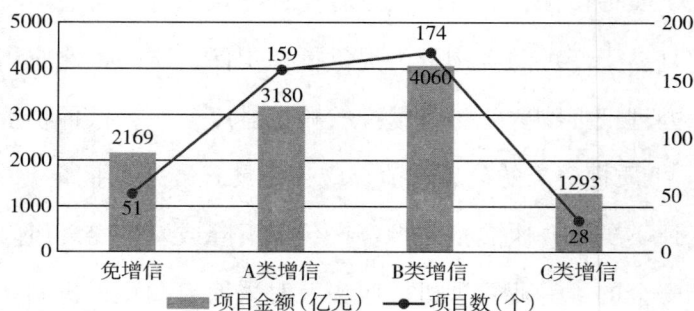

图15　险资基础设施投资的增信方式

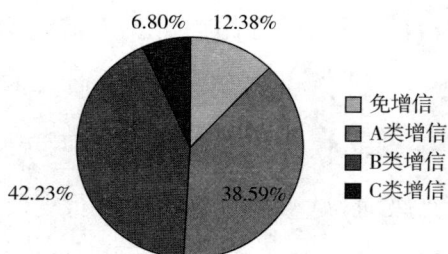

图16　险资基础设施投资项目中不同增信方式占比

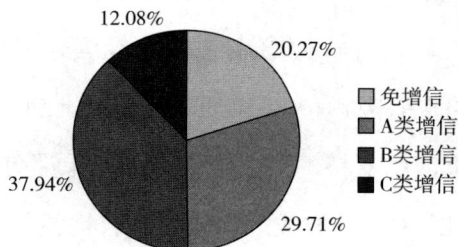

图17　险资基础设施投资金额中不同增信方式占比

从走势看，2010～2014年A类增信占比持续上升，B类增信占比则下降。进入2015年之后情况出现逆转，受与银行跨行同业竞争加剧等因素影响，期望让银行提供担保变得越来越困难，A类增信随之减少，依靠企业提供担保的B类增信增加。其间，A类增信占比由2014年的51%下降到2016年的23%，B类增信占比则由2014年的28%提高到2016年的55%，成为最主要的增信方式。另外，C类增信"门槛"标准较高，且在实施时还由于保险资管机构不被视为金融机构而使有关政策难以落实，因此占比相对较小。

近年来，免增信项目呈上升趋势，2016年占比达到19%。2017年颁布的《中国保监会关于债权投资计划投资重大工程有关事项的通知》（保监资金〔2017〕135号）规定，债权投资计划投资经国务院或国务院投资主管部门核准的重大工程，且偿债主体具有AAA级长期信用级别的，可免于信用增级。随着该通知的实施，免增信项目进一步增加。

5. 融资主体

截至2016年底，累计417个债权投资项目中，偿债主体为政府部门的17个（中央5个，省级12个），政府融资平台的251个（省级130个，地市级112个，县级9个），国有企业及其子公司的147个（央企85个，地方国企62个），民营企业的2个（参见图18）[①]，分别占比4.1%、60.2%、35.3%和0.5%。可见，融资主体主要是政府融资平台和国有企业及其子公司。在2014年以前融资主体主要为地方融资平台。2014年，《国务院关于加强地方政府性债务管理的意见（国发〔2014〕43号）颁布后，地方投融资平台的债务融资受到很多限制，其作为偿债主体的项目所占比例随之减少，由2014年的72.5%下降到2016年底的58.1%（项目数量从81个下降为38个），企业类融资主体的项目则由2014年

---

① 2013年平安投资内蒙古伊泰煤炭股份公司30亿元，2016年光大永明投资三浦威特园区发展公司（属华夏幸福子公司）10亿元。

的27.5%提高到2016年的41.9%。且政府类融资主体（含政府部门和政府融资平台）位阶逐步向下转移。政府部门2012年之前均为中央，2013年后均为省级；政府融资平台2013年前均为省级，2014年后地市级成为主力，县级也有逐步增多的趋势。

（个）

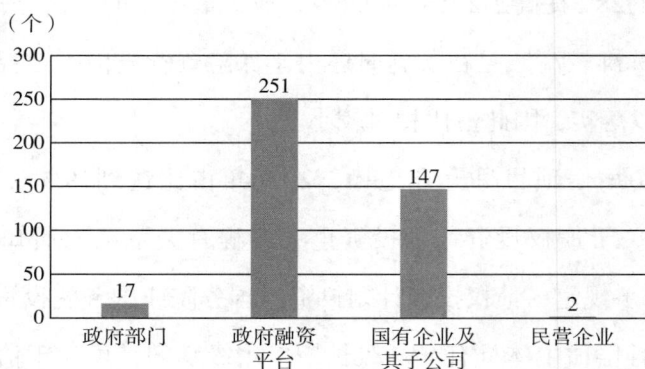

图18　不同融资主体的项目数

6. 投资主体

近年来保险资管快速发展，已形成较为完备的保险资管主体体系。2017年7月底，各类保险资管主体超过200家，包括24家综合保险资管机构，13家专业性资管机构，7家养老金管理公司，1家财富管理公司，11家香港保险资管子公司，10家保险私募基金，10家保险系证券投资基金公司，以及173家保险公司内部资产管理中心或部门。

截至2016年底，共有26家保险资管主体投资基础设施。居前八位的累计投资349个项目共10243亿元，项目数和投资额均占约80%。其中平安资产投资92项，共3078亿元，分别占项目数量和投资额的21%和24%。在股权投资中，人保系主体最多，共投资8个项目，共415亿元，分别占股权投资项目数量和投资额的40%和23.7%（参见图19）。

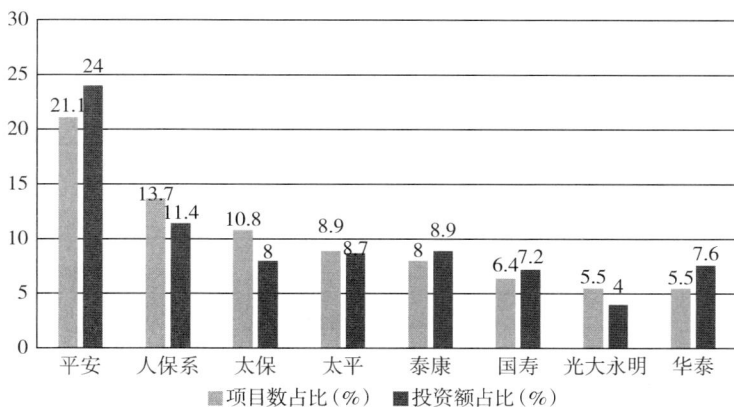

图19　险资基础设施投资前八位的投资主体

注：数据为截至2016年底累计投资项目。人保系包括人保资产和人保资本。

7. 单体投资规模

截至2016年底，累计投资项目单体平均投资29.4亿元。2014年项目数大幅增加，但当年投资额与2013年基本持平，单体投资额随之下降。2016年单体投资额25.6亿元，与2015年相比，项目数增加了28个，而单体投资额下降了5亿元（参见图20）。

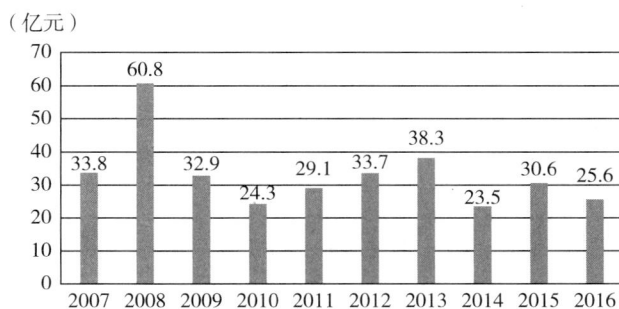

图20　险资基础设施投资单体投资额

单体平均投资额在不同的投资领域、地域以及投资方式中有所差异。截至2016年底的累计投资项目中，交通领域单体平均投资33.8亿元，能源领域24.8亿元，市政领域22.7亿元。从地域看，东部单体平均投资30.1亿元，中部为22.3亿元，西部为21.7亿元，东北为18.7亿元，跨地区债权或对央企股权的单体投资最大为74.1亿元。从投资方式看，债权单体投资平均为26.6亿元，股权投资远高于债权，为87.6亿元。在股权投资项目中，3个纯股权单体投资额为101.6亿元，17个明股实债为85.2亿元。

8. 投资期限和收益率

截至2016年底，累计417个债权投资项目投资期限平均为7.3年，平均收益率为6.48%。从债权主要投资行业看，投资期限与收益率相差不大。其中煤炭行业收益率最高，为6.68%，投资期限平均为7.1年；铁路行业平均收益率最低，为6.30%，投资期限为8.3年（参见图21）。

另外，17个明股实债项目平均投资期限为8.4年，平均收益率为6.66%。与债权投资计划相比，期限长1.1年，收益率高18个bp。除泰康资产的中石油西部管道的期限长为20年外，其余均为5~10年。

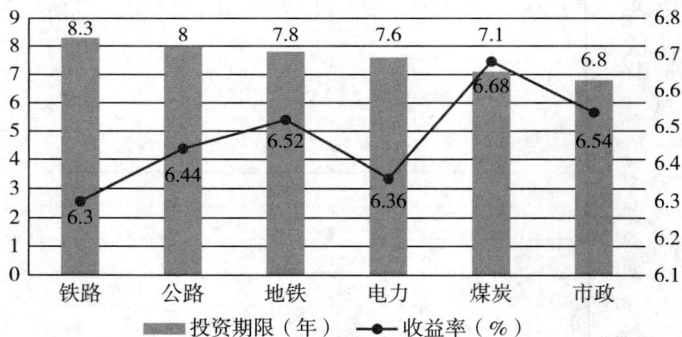

图21　险资债权主要投资行业的投资期限与收益率

2007~2016年，险资基础设施收益率在5.7%~7.3%小幅波动，10年平均为6.5%，与同期保险资金运用整体收益率相比，平均水平要高0.8个百分点，且波动幅度小得多（参见图22）。

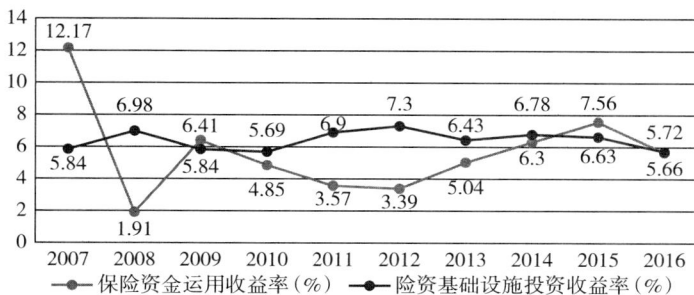

图22　保险资金整体运用收益率与险资基础设施投资收益率比较

（三）寿险资金有望成为"一带一路"基础设施建设资金的重要提供者

1. "一带一路"建设给寿险资金全球化配置带来机遇

首先，"一带一路"基础设施建设融资需求巨大。 "一带一路"建设旨在加强丝绸之路沿线国家的互通互联。这可以帮助各国应对落后的物质性和社会性基础设施挑战，推动经济全球化进程，促进全球增长，创造大量的就业，助推世界经济可持续发展。基础设施互联互通是"一带一路"建设优先领域。许多"一带一路"沿线国家与地区的物质性与社会性基础设施的建设滞后于发展的需要，不同程度面临融资的困难，迫切需要金融的支持。

根据国务院发展研究中心"'一带一路'设施联通研究"课题组的估算，2016～2020年"一带一路"沿线64个国家基础设施合意投资需求至少在10.6万亿美元以上。此外，考虑到"一带一路"建设的开放性，目前已有140多个国家和80多个国际组织积极支持和参与"一带一路"建设，其基础设施投资需求将进一步上升。满足如此巨额的投资，仅依靠本地区内部的金融资源远远不够，必须在充分利用内部金融资源的基础上，整合全球可获得的融资渠道。

其次，寿险资金是"一带一路"基础设施建设的重要金融资源。 对于"一带一路"基础设施建设而言，可以利用的资金主要包括沿线国家内部的金融资源、沿线国家之间的金融资源互通以及国际金融资源。寿险资金则是"一带一路"基础设施建设的重要金融资源。首先，"一带一路"沿线国家寿险资金是各国内部金融资源的重要组成部分，是其发展国内基础设施的重要资金来源。其次，"一带一路"沿线国家寿险资金是各国之间金融资源互通的重要参与者，为金融资源的互通与整合以及实现整个区域的设施联通提供了良好的资金基础。最后，大型寿险公司，尤其是跨国寿险集团是国际金融资源的重要提供者。这些机构投资者可以主要成为"一带一路"基础设施项目的财务投资者，寻求通过早期参与项目，实现资金的合理回报。

最后，"一带一路"为寿险资金全球化配置带来机遇。多元化、国际化保险资产配置是寿险资金运用发展的重要方向。"一带一路"为各国保险资金境外投资提供了新的路径。寿险公司可以借助"一带一路"建设拓展保险境外投资业务，利用大量基础设施建设融资带来的投资机遇，在更广阔的空间、更多的投资机会中进行投资资产组合配置，分散投资风险，获取更稳定的投资收益。

2. 中国寿险资金参与"一带一路"建设的现状

在政策的引导和支持下，中国保险资金（主要是寿险资金）积极参与长周期、大规模的"一带一路"基础设施项目。一方面，支持中国境内"一带一路"重点区域的道路、港口、油气管道、通信等重点项目和沿线省份的园区建设，如连霍国道主线、糯扎渡水电站、贵阳轨道交通和西安保税区基础设施等重点项目。另一方面，积极稳妥参与境外交通、能源管道等基础设施建设，探索投资境外油气产业园和中外产业合作基地。在中蒙俄经济走廊、中巴经济走廊能源合作及中哈产能和投资合作等重大项目中，保险资金都在积极参与、主动发挥作用。

截至2017年底，中国保险资金支持"一带一路"建设投资规模达8568.26亿元人民币（其中绝大部分为寿险资金）。此外，成立总规模3000亿元的中国保险投资基金，主要投向包括"一带一路"在内的国家战略项目。中国保险投资基金不仅有利于创新保险资金运用方式，提高资金的运作效率，也通过构建行业投资平台，更好地推动了保险资金有序集中服务"一带一路"的建设，开展重大基础设施项目投资。

（四）寿险资金不断拓展支持实体经济新领域

近年来，寿险资金不断拓展支持实体经济的新兴领域，如参与不良资产处置。保险机构作为重要的长期资金提供方，在有效防范风险的前提下审慎参与不良资产市场化处置，既可以缓解长期保险资金的配置压力，又可以促进保险资金更好地服务实体经济。

1. 保险机构参与不良资产处置具有期限匹配的优势

保险机构（尤其是寿险公司）的负债期限较长，这使得保险资金期限较长，与不良资产处置业务周期较长的特点较为匹配，具有匹配不良资产跨周期处置的优势。

不良资产处置具有跨周期的属性，即在经济下行时不良资产供给增加，也是不良资产投资的建仓期，随着经济复苏，不良资产估值上升，投资人可获取跨周期溢价。保险公司，尤其是寿险公司长期负债形成的长期属性的资金与不良资产处置业务周期较长的特点较为匹配。因此，寿险资金的长期性优势使其在不良资产处置中具有相当的潜在优势，能为不良资产的跨周期处置提供长期稳定的资金保障。寿险资金以长期投资为主，可以成为不良资产处置市场中重要的机构投资者之一，秉承长期投资、价值投资、稳健投资的投资理念，成为不良资产处置市场中的重要资金提供方。同时，不良资产处置业务的跨周期特征也有利于缓解长期保险资金的配置压力，有利于保险资金更好地服务实体经济。

2. 保险机构参与不良资产处置的路径

近年来，在政策的引导下，保险机构主要以间接和直接两种路径参与不良资产处置（参见表3），正逐渐成为不良资产处置市场的重要主体。

表3　　　　　　　　　　保险机构参与不良资产处置的路径与方式

参与路径	具体参与方式
间接	投资资管、信托等金融机构发行的不良资产证券化产品
	以有限合伙的形式投资不良资产私募股权基金
	设立或入股地方资产管理公司
直接	保险机构发行债权投资计划包
	设立债转股实施机构
	设立专项债转股基金
	直接收购不良资产

资料来源：曹德云：《保险机构可布局不良资产处置领域》，在"2017年中国金融论坛"的演讲，2017年6月8日。

险资以间接的路径参与不良资产业务处置，包括三种方式。

一是投资资管、信托等金融机构发行的不良资产证券化产品。保险机构可以与专业的资产管理机构合作，投资以不良资产为基础资产的金融产品。投资不良资产证券化产品收益稳定、抵质押充足、资产质量好，有利于在降低投资风险的情况下获取相当的收益。目前保险机构作为投资者参与不良资产证券化尚存在一定的政策障碍，这种方式还没有实质性启动。

二是以有限合伙的形式投资不良资产私募股权基金。不良资产处置业务对投资管理团队的专业度有着较高的要求，险资可以与资深资产管理人合作，作为有限合伙人投资不良资产私募股权基金。如国寿集团作为有限合伙人投资广州鑫汇产业投资基金合伙企业，参与收购招商银行不良资产包。保险机构投资不良资产私募股权基金，一方面可以利用专业投资管理人在信息获取、估值定价、行业研究及法律运用等方面的综合能力，使险资通过外部力量获取不良资产投资收益；另一方面可以以产业链整合为目标，寻找保险机构上下游产业链上的特定投资机会，更好地整合资源，实现协同效应。

三是设立或入股地方资产管理公司。截至2017年底，国内不良资产管理机构包括4大国有资产管理公司、地方资产管理公司以及民营非持牌资产管理公司等，持牌机构数量超过60家，非持牌机构达200多家。特别是2016年10月银监会发函允许地方增设资产管理公司后，不良资产处置机构的牌照持有受到广泛关注。目前地方资产管理公司已获得了四大国有资产管理公司最基本的处置功能，能够发挥积极作用并具备地方资源获取的比较优势。险资设立或入股地方资产管理公司是其参与不良资产市场的重要路径。近年来，幸福人寿、中国平安先后参与投资多家地方资产管理公司。保险机构与地方合作，设立或入股地方资产管理公司，可以更容易获取不良资产业的资源，同时还可以利用地方资产管理公司的专业团队参与不良债务处置市场。

保险机构直接参与不良资产处置的方式包括：

一是保险资产管理机构可探索资产支持计划。保险资管机构可探索以不良贷款、非银金融机构不良资产以及企业应收账款坏账为基础资产的资产支持计划，以活跃资产支持计划业务，把握不良资产处置的直接机会。

二是探索债转股相关业务。保险资产管理机构发挥比较优势，探索进入债转股市场。

三是保险机构直接收购不良资产包进行处置。保险机构直接收购不良资产包进行处置需要内部有专业的投资管理团队，具备不良资产处置全流程的业务能力。相比而言，此种方式难度较大，对公司的要求更高。

险资直接参与不良资产处置目前主要体现为保险机构参与债转股。目前保险机构整体上对于债转股非常审慎，主要是中国人寿资产管理公司实施了五个债转股项目。截至2017年底，国寿共实施川气东送公司、陕煤集团、中国重工、中国华能和黄河基金等五单债转股项目，总规模为500亿元。

五、寿险资金支持实体经济取得积极成效

我国寿险资金通过投资国家重大项目、支持地方经济发展和助力民生工程建设等方式支持实体经发展，取得了积极的成效，包括主动服务国家供给侧结构性改革、积极支持"一带一路"倡议和国家区域发展战略、积极参与PPP项目和重大工程建设、支持军民融合发展和制造业转型升级。

（一）主动服务国家供给侧结构性改革

近年来，保险监管部门积极引导保险资金服务供给侧结构性改革。围绕供给侧结构性改革和"去产能、去库存、去杠杆、降成本、补短板"五大重点任务，积极发挥保险资金融通和引导作用。支持保险资产管理机构发起设立去产能并购重组基金，促进钢铁、煤炭等行业加快转型发展和实现脱困升级。支持保险资金发起设立债转股实施机构，开展市场化债转股业务。支持保险资产管理机构开展不良资产处置等特殊机会投资业务、发起设立专项债转股基金等。截至2017年8月末，累计注册永续债14项，规模达808亿元。目前，保险资金参与了陕西煤业化工集团有限责任公司100亿元债转股项目，中船重工20亿元债转股项目。

（二）积极支持"一带一路"倡议

近年来，在监管部门的政策引导下，保险机构发挥保险资金长期稳定优势，积极参与长周期、大规模的"一带一路"基础设施项目。保险资金是支持实体经济发展的重要力量，具有长期性、稳定性的特点，与"一带一路"基础设施建设项目资金需求大、建设周期长、收益稳定的特点非常匹配。保险资金服务"一带一路"，可以通过债权、股权、股债结合、股权投资计划、资产支持计划和私募基金等方式，以及通过投资亚洲基础设施投资银行、丝路基金和

其他金融机构推出的金融产品等途径，直接或间接投资"一带一路"重大投资项目，促进共同发展、共同繁荣。一方面，支持境内"一带一路"重点区域的道路、港口、油气管道、通信等重点项目和沿线省份的园区建设，如连霍国道主线、糯扎渡水电站、贵阳轨道交通和西安保税区基础设施等重点项目。另一方面，积极稳妥参与境外交通、能源管道等基础设施建设，探索投资境外油气产业园和中外产业合作基地。为了支持"一带一路"建设，保险监管部门推动保险机构不断提升境外投资能力，支持保险资金参与"一带一路"沿线国家和地区的重大基础设施、重要资源开发、关键产业合作和金融合作。支持保险资金为"一带一路"框架内的经贸合作和双边、多边的互联互通提供投融资支持，通过股权、债权、股债结合、基金等形式为大型投资项目提供长期资金支撑。鼓励中资保险机构"走出去"，在"一带一路"沿线国家或地区布局，为"一带一路"建设提供保险保障服务。

（三）积极支持国家区域发展战略

近年来，监管部门鼓励保险资金服务京津冀协同发展、长江经济带以及西部开发、东北振兴、中部崛起、东部率先等区域发展。支持保险资金对接国家自贸区建设和粤港澳大湾区等城市群发展的重点项目和工程。积极引导和支持保险资金参与雄安新区建设，探索新的投融资机制，对于新区的交通基础设施、水利、生态、能源、公共服务等重大项目给予长期资金支持。截至2017年底，保险资金支持支持长江经济带和京津冀协同发展战略投资规模分别达3652.48亿元和1567.99亿元；支持清洁能源、资源节约与污染防治等绿色产业规模达6676.35亿元。

（四）积极参与PPP项目和重大工程建设

近年来，保险监管部门推进保险资金参与PPP项目和重大工程建设。支持符合条件的保险资产管理公司等专业管理机构，作为受托人发起设立基础设施投资计划，募集保险资金投资符合条件的PPP项目。在风险可控的前提下，调整PPP项目公司提供融资的主体资质、信用增级等监管要求，推动PPP项目融资模式创新。鼓励保险资金投资关系国计民生的各类基础设施项目和民生工程，逐步完善投资计划监管标准，放宽信用增级要求和担保主体范围，扩大免增信融资主体数量，创新交易结构，精准支持对宏观经济和区域经济具有重要带动作用的重点项目和工程。

近年来，保险监管部门陆续印发《关于保险资金投资政府和社会资本合作项目有关事项的通知》《关于债权计划投资重大工程有关事项的通知》等系列配套文件，从技术细节上明确了具体支持政策，如优化投资渠道、投资方式、主体资质、信用增级等方面的监管要求。截至2017年底，累计发起设立债权投资计划和股权投资计划843项，合计备案（注册）规模20754.14亿元。

（五）支持军民融合发展和制造业转型升级

近年来，保险监管部门鼓励保险资金服务军民融合发展，积极探索保险资金参与军工产融合作模式，支持保险机构和军工企业共同发起设立保险军民融合发展基金。如人保资产–中国航天军民融合发展基金股权投资计划（一期），规模50亿元。同时，鼓励保险资产管理机构发起设立支持制造业创新发展、兼并重组和转型升级的债权计划、股权计划和股权投资基金等金融产品，更好服务制造业转型升级。如华泰–中国商飞债权投资计划，规模150亿元，支持我国大飞机建设项目。

第三章 寿险资金支持实体经济的挑战、风险与政策障碍

寿险资金支持实体经济面临的挑战包括：寿险发展不充分以及发展方式转型不到位不利于寿险资金支持实体经济，不规范行为弱化了寿险资金支持实体经济的效果，寿险资金对民营企业支持偏弱不利于转变经济发展方式。寿险资金支持实体经济中存在资产负债不匹配风险、信用风险、跨市场跨领域风险、增加地方政府隐性债务等风险。另外，寿险资金在参与"一带一路"以及参与不良资产处置等新兴领域投资中还存在新的风险。寿险资金支持实体经济尚存在一些政策障碍，包括基础设施债权计划相关的管理规则有待完善，保险资金投资股权的范围有待进一步放开，不动产抵押登记的政策有待完善，投资养老健康产业的政策有待完善，参与PPP存在制约因素，参与不良资产处置的政策环境有待完善，以及另类投资的流动性对冲机制有待健全。

一、寿险资金支持实体经济面临的挑战

（一）寿险发展不充分不利于寿险资金支持实体经济

我国寿险业尚发展不足，2017年末，保险业资产总量16.75万亿元（其中寿险公司总资产13.21万亿元，约占保险业资产总量的79%）（参见图1），保险

资产约占银行业金融机构资产的6.6%（参见图2），在金融业资产中的比重相对较低，远远低于2016年29个经济体保险业资产占银行业资产的比例（平均为21.3%）（参见图3），这意味着保险业，尤其是寿险业在金融资产中所占的比例有待进一步提升。

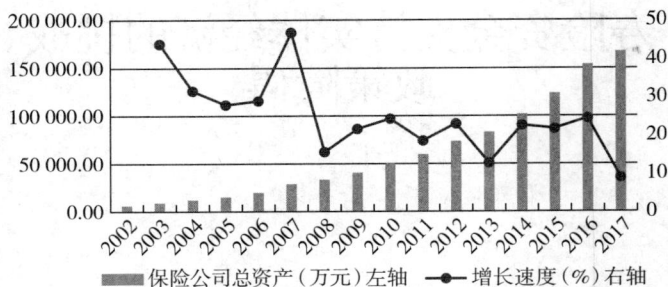

图1　我国保险公司总资产及其增长趋势

资料来源：Wind资讯、中国保监会。

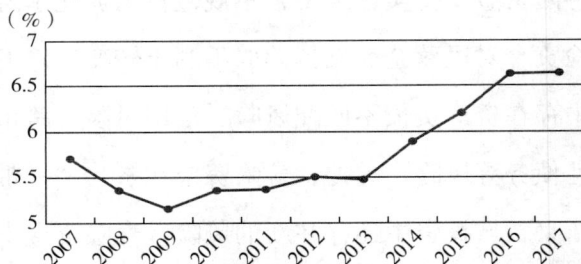

图2　近年来我国保险资产与银行业金融机构资产的比例

资料来源：Wind资讯、中国保监会、中国银监会。

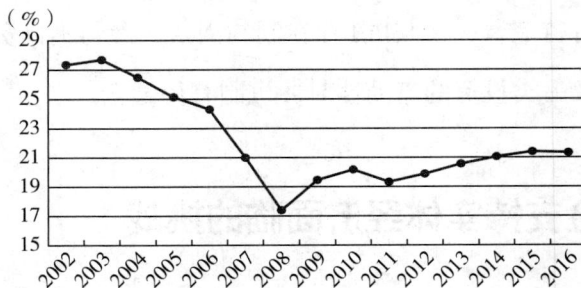

图3　29个经济体保险资产与银行业金融机构资产的比例

注：29个经济体包括阿根廷、澳大利亚、比利时、巴西、加拿大、开曼群岛、智利、中国、法国、德国、中国香港、印度、印度尼西亚、爱尔兰、意大利、日本、韩国、卢森堡、墨西哥、荷兰、俄罗斯、沙特阿拉伯、新加坡、南非、西班牙、瑞士、土耳其、英国、美国。

资料来源：各国国家资产负债表与其他数据；FSB计算。

同时，2017年，我国保险深度为4.42%，保险密度为2646元（参见图4）。与国际比较，我国保险业发展水平虽然高于新兴市场，但仍相对较低（参见表1）。保险深度和保险密度不仅低于全球平均水平，更是低于主要发达经济体的平均水平。

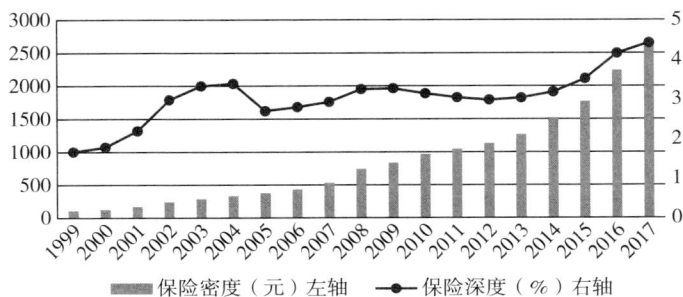

图4　我国保险密度、保险深度增长趋势（1999~2017）

资料来源：Wind资讯、中国保监会。

表1　　　　　　　　　　　　保险业发展水平的国际比较

	保险深度（%）	保险密度（美元）
全球	6.3	638
发达市场	8	3505
新兴市场	3.2	149
新兴市场（除中国外）	2.6	97
经合组织	7.5	2757
G7	7.9	3665
欧元区	7.3	2528
欧盟	7.4	2383
欧盟15国	7.9	2911
北美自贸区	7.1	3049
东盟	3.4	136
中国（2017年数据）	4.42	407

注：除中国外，其他为2016年数据。

资料来源：Swiss Re. World insurance in 2016: the China growth engine steams ahead. Sigma No.3,2017.

寿险资金是寿险业支持实体经济发展的基础。寿险业发展不充分不利于积聚期限长、稳定性高的资金，从而制约了寿险资金支持实体经济的广度和深度。

（二）寿险发展方式转型不到位不利于寿险资金支持实体经济

很长一段时间以来，寿险业以高负债成本争夺储蓄，倒逼高风险投资。高结算利率容易引发利差损风险，高渠道费用易产生费差损风险，这种发展模式不可持续。同时，理财为主的产品结构难以彰显寿险业的价值，难以形成行业核心竞争力。寿险投资活动主要基于负债活动展开，寿险转型不到位造成负债结构不合理，不利于寿险资金支持实体经济。

2017年以来，随着监管力度持续加强，以万能险产品为代表的中短存续期产品受到严格限制。受此影响，各大寿险公司纷纷调整保费结构，主要做法是提高保障型产品的原保费收入占比，压缩万能险与投连险等险种，拉长了承保端的久期，提高期交占比，由趸交业务向期交业务转型。具体表现为：一是相对于万能险和投资联结保险业务，普通寿险业务与分红险寿险业务的原保险保费收入增长更快。2017年，寿险公司普通寿险业务原保险保费收入12936.48亿元，同比增长23.77%，占寿险公司全部业务的49.68%，同比上升1.50个百分点；分红寿险业务原保险保费收入8403.20亿元，同比增长22.14%，占寿险公司全部业务的32.27%，同比上升0.56个百分点。

二是保户投资款和独立账户本年新增交费大幅下降。2017年，未计入保险合同核算的保户投资款和独立账户本年新增交费6362.78亿元，同比下降50.29%。

三是新单保费与新单期交保费大幅增加。2017年，寿险公司人身险业务新单原保险保费收入15355.12亿元，同比增长10.66%，占寿险公司全部业务的比例为58.97%。其中，新单期交原保险保费收入[1]5772.17亿元，同比增长35.71%，占新单原保险保费收入的37.59%。

四是新单期交保费的结构不断优化。在新单期交原保险保费收入[2]中，3

---

[1] 这里的新单期交原保险保费收入为财务数据。
[2] 这里的不同缴费期限的原保险保费收入为业务数据。

年期以下154.13亿元，占比2.60%，同比上升1.70个百分点；3至5年期1776.95亿元，占比29.93%，同比下降2.22个百分点；5至10年期918.90亿元，占比15.48%，同比上升0.49个百分点；10年期及以上3087.04亿元，占比52.00%，同比上升0.03个百分点。

最后，渠道结构进一步优化。业务的转型也带来了渠道结构的变化，突出表现是个人代理业务增长迅速，银邮代理业务增速下降。2017年，个人代理业务原保险保费收入13065.64亿元，同比增长30.43%，占寿险公司业务总量的50.18%，同比上升4.00个百分点；寿险公司银邮代理业务原保险保费收入10584.02亿元，同比增长10.53%，占寿险公司业务总量的40.65%，同比下降3.50个百分点（参见表2）。

表2　　　　　　　　　　2017年寿险公司各渠道业务情况表　　　　　　　单位：亿元、%

业务渠道	原保险保费收入	同比增长	占比	占比较去年同期增长（百分点）
银邮代理	10584.02	10.53	40.65	−3.50
个人代理	13065.64	30.43	50.18	4.00
公司直销	1751.89	8.43	6.73	−0.72
专业代理	179.65	48.64	0.69	0.13
其他兼业代理	274.11	15.09	1.05	−0.05
保险经纪	184.24	47.22	0.71	0.13
合计	26039.55	20.04	100.00	—

资料来源：中国保监会。

尽管寿险业转型取得了上述成绩，但整体来看转型仍然不到位，表现为以下几方面。

一是趸交保费的占比仍然较高。趸交保费虽然可以在短期内快速地提升保费收入规模，但可持续性差，在保费收入达到了一定的规模之后将面临继续增长的瓶颈。且一些保险公司大都通过银保渠道获取趸交保费，渠道受金融环境与政策的影响比较大，造成趸交保费的业务波动较大，从而不利于形成稳定的寿险资金。

二是产品结构仍然不合理。长期性、保障型产品发展仍然不足。特别是为死亡风险提供财务保障人寿保险、为病残风险提供财务保障的健康保险以及为长寿风险提供财务保障的养老年金险都有待发展。

三是渠道价值有待提升。对于银保渠道，银行与保险公司之间的合作层次浅，向期交、保障性业务的转型难度大。对于个险渠道，虽然代理人数量有大幅度的攀升，但人均产能与销售效率有待提高，销售行为有待规范。

寿险发展方式转型不到位，不利于积聚长期、稳定的寿险资金，从而不利于支持实体经济的发展。

（三）不规范行为弱化了寿险资金支持实体经济的效果

一是产品多层嵌套和监管套利问题弱化了对实体经济的支持。近年来，随着金融领域的不断创新，金融产品日趋复杂，杠杆高、嵌套多、投资链条长、交易不透明、监管套利等现象较为严重，这种情况已经蔓延到保险资金运用领域。部分保险资金通过投资信托、私募基金等产品违规开展多层嵌套、通道等业务，模糊资金真实流向，掩盖了风险真实状况。比如，有的保险机构将资金投向信托计划、银行理财等金融产品，再由信托、银行等将这些资金投向其他金融产品，增加了杠杆，减少了透明度，加大了风险，甚至部分机构自身发行的私募股权投资基金、股权投资计划等保险资管产品也不同程度地存在多层嵌套的现象，不仅存在较大的风险隐患，而且不符合去杠杆、消嵌套、挤泡沫的监管方向，从而弱化了寿险资金支持实体经济的效果。

《关于规范金融机构资产管理业务的指导意见》明确提出打破刚性兑付、规范资金池、消除多层嵌套，对非标资产明确禁止期限错配，有利于规范以各类保险资管产品为代表的非标资产投资，但资管新规也给非标资产和另类投资带来一定的挑战。在短期可能会造成保险资管产品规模的萎缩，通道业务和嵌套受限后各类型非标资产将出现明显收缩，保险资金投资非标资产的增速有可能出现下滑，从而对投资收益率负面影响可能较大。

二是非理性举牌与激进投资不利于寿险资金支持实体经济。近年来，由于万能险的发展出现异化、资本市场的相关规则有待完善以及金融跨界与联动带来一定的监管空白等原因，寿险资金在支持实体经济中出现了非理性举牌、与一致行动人非友好投资、非理性跨境跨领域大额投资和并购、激进经营和激进投资等问题，一定程度上弱化了对实体经济的支持。

（四）寿险投资的结构性问题不利于转变经济发展方式

截至2017年底，我国民营企业数量达2726.3万家，个体工商户6579.3万户，注册资本超过165万亿元，民营经济对国家财政收入的贡献占比超过50%；GDP、固定资产投资和对外直接投资占比均超过60%；技术创新和新产品占比超过70%；吸纳城镇就业超过了80%；对新增就业贡献的占比超过90%。因此，民营企业是转变经济发展方式的主体。但目前寿险资金的另类投资主要投向地方政府与相关的国有企业，对民营企业的支持偏弱，这显然不利于支持民营企业融资，从而不利于中国经济发展方式的转型。另外，目前寿险资金以债权型投资为主，股权型投资偏少，这种结构性问题也不利于转变经济发展方式。

二、寿险资金支持实体经济中的主要风险

（一）资产负债不匹配风险

一是负债端成本高企倒逼投资端提升风险偏好。近年来我国寿险负债端的成本不断提升，2017年以来，负债端融资成本尽管有所下降，但仍在5%以上，相对于优质安全资产可选择的资金供应渠道而言依然偏高，"资产荒"的情况仍然存在。在负债端保单成本高位和资产端优质资产难觅等因素的影响下，保险公司加大收益高、流动性低、期限长的投资，投资组合的市场风险和信用风

险有所增加。

二是期限不匹配。一方面，存在"长钱短配"现象。这主要体现为我国寿险长期资金的价值没有得到应有的体现。我国资本市场缺乏长期投资品种，长期资产配置难，长期寿险资金不得不被动配置短期限资产，牺牲了投资收益，增加了短期波动性。另一方面，也存在"短钱长配"现象。过去一段时间，部分中小寿险公司中短期保险理财产品规模大，业务结构单一、负债成本相对较高。为获取高收益，这些短期资金主要投向收益高、流动性低、期限较长的不动产、基础设施、信托等另类资产，"短钱长配"现象凸显。

三是流动性风险。负债端的业务结构调整或满期给付引发流动性告急和偿付能力不足等风险。自2016年以来，保监会加强对中短存续期产品的监管力度。这有利于抑制部分市场主体的短期行为，彰显保险的保障功能，但也使得部分寿险公司原来隐藏的现金流风险显性化。一方面，中短存续期产品面临退保和满期给付双重压力。2017年，寿险公司退保金6117.93亿元，同比增长37.25%。退保率6.52%，比去年同期增加0.92个百分点。同时，寿险业务给付金额4574.89亿元。退保和满期给付的增加带来大量的现金流出。另一方面，业务收入急速收缩，这使得之前依赖新单现金流入补足给付缺口的模式难以持续，造成一些公司面临较为严重的现金流风险压力。2017年行业经营活动产生的现金流量净额6330.75亿元，同比下降65.12%。在这种状况下，另类投资比例增加进一步加大了流动性风险。另类投资作为非标资产，流动性较差，交易不活跃，变现周期较长，加剧了一些公司面临的现金流不足的风险。

（二）信用风险

信用风险持续暴露使行业面临较大的风险隐患。近两年债券市场违约事件频发，在经济转型、去杠杆和打破刚性兑付背景下，保险资金运用面临的信用风险加大。近年来受到宏观经济下行、债券市场波动等影响，债券违约进入多发期，某些行业积累的信用风险开始显现。2016年共有35家企业的79只债券发生兑付危机，涉及资金398.9亿元，较2015年的117.1亿元大幅增加。2017年共有40只债券发生违约，涉及发行人共17家，违约金额合计188.20亿元，约为2016年债券违约规模的一半。从违约主体、债券数量以及违约金额来看，2017年债券市场信用风险的暴露频率均低于2016年的水平。在金融监管趋严的大环境下，货币政策仍将维持稳健中性，企业整体的融资环境将继续维持偏紧格局。因此，2018年债券市场信用风险或较2017年整体抬升。同时，40%以上的信用债是地方政府债务，随着地方政府债务压力的上升，潜在的地方信用风险可能会释放。

在上述背景下，另类投资的信用风险加大。尽管寿险资金投资实体经济至今没有出现兑付危机，但信用风险已经开始显现。过去在信用扩张期，出现集中违约的可能性较低，未来信用扩张速度减慢后，由于非标产品的流动性较弱，集中违约的风险加大。

同时，寿险资金支持实体经济主要通过债权计划，非标产品结构日趋复杂，潜在信用风险增加，这也增加了保险资金运用行业整体面临的信用风险隐患。

信用违约风险增大会降低持仓信用产品的信用评级，从而增加最低资本要求，直接影响保险公司的当期损益和当期偿付能力。同时，国内市场上信用类产品流动性差，一旦出现信用风险，处置手段非常有限，目前来说，除了通过法律诉讼，没有其他降低损失的方法。因此，信用风险一旦爆发，对行业的影响较大。

（三）跨市场跨领域风险

随着保险资金参与金融市场和服务实体经济的广度、深度不断提升，股市、债市、汇市、利率等市场波动对保险资金影响增大，保险资金运用已经与经济金融风险深刻交织交融在一起，外部各类市场风险的冲击显著增强。特别是一些非标产品通过层层嵌套变相增加杠杆，保险资金购买这些产品可能存在底层资产模糊、突破资金运用监管比例或范围的情况，加剧了风险跨行业、跨市场的传递。

同时，由于金融产品由简变繁，交易环节缺乏透明度、投资链条延长，风险更加隐蔽。一些跨领域的投资行为，从局部看是合规的、风险可控的，但从整体看，风险跨产品、跨行业、跨监管传染叠加，风险识别应对难度加大。

（四）增加地方政府隐性债务风险

一些寿险资金的投资背后存在地方政府担保，变相增加了地方政府隐性债务风险。比如，一些股权计划中存在"明股实债"等不规范行为，一定程度上成为新增地方政府债务。原因在于，"名股实债"虽然从形式上看是投资人以股权的方式投资于被投资企业，但该业务在实际操作的过程中却蕴含着大量具有债权属性的条款约定。和一般的股权形式投资相比，"名股实债"可以获取预先约定的固定收益，且融资方一般承诺本金优先退出。而承诺方式一般有两种：一是设置明确的预期回报，且每年定期向投资人支付固定投资回报；二是约定到期、强制性由被投资企业或关联第三方赎回投资本金。"名股实债"可能使得数据失真，宏观的风险管理判断失真和措施着力点错位，在微观激励约束机制不尽合理，特别是有所软化的环境下，加剧债务不透明的过度积累，埋下风险隐患。

（五）境外投资的风险

寿险资金在参与"一带一路"基础设施建设过程中，存在一定的境外投资风险。对于基础设施投融资而言，首先要有可投的项目，然后才有融资及后续业务的开展。寿险资金参与"一带一路"建设的关键在于挖掘与培育优质项目。大部分寿险保单要求保险公司提供最低保证收益，这就决定了寿险资金必须投资于有良好发展预期、能带来稳定现金流的优质项目。现实中，"一带一路"沿线基础设施项目中的优质项目主要集中发展基础较好的国家和地区，而那些亟须通过改善基础设施挖掘发展潜力的国家和地区优质项目缺乏，受资金短缺的束缚较为严重。虽然这些国家和地区的基础设施潜在投资项目众多，但缺乏优质项目是无法回避的难题，这是寿险资金参与"一带一路"建设的最大挑战，具体包括以下三个方面。

首先，沿线国家的发展环境差异大。"一带一路"沿线国家和地区在政治制度、经济社会体制和发展程度、法律体系和政策体系、文化和宗教等方面均存在显著差异，由于透明度不足及语言多元的原因，外部资本在进入各国国内基础设施领域时往往心存疑虑，要花大量的精力和财力去了解东道国的投资环境。即便做了充分准备，在进入后也难以避免水土不服的问题。而且由于多方面的差异，国家之间协调的难度很大（个别跨境基础设施项目历时20多年仍没有得到有效协调），难以通过国家间的合作为外部资本的投资行为提供有效保障。这些问题与基础设施项目固有的投资规模大、回报周期长等问题叠加，进一步提升了吸引市场资金进入的难度。这些问题在经济不发达、政治不稳定、法制不健全的国家表现尤为明显。

第二，缺乏可靠稳定的盈利模式。基础设施投资的盈利主要来源于三个方面，一是使用者付费，二是在因基础设施改善提高的财政收入中安排资金进行支付，三是因基础设施改善带来的周边区域商业升值。第三种来源是中国发展基础设施的重要经验。这三种盈利模式都存在一定的风险。对于基础设施的建设方、运营方而言，使用者付费模式存在市场发展低于预期的经营风险。在经济欠发达地区，市场发展低于预期的可能性较大。财政资金支付模式则受制于东道国的整体财政能力。"一带一路"沿线很多国家均存在严重的财政赤字，债务违约风险较高。周边区域商业升值模式的风险在于东道国的土地制度，对于土地私有制的国家，周边土地并不一定能提供给基础设施建设运营方开发，第三方开发的收益也不一定会与其分享。现实中，"一带一路"沿线国家基础设施的债务违约率较高，有的国际咨询机构甚至将有些国家列入高风险债务人。

第三，**地缘政治风险较大**。"一带一路"沿线部分国家和地区具有独特的资源能源和区位，处于大国利益角逐的中心地带，政治经济形势十分复杂，国际形势特别是域外大国势必影响这些国家的政策。虽然"一带一路"沿线国家在改善基础设施、实现更好发展方面拥有共同的愿望，但并不排除其与其他利益集团之间也存在难以割舍的利益诉求（包括政治、军事、经济），从而给本地区基础设施建设带来不确定性，增加投资风险。

为解决上述问题，将规模庞大的基础设施投资需求变为真实的投资行为，参与"一带一路"基础设施建设的各类主体既要通过分析研究挖掘具有发展潜力的优质项目，更要在改善投资环境、提升域内基础设施项目对市场资金吸引力方面共同努力，形成"投资环境改善→优质项目增多→融资渠道拓宽→经济快速发展→投资环境进一步改善"的良性循环。

（六）拓展新兴领域的风险

寿险资金在拓展支持实体经济的新兴领域，也存在一定的风险。以参与不良资产处置为例，保险机构面临的潜在风险包括：一是不良资产处置方式自身可能带来的潜在风险；二是不良资产处置市场存在的问题诱发风险；三是保险机构风险防范与控制能力不足带来的风险。

首先，不良资产处置方式自身可能带来潜在风险。所有的不良资产处置方式本身是为了化解金融风险，但如果运用不当，则可能出现诱发甚至放大金融风险的"非意图后果"。以不良资产证券化为例，其目的是为了分散风险，以避免危机的爆发。但实际上，不良资产证券化是将单个银行的风险转化和分散为整个金融市场风险，相应债务工具转变为衍生产品工具，与实体经济的关联性下降。且资产证券化产品将资本市场和货币市场相结合，业务链条较长，涉及多个监管部门。如果在不良资产证券化发行过程中出现监管缺位或过度证券化，反而可能导致资产价格的泡沫和失真，继而引发更大系统性风险的爆发[1]。

债转股也是如此。其本意是降低企业杠杆率，促进企业更好发展。但债转股在实施过程中有可能被异化，并带来多方面的风险[2]。一是政策意图被扭曲的风险。如果企业把这次债转股误解成政策性"免费午餐"，期望政府对可能发生的损失兜底，就没有动力改善经营，可能还会强化原来不合理的产品和产业结构。二是债务重组后企业经营效益降低的风险。债转股本身只是调整了企业的资本结构，使债务比例降低、股权比例提高，而企业的资产结构和运营效率可能并不会发生质的变化。如果重组后企业不能有效运作资产、提高经营效益，不仅股东权益得不到保障，还会引发一系列经济风险。三是企业道德或社会信用风险。不适当的债转股容易变为企业的逃债途径，冲击"借债还钱"的市场信念。

其次，不良资产处置市场存在的问题处置不当会诱发风险。我国不良资产处置市场尚不健全，发展过程中存在着各种问题，从而构成保险机构参与不良资产处置的风险。以不良资产证券化为例，目前尚处于初期试点阶段，存在估值不准确、流动性较低、投资者群体及市场成熟度有待提高、法律机制不完善等问题。又比如，由于存在信息不对称、资本市场退出机制不完善，债转股同样存在项目筛选、转股企业的管理与运营以及从转股企业中退出等问题与风险。这些问题如果处理不好，也会导致风险的产生。

最后，保险机构防范与控制能力不足带来风险。保险机构此前的资金运

---

　　[1]　高蓓、张明："不良资产处置与不良资产证券化：国际经验及中国前景"，载于《国际经济评论》，2018年第1期。

　　[2]　余玉苗、刘国升："用债转股促进企业更好发展"，载于《人民日报》，2017年1月9日。

用范围不包括参与不良资产处置业务，因此，险资目前对于不良资产的风险识别、控制和管理能力相对有限。对于发展前景良好但遇到暂时困难的优质企业，银行可以通过展期贷款、以新还旧的方式来帮助企业渡过难关；而对于高负债企业的问题债务，投资风险可能偏高。此外，相对于新增债务，存量债务的信息不对称更为突出，涉及的法律关系也较为复杂。因此，不良资产处置的投资、法律、信用等风险较高①。具体来说，保险机构参与不良资产处置存在以下难题与风险：**一是在信息获取方面**，资产管理人对资产历史情况存在盲区、复杂的债权抵押物和担保关系使得尽调较难进行、银行没有动力分享信息等因素都会导致信息获取不对称。**二是在估值定价方面**，不良资产的特性不同于一般资产，即使是抵押物也会受到法律瑕疵和还款意愿等因素的影响，从而影响到资产估值、定价和买入，最终可能影响到利润空间。**三是在行业研究方面**，抵押物的价值受到经济、利率、行业的影响，因此对经济走势、不良贷款趋势、不动产价值的总体判断需要较高的研究水平，实际过程中还可能需要研究特定区域与特定行业。**四是在法律运用方面**，不良资产的法律关系一般较复杂，各地法制环境也不尽相同；运用法律手段处置不良资产流程较长、环节较多。因此，不良资产投资对法律运用也有着较高要求。

面对不良资产处置的上述诸多难题和风险，保险机构如果不能有效提高风险防范与控制能力，则将给自身带来风险。以债转股为例，拟实施债转股企业的主要诉求是增加权益资本、降低有息负债，进而降低企业的杠杆和利息负担，为转型发展奠定基础。但债转股的企业通常都陷入困境，如果仅仅是注入资金，而没有有效转变企业既有的经营机制，将导致保险机构的股权投资面临较大的改制风险、定价风险和退出风险，这显然与保险资金风险偏好程度较低的属性相冲突。

---

① 魏瑄："关于保险资金参与市场化银行债转股的初步分析"，载于《中国保险资产管理》，2016年第6期。

三、寿险资金支持实体经济存在的政策障碍

（一）基础设施债权计划相关的管理规则有待完善

《保险资金间接投资基础设施项目管理办法》已于2016年8月1日正式实施，但是配套的《基础设施债权投资计划管理暂行规定》一直没有完成重新修订工作，一些管理规则有待完善，以适应保险资金投资实体经济的现实需要。这主要体现在以下两个方面。

第一，融资主体免于增信的条件有待完善。根据《基础设施债权投资计划管理暂行规定》，债权投资计划的增信要求标准高，方式手段要求严。保险债权投资计划这一产品形式与银行开发贷、经营贷或项目融资等产品相类似。在项目运作中保险债权投资计划与银行形成了一定的竞争关系，尤其是在部分优质项目中银行常常直接提供贷款以获取息差，而不倾向于为保险债权投资计划提供融资担保以赚取担保费。可见，在当前银保关系以及加强地方政府投融资平台、大型企业担保管理的背景下，A类和B类增信（约占90%）变得更加困难，成为制约保险资金投资基础设施的重要因素。虽然《基础设施债权投资计划管理暂行规定》也规定了免增信条件，但要求太苛刻，在实践中很少能达到免增信的要求。

为支持保险资金投资关系国计民生的重大工程，进一步服务实体经济，《中国保监会关于债权投资计划投资重大工程有关事项的通知》（保监资金〔2017〕135号）规定，"债权投资计划投资经国务院或国务院投资主管部门核准的重大工程，且偿债主体具有AAA级长期信用级别的，可免于信用增级。"但在实践中很少有项目根据该通知的精神免于信用增级。

因此，为了支持保险资金投资基础设施，有必要在控制风险的基础上适当降低免于增信的标准，并予以明确。

第二，投资计划资金用途有待拓宽。根据2012年的《基础设施债权投资计划管理暂行规定》，基础设施债权投资计划资金只能投资于一个或者同类型的一组基础设施项目。随着国内基础设施建设的逐步饱和，而国企改革、供给侧结构性改革持续深化，基础设施项目新增融资需求出现下降趋势，企业的重组、并购融资需求增加。由于债权投资计划在资金使用用途上的限制，保险资产管理机构不得不借助信托等其他通道，满足这些新增的重组、并购融资需求，不但限制了债权投资计划产品本身的发展，而且增加了融资主体的成本。因此，除项目融资外，债权投资计划资金的用途有待进一步拓宽，比如，可以进一步拓展其在企业并购重组、补充营运资金、偿还债务等方面的用途。

（二）保险资金投资股权的范围有待进一步放开

第一，间接投资股权的范围有待放开。根据《保险资金投资股权暂行办法》的规定，"间接投资股权，是指保险公司可投资股权投资管理机构发起设立的股权投资基金等相关金融产品。"实践中，为控制风险，私募基金存在多种投资方式，既包括股权投资，也包括以委托贷款等形式的债权投资。目前，基金业协会对私募基金实行分类备案，备案为股权投资基金管理人的投资机构仅能发起设立以股权为主的私募基金，备案为其他类基金管理人的投资机构能发起设立以债权为主的私募基金。但目前，间接投资股权的范围仅限于股权投资基金，如果范围进一步放开，允许保险资金投资备案为其他类基金管理的投资机构发起设立的投资基金，则保险资金可以进一步投资于以债权为主的私募基金。

第二，直接投资股权的范围有待进一步放开。2010年，《保险资金投资股权暂行办法》规定，"保险资金直接投资股权，仅限于保险类企业、非保险类金融企业和与保险业务相关的养老、医疗、汽车服务等企业的股权。"2012年，《关于保险资金投资股权和不动产有关问题的通知》对于保险资金直接投资股权的范围，增加了能源企业、资源企业和与保险业务相关的现代农业企业、新型商贸流通企业的股权。由于保险资金的直接投资股权仅限于上述范围，对装备及制造、大消费、媒体信息及通信服务等行业企业尚未纳入可以直接投资股权的范围。这些行业涵盖众多发展前景良好、财务指标健康、风险收益比较高的投资标的，不乏国内产业转型升级的重要领军企业。因此，基于安全、价值投资原则，有必要适度放开直接股权投资范围。

第三，放松对保险股权投资的审批制。目前保险股权投资计划和保险私募基金产品都还需要保监会的审批，虽然有利于防范风险，但在一定程度上降低了保险股权投资的效率。因此，随着市场主体自身风险防范意识和能力的加强，监管部门可以考虑适时放宽股权投资产品的审批权限，改为保险资产管理行业协会备案制度，以提高效率。

（三）不动产抵押登记的政策有待完善

目前由于政策限制，保险机构无法通过不动产抵押担保方式保障其债权实现，从而限制了保险资金服务实体经济手段和空间。

依据《中华人民共和国物权法》《中华人民共和国担保法》的相关规定，"国有建设用地使用权"是法律允许的"可抵押财产"，只要债务人或第三人同意提供土地使用权抵押担保，对债务人拥有合法债权的"债权人"就可以作为"抵押权人"申请土地抵押登记。保险资产管理公司作为不动产相关项目的合法债权人，理论上当然可以作为土地使用权抵押权人请办理土地抵押登记。然而，根据《国土资源部关于规范土地登记的意见》（国土资发〔2012〕134号，以下简称"国土部134号文"）第五条的相关规定"依据相关法律、法规规定，经中国银行业监督管理委员会批准取得《金融许可证》金融机构、经省级人民政府主管部门批准设立的小额贷款公司等可以作为放贷人申请土地抵押登记"。这样，在实践中，国土资源部门认定，只有持有中国银监会颁发的《金融许可证》的金融机构（比如银行、信托公司等）、小额贷款公司或者经营范围中有"贷款"字样的企业，才能作为土地使用权抵押权人。而因保险资产管理公司既无中国银监会颁发的《金融许可证》，其经营范围中又不包括"贷款"，其不属于国土部 134 号文确规定的可以申请土地抵押登记的放贷人，从而使得保险资金通过债权或股权等方式直接或间接投资于不动产相关项目时，多地国土部门不认可保险资产管理公司作为土地使用权抵押权人申请土地抵押登记。

（四）投资养老健康产业的政策有待完善

近年来，国家政策支持保险资金投资养老健康产业。《国务院关于加快发展养老服务业的若干意见》（国发〔2013〕35号）提出，"逐步放宽限制，鼓励和支持保险资金投资养老服务领域。"《国务院关于促进健康服务业发展的若干意见》（国发〔2013〕40号）提出，"鼓励企业、慈善机构、基金会、商业保险机构等以出资新建、参与改制、托管、公办民营等多种形式投资医疗服务业。"国家发展改革委、中国保监会《关于保险业支持重大工程建设有关事项的指导意见》（发改投资〔2015〕2179号）提出，"鼓励设立不动产、基础设施、养老等专业保险资产管理机构，支持保险资金进行养老、医疗、健康等相关领域的股权和不动产投资。"

养老和健康产业投资拉动经济作用明显，与养老健康保险业务具有契合性，但保险机构投资养老健康服务产业相配套的具体实施细则和优惠政策尚不完善，保险机构投资养老健康产业面临市场准入、土地和财税政策等方面障碍。如对于养老实体产业的用地性质还没有明确地位；我国的养老机构可以享受减免营业税、所得税等优惠政策，但通常仅限于福利性、非营利性的养老服务机构，而对于营利性的养老服务行业优惠政策并不明显；养老服务产业的进入标准、配套设施和专业服务等均尚未形成完善而统一的行业标准，与之相关的监管制度同样存在缺失，造使得保险公司投资养老服务产业的实践工作还存在着诸多不确定性，需要进一步完善发展。

（五）参与PPP存在制约因素

一方面，PPP项目的现金流量水平有限制约了寿险资金股权投资的积极性。PPP融资的典型特点是有限追索或无追索项目融资，关注的重点是项目未来的现金流量水平。但由于我国特许经营模式未来使用者付费的市场容量、收费机制、排他性机制等不明确，政府付费也存在着政府的换届和信用等问题，使得对PPP未来十年、二十年甚至三十年的长期现金流量的预期困难，没有信心，这使得股权投资很困难，并导致PPP从一种股权投资演变成一种必须给出合理回报水平，而且在一定时期之内地方政府必须接手的投资模式。这使得股权投资变成一定的回报、一定的期限的债务融资，实际操作中演变成各种名目的明股实债，成为地方政府的或有债务，增加了地方政府的债务，从而成为被限制和清理的对象，从而制约了保险资金对PPP项目参与。

另一方面，寿险资金参与政府与社会资本合作（PPP）相关的平等契约关系、风险保障机制等缺少法律保障，影响保险机构投资积极性。

（六）参与不良资产处置的政策环境有待完善

首先，参与不良资产证券化的政策需要进一步完善。虽然相关部门出台了推进险资参与资产证券化的规定，但是监管机构目前尚没有放开保险机构作为投资者参与不良资产证券化。按照保监会2012年发布的《关于保险资金投资有关金融产品的通知》（保监发〔2012〕91号），保险资金投资的信贷资产支持证券，入池基础资产限于正常类和关注类的贷款，且按照孰低原则，产品信用等级不低于国内信用评级机构评定的A级或相当于A级的信用级别，这对于不良资产来说很难达到。

2017年5月，中国保监会发布《关于保险业支持实体经济发展的指导意见》（保监发〔2017〕42号），提出"支持保险资产管理机构开展不良资产处置等特殊机会投资业务、发起设立专项债转股基金等"，很大程度上为保险资金未来直接投资不良资产证券化产品扫清了一定的政策障碍，但具体涉及操作层面的政策还需要进一步明确。

因此，未来还需要相关部门放开保险机构参与不良资产证券化的政策，并对不良资产的评级、风险管控等作出明确的规定，完善相关的法律法规。

其次，参与债转股的政策尚不配套。 一是国有股权交易进场的刚性规定不利于债转股的实施。目前债转股的主要合作对象是周期性行业的大型国有企业。根据国资委2016年6月发布的《企业国有资产交易监督管理办法》相关规定，对国有企业增资都要进场交易，该办法中虽然规定"企业债权转为股权"时可以协议增资，但目前实际操作中相当部分债转股是先入股再置换债务，这种情况下严格按规定也需进场。由于债转股是一个综合交易安排，主要的工作在于方案设计和条款安排，最后完成增资只是一个结果，如果均需进场挂牌交易的话，将不能确保与企业完成大量前期工作的机构必然能摘到牌，从而不利于机构参与债转股。

二是国有股权交易评估的规则有待完善。国资委2005年发布的《企业国有资产评估管理暂行办法》规定，国有资产转让、非上市公司国有股东股权比例变动必须进行评估。资产评估在实际操作过程中，涉及评估对象复杂、存在估值风险、程序烦琐、评估时间不确定等问题，给投资机构带来较大的不确定性，并影响项目进程。此外，办法还规定评估值不能低于净资产，而进行债转股的企业多数是比较困难的企业，其价值有可能低于账面净资产，不符合市场化定价的原则。

三是税收规则有待完善。目前对于企业股权投资，投资机构只有在直接入股企业的情况下才能享受免所得税政策，如果通过金融产品来投资，就面临双重征税的问题。实践中，考虑到分散投资风险、减轻投后管理压力等因素，保险机构更多情况下是以产品形式进行债转股投资，双重征税加重了债转股企业的综合成本。

四是上市公司市场化债转股与现有规定存在一定的矛盾。参与上市公司市场化债转股的保险机构，通常希望获得上市公司股份，以在资本市场实现退出，但这与现有的相关规定存在一定的冲突。

首先，发行规模和发行股价受再融资新规限制。2017年2月，证监会发布再融资新规，明确非公开发行的规模上限为总股本的20%；并需以发行期首日为定价基准日，发行价格随行就市。这导致投资者难以履行内部决策流程，增加了投资者参与市场化债转股的不确定性。

其次，募集资金用于偿还贷款的监管较严。目前监管机构要求上市公司再融资募集资金全部偿还银行贷款必须同时满足两个条件：投资者锁定三年，且还贷规模上限应通过严格公式测算。这对投资者参与债转股的意愿产生了较大限制。此外，再融资募集资金用于还贷的审核节奏缓慢，难以匹配债转股企业的时间要求。

最后，债权无法纳入发行股份购买资产标的。根据《上市公司重大资产重组管理办法》规定，发行股份购买的资产必须是经营性资产，因此即便有利于改善持续盈利能力，上市公司也无法直接发行股份购买债权。

第四章　寿险资金支持实体经济的国际经验、教训和发展动向

　　尽管由于国情不同，不存在放之四海而皆准的国际经验，但在那些拥有较长寿险业发展历史的国家中，寿险投资服务实体经济过程中所表现出来的一些经验和教训具有共性特征，值得我国参考借鉴；一些新的发展动向更应引起我国的关注和反思。

一、国际经验

（一）寿险公司以规模大、期限长等鲜明特点成为实体经济投资领域的重要力量

　　拥有发达的金融体系是发达国家的一个普遍特征，其中，保险公司，特别是寿险公司往往成为发达国家经济增长的一股重要力量，为各类融资活动提供了不可替代的资金来源。不可替代性主要体现在规模大和投资期限长两个方面。

　　其一，资金规模大。在2011年末，OECD国家的机构投资者拥有的资产总量超过70万亿美元，其中，保险公司是仅次于各类投资基金的第二大机构投资者，总资产高达24.3万亿美元，且呈现上升态势（见图1）。不少国家保险业总

资产甚至远远超过了GDP的规模，例如，卢森堡保险业总资产为GDP的2.6倍，丹麦为1.2倍，英国则大致持平（见表1）。在保险业总资产中，寿险业占据绝大部分份额。以欧洲为例，2013年末欧洲寿险业总资产为6.9万亿欧元，占GDP的比重为53.1%；非寿险业资产为1.5万亿欧元，占GDP的比重为11.6%。

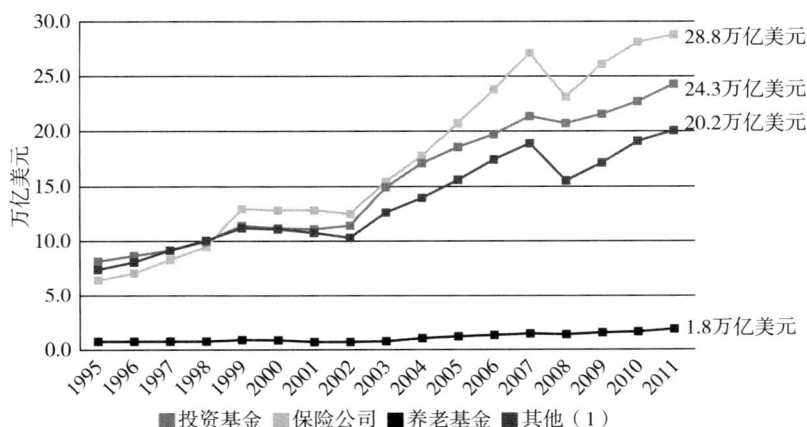

图1　1995～2011年OECD国家四类机构投资者的总资产变化

资料来源：转引自Della Croce, R. and J. Yermo（2013）。

表1　　2011年末部分OECD国家保险业总资产占GDP的比重

国家	保险业总资产占GDP的比重（%）
卢森堡	263.6
丹麦	124.8
爱尔兰	120.5
英国	103.2
法国	91.7
瑞典	85.5
日本	75.9
加拿大	73.3
瑞士	72.5
荷兰	68.9

资料来源：转引自Della Croce, R. and J. Yermo（2013）。

其二，投资期限长。由于寿险公司的负债期限普遍较长，为了资产负债匹配需要，资产期限也普遍较长。表2列示了日本、德国、英国、美国近年来大型寿险公司的资产负债久期，可以发现，平均资产久期都在10年以上。有研究显示，2012年全球所有长期投资者配置在长期资产方面的投资规模总计在2.43万亿欧元左右，其中约60%左右由养老基金和保险公司所持有[①]。

表2　　　　　　近年来4个发达国家大型寿险公司的资产负债平均久期

国家	数据时间	资产平均久期（年）	负债平均久期（年）
日本	2016年3月底	12.3	14.0
德国	2013年12月底	10.0	20.2
英国	2013年12月底	12.0	11.5
美国	2015年12月底	10.5	11.3

资料来源：Bank of Japan（2017）。

（二）寿险投资活动主要基于负债活动展开，以资产负债匹配为根本指导原则

保险公司从事的是典型的负债驱动资产型投资。在很大程度上，有什么样的保险产品组合，就有什么样的资产配置组合。确保资产负债匹配可以说是保险投资的首要原则。

以美国为例，在20世纪40年代之前，由于寿险公司的主要产品是定期寿险，相应的，投资组合由政府债券为主导。此后，随着承保的风险类型由死亡风险为主逐渐向生存风险、长寿风险转移，向客户提供更高的回报率越来越成为业务的诉求之一，在负债端，终身寿险、年金保险、投资联结保险替代定期寿险成为保险产品主流；在资产端，保险公司也相应地将投资更多地配置在风险更高、收益更大的领域，包括垃圾债券、商业地产贷款、股票等。此外，对于不同规模的保险公司而言，受到营销能力、市场定位等因素的影响，产品组合存在差异，资产负债匹配的需要以及对久期以及流动性风险的考虑有所不同，因而投资组合也存在较大差异。在美国，这种差异主要表现为小保险公司

① 资料来源：INREV RESEARCH & MARKET INFORMATION，"REAL ESTATE AS A LONG-TERM INVESTMENT: The impact of regulatory change on long-term investing strategiesand on the real economy"，2013，http://www.europeanrealestateforum.eu/wp-content/uploads/2013/09/INREV_Real_Estate_as_a_Long-Term_Investment_20130408.pdf。

相比大保险公司持有更多的现金和短期投资（见表3）。

表3　　　　　　　　　**2014年美国大型和小型保险公司的投资组合差异**

	小型保险公司	大型保险公司	行业平均
债券投资比例（%）	69	80	67
股票投资比例（%）	10	9	12
现金和短期资产投资比例（%）	17	1	4

注释：小保险公司是指现金和投资资产的账面价值低于2.5亿美元的保险公司；大型保险公司则是指现金和投资资产金额超过10亿美元的保险公司。

资料来源：NAIC, http://www.naic.org/capital_markets_archive/151201.htm, 2015.

很多情况下，资产负债匹配原则对保险投资的影响远远超过其他金融机构。例如，2014年，由于量化宽松政策的实施，长期欧元债券收益率大幅下跌，然而有研究显示，2014年德国保险公司对政府债券的需求快速上升，显然，这一资产配置的调整与对回报率的追求无关，而与对资产久期的追求有关。相反，德国投资基金、银行、家庭等部门都没有发现类似的资产配置调整①。日本也发生了类似情况。根据日本央行的统计，2004-2011年，日本寿险公司持续增加对日本国债的投资，特别是增加了对10年期以上超长期国债的投资比重，2011年末在超长期国债上的投资份额已经超过了40%，背后的主要驱动力在于资产负债的期限匹配，而非收益率的追求。

（三）寿险投资对宏观经济大势和政策走向保持高度敏感，灵活调整投资方向和投资组合配置

不管是出于追求自身回报还是确保投资业务有效支持负债业务考虑，都要求保险投资必须遵循宏观大势，积极响应实体经济提出的各项需求。这也就意味着，即使在美国这样市场体系高度发达的国家里，保险投资活动的开展也不是绝对意义上市场独自决策的结果，而是不同程度受到政府政策的引导。

例如，20世纪四五十年代，随着美国经济的繁荣和工业化进程的推进，寿

---

① 资料来源：Dietrich Domanski, Hyun Song Shin andVladyslav Sushko, "The hunt for duration:not waving butdrowning?", BIS Working PapersNo 519, 2015。

险公司显著降低了对政府债券和农业按揭的持有，提高了对非农业按揭、特别是私募公司债券的持有，这一调整体现了寿险业对宏观经济走势的高度敏感。

另外一个例子是，美国寿险业积极参与住房金融体系建设。美国的住房金融体系具有很强的政策性特征，在一级和二级市场政府和金融机构密切合作，共同扮演着不可替代的角色。在一级市场，1932年，美国建立了联邦住房贷款银行系统（Federal Home Loan Bank System,简称FHLBs），FHLBs属于政府支持机构，由1家总行和12家分行组成，每一家分行负责4~5个州的业务。联邦住房贷款银行并非直接向个人贷款，而是在金融机构申请成为FHLB会员后，通过向金融机构提供低成本融资的方式使得前者能够向后者发放更便宜的按揭贷款。保险公司在FHLB系统里非常活跃，主要通过三种方式介入：其一，向FHLB借款；其二，投资于FHLB发行的债券；其三，持有本地FHLB分行的股权。根据NAIC的统计，在一般的FHLB分行里，保险公司占会员数量的5%，贷款额的10%（见表4）。在一级市场之外,美国住房金融体系还拥有发达的二级市场，即住房抵押贷款证券化市场，二级市场80%以上的抵押贷款支持证券都是由房利美和房地美这两大政府支持企业发行的，寿险公司是住房抵押贷款证券化市场重要的投资者。图2表明，几乎在整个20世纪，按揭贷款都是美国寿险公司资产配置中非常重要的投资方向。通过对住房金融一级和二级市场的积极参与，寿险公司在解决美国居民的住房问题以及推动美国房地产市场的发展方面发挥了非常重要的作用。

表4　　　　　　　2011年末联邦住房贷款银行（FHLB）会员情况

会员类别	会员数量	持有的监管资本金额（百万美元）	会员借款人数量	全部借款金额（百万美元）	平均借款金额（百万美元）
商业银行	5424	22605	3605	208233	38.4
储贷机构	1067	8281	779	95470	89.5
信用社	1063	2519	401	22815	21.5
保险公司	234	3387	100	46150	197.2
社区开发性金融机构	7	3	3	6	1
全部会员	7795	36795	4888	372674	47.8

资料来源：http://www.naic.org/capital_markets_archive/121214.htm

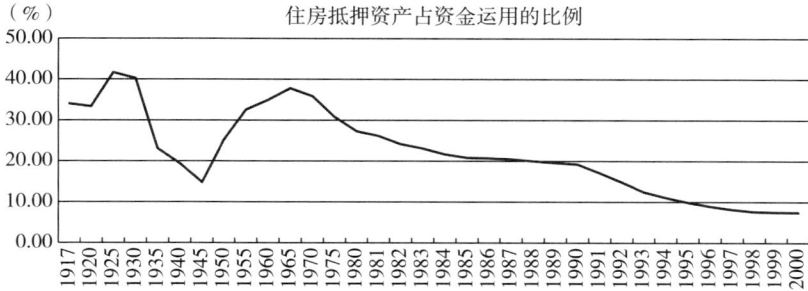

图2　美国寿险公司住房抵押资产占资金运用的比例

（四）寿险投资与资本市场保持密切互动，对资本市场深化做出积极贡献

对于不同的国家而言，有时寿险业发展走在资本市场发展前面；有时则滞后。不论哪一种情况，多数国家的经验都表明，资本市场和寿险投资是相生相合、相互促进的关系，寿险投资离不开健全的资本市场和丰富的金融产品，同样地，资本市场的深化也需要借助寿险公司这类长期机构投资者的力量。

国际共性特征是，资本市场是寿险公司资金配置的主要渠道，但各国投资组合的具体状况存在一定差别，与资本市场的特征密切相关。例如，欧盟地区的寿险公司大量投资于国债，Domanski等人的研究（2015）表明，保险公司是欧元区政府债券的最大持有者。2014年欧元区政府债券的40%由保险公司持有。相反，美国寿险公司则更多投资于公司债券和股票。Cummins and Weiss（2010）的研究表明，2009年末，寿险投资约占美国公司债券和外国债券市场总投资的16.7%，公司股票市值的6.2%。欧美之间的差别主要体现了二者金融体系的差别：美国是典型的资本市场主导的金融体系，融资主要通过股票和债券市场进行，相应地，寿险投资大量配置在股票和公司债券领域；欧洲则是以银行贷款为主导的金融体系，企业与银行有紧密的关系，股票和公司债券市场相对不发达，因此寿险公司的投资主要集中于政府债券。不过，近年来，随着机构投资者的快速发展，投资多元化的需求日益旺盛，加速了欧洲地区公司债券市场的发展，也推动了寿险公司在公司债券领域的资产配置。

以寿险公司为代表的机构投资者对各国资本市场深化所发挥的作用是极其关键的。以美国公司债券市场为例。以往，美国公司债券的发行门槛偏高，主要由大投资银行和大企业所主导，从发行到定价都缺乏充分竞争，小企业很难发债。到了20世纪70年代，由于机构投资者的兴起，情况发生了变化。由于机构投资者追求更高的回报率，因而专注于交易而非证券发行和承销的新型投资银行兴起，并与机构投资者建立了紧密的联系，同时鼓励企业直接向机构投资者发行证券，从而增加了发行程序的竞争程度，降低了发行和交易成本。小企业和低信用级别的企业也因此得以进入债券市场发债。由此，保险公司、养老基金等机构投资者的介入大大推动了美国公司债券市场的扩容。类似的例子发生在英国，由于保险公司、养老基金等大量、稳定、长期资金的进入，推动其股票市场成为全球规模最大、流动性最高的市场之一。可以说，美国和英国之所以拥有全球最发达的资本市场体系，以保险公司和养老基金为代表的机构投资者功不可没。

二、国际教训

（一）保险资产和负债业务均应稳健经营，切忌过度激进

由于保险特殊的业务性质（如建立在大数法则基础上、涉及大量公众利益），稳健经营对个体公司和整个行业而言均十分重要。稳健经营既包括负债业务，也包括资产业务，如果整个经营模式背离了稳健原则，过度激进，即使资产负债相匹配，也会使公司陷入危险境地，甚至对整个行业乃至金融体系的稳定造成冲击。

国际上有不少寿险公司破产的案例（参见表5）。这些案例虽然具体背景和细节有所差异，但大多可以归咎于共同的原因，即违背了稳健经营原则。当一

家寿险公司采取激进的手段开展竞争，推出激进的保险产品，如给予客户过度慷慨的保证回报率；过低的退保惩罚，允许保单持有人在合同到期日之前就轻易抽回资金等，往往同时需要采取激进的投资策略加以配合，如在按揭、房地产等高风险资产方面过度投资。在激进的经营模式下，内外部因素的变化很容易产生连锁反应，造成寿险公司偿付能力和流动性两方面的压力，最终导致经营失败。

表5　　　　　　　　　几个著名的寿险业破产案例

破产主体	破产时间	破产原因
美国Executive life insurance company（ELIC）	1991年	负债业务：经营大量非传统的年金业务，向客户提供明显高于市场同业的保证回报率；不少产品可以退保，但收取很低的退保费用。 投资业务：资产配置集中度很高，垃圾债券的投资比例显著高于同业；负债业务的保证回报率高度依赖于垃圾债券的表现。随着1990年代美国经济走向萧条，垃圾债券价值下跌
美国Mutual Benefit Life Insurance Company（MBL）	1991年	负债业务：在20世纪80年代，大量进行商业地产按揭以及其他一些房地产投资，投资比例远高于同业。随着80年代全国性的商业地产市场萧条，揭违约率升高，资产价值大幅下滑，从而影响偿付能力
加拿大Confederation Life Insurance Company（Confed）	1994年	负债业务：在其大部分历史上，都是一个保守、传统的相互保险公司。在20世纪80年代早期，公司新的管理层为了谋求更快速的增长，开始发展更激进的保险业务，希望把公司转变为一个金融综合集团。 资产业务：投资组合中，商业按揭贷款和其他房地产投资二者合计占比超过70%。随着加拿大房地产市场陷入严重萧条，不良资产和商业按揭的违约率在1993年和1994年早期大幅上升
8家日本寿险公司	20世纪90年代末和21世纪初	负债业务：为了吸引保单持有人，寿险公司以很高的保障利率出售合同，提供给保单持有人的最低保障利率完全与保险公司的资产回报率脱钩。 资产业务：寿险公司显著增加在股票和房地产等高风险资产方面的配置比例。随着90年代初泡沫经济的破灭以及日本央行下调利率，泡沫时代销售的高预定利率保单形成了大量利差损，直接导致几大寿险公司的破产倒闭

（二）寿险投资离不开有效监管，缺乏有效监管很容易出现严重问题

寿险业是需要严格监管的行业，同时也是高度依赖市场创新的行业。如何

在控制风险和鼓励创新之间保持平衡，对所有监管机构都是一道难题。不过，以往的案例表明，尽管在如何把握监管的力度和方式方面还存在很多探讨的空间，但所谓"最少的监管就是最好的监管"的说法并不完全适用于寿险业，在缺乏有效监管，存在大量监管空白和监管套利的情况下，市场竞争很容易偏离正常的轨道，产生大量问题，甚至酿成系统性风险的大爆发。美国的两个例子足以佐证缺乏有效监管所可能导致的严重后果。

第一个例子发生在寿险业发展的早期。19世纪末20世纪初，美国多数州已经开始实施保险监管，但完善的监管体系尚未建立。当时美国寿险公司发展很快，积累了大量资金，从事了很多投资，包括购买银行和其他公司的控股权。保险业实力增强的同时伴随着许多问题，包括管理失误、欺诈、腐败等案例频出，导致1905年在纽约开始了阿姆斯特朗调查。调查揭示了保险业存在的许多问题，最终新的保险监管规则出台，包括禁止保险公司投资并持有普通股、承销债券等。

第二个例子发生在2008年国际金融危机。美国国际集团（AIG）作为当时世界上最大的保险集团，被认为是此次危机的重要制造者之一。AIG的问题是多种因素综合作用的结果，其中一个关键因素在于美国金融监管体系的失效，即尽管美国存在不同的金融监管机构，但缺乏一个对大型的、复杂的、全球性金融集团进行整体监管的机构。AIG的问题揭示了宏观审慎监管的必要性。

三、国际发展动向

（一）寿险公司正以更加积极的态度介入基础设施、新创企业等另类投资领域，另类资产占比显著增加

对于寿险公司而言，另类投资是指股票、债券等传统投资之外的新型投资

渠道，包括基础设施、PE/VC、对冲基金、房地产基金等[①]。2008年国际金融危机以来，由于长期的低利率环境以及股票、债券公开市场投资不确定性的加剧，全球范围内寿险投资的一个明显动向是显著增加了在另类资产上的配置比例，以期获取更高回报率，同时提高投资的多样化程度，熨平短期波动，降低风险。根据2017年由"欧洲保险（ Insurance Europe ）"所做的一次覆盖欧盟11个国家的调查显示，欧洲保险公司对基础设施投资的兴趣不断增长，几大欧洲保险公司已经公开承诺会提高对基础设施的投资力度，未来年度投资总额将合计为500亿欧元左右。在美国的法定报告制度中，非传统投资被归类于Schedule BA资产中。统计显示（参见图3），尽管自2008年以来，美国保险公司向债券的配置比例保持相对稳定，约为72%，但现金及短期债券的投资比例已经从2008年的6.5%下降为2013年的4.1%；与此同时，向Schedule BA资产的配置比例从2008年的3.8%提高到2013年的和5.4%，其中寿险公司Schedule BA资产的配置比例从3.5%提高到4.3%。

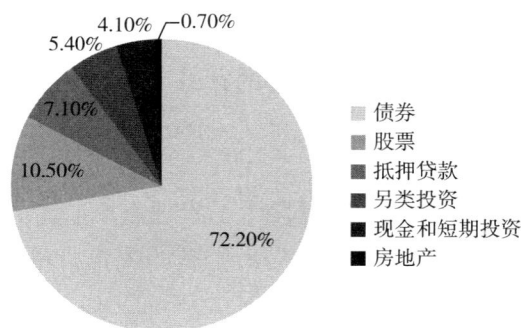

4.10% 0.70%
5.40%
7.10%
10.50%
72.20%

债券
股票
抵押贷款
另类投资
现金和短期投资
房地产

图3　2013年美国保险业一般账户资产配置

资料来源：Sneed（2015）。

---

① 在美国，对另类资产的一种定义是："另类资产是指那些没有在任何全国性的交易所或OTC市场挂牌的资产，或者其报价无法从公开财经刊物、交易所或者NASDAQ处获得的资产。这些投资经常不处在任何联邦或者州监管之下，在投资策略上比注册的投资公司有更大的灵活性。"引自AICPA，"Alternative Investments in Employee Benefit Plans"，Jan.2009。

（二）越来越多地寿险公司投资保险科技，以改善风险管理，提高投资组合回报率

近年来，区块链、人工智能、大数据、云计算等新兴科技一日千里，并快速运用到保险领域，对整个行业的发展正在造成颠覆性影响，甚至出现了保险科技这一专有名词。所谓保险科技（InsurTech），是指将不同的科技手段运用到保险经营的各个环节以提升营运效率的一种做法。2014～2016年，全球保险科技领域的投资，不论是交易数量还是交易金额都翻了一番，2016年投资总额达到17亿美元。目前保险科技的投资者大多来自保险业以外，但保险公司通过其内部的风险投资部门开展的投资活动正逐年提高。例如，2014年全部保险科技交易活动中，来自保险公司的投资只占3%，2015年提高到12%，2016年进一步跃升为14%[①]。

保险科技除了应用在产品设计、定价、销售、理赔等环节之外，在投资活动中也大有可为。主要原因在于，保险投资活动正变得更为复杂。其一，在持续低利率以及资本市场波动率不断上升的背景下，以往传统的投资组合构建方式，例如6:4的债权/股权分配比例，已经变得日趋过时。其二，另类资产配置比例的提高意味着资产组合构建的方式更为复杂。其三，偿付能力Ⅱ等新的监管规则对保险公司信息基础设施建设提出了新的要求，例如新监管规则实施了"穿透"原则，要求保险公司提供关于最底层投资者的基础资料，即使他们被包含在基金或者基金的基金中。由于上述新变化，保险公司需要采用比以往更加动态、更加复杂的方法来进行资产负债匹配，需要更及时、准确的数据以及快速、高效的资产组合构建能力加以支持。新的保险科技的发展有利于帮助保险公司更好地开展投资管理，以适应新形势发展的需要。

---

① 资料来源：http://www.ftchinese.com/story/001072018。

（三）保险业与系统性风险的相关性呈现上升趋势，如何防控资产和负债业务风险、维持行业稳定成为巨大挑战

以往，普遍的共识是，保险业并非是系统性风险的来源，反而是维持经济和金融体系稳定的一股重要力量。Bobtcheff、Chaney和Gollier（2016）对1960～2008年美国各行业的波动率进行了计算，发现保险业的波动率只有GDP波动率的20%，而投资银行波动率则为GDP波动率的几乎2倍，商业银行则介于保险业和投行业之间（见图4）。由此可见，保险业是美国经济的重要稳定力量。

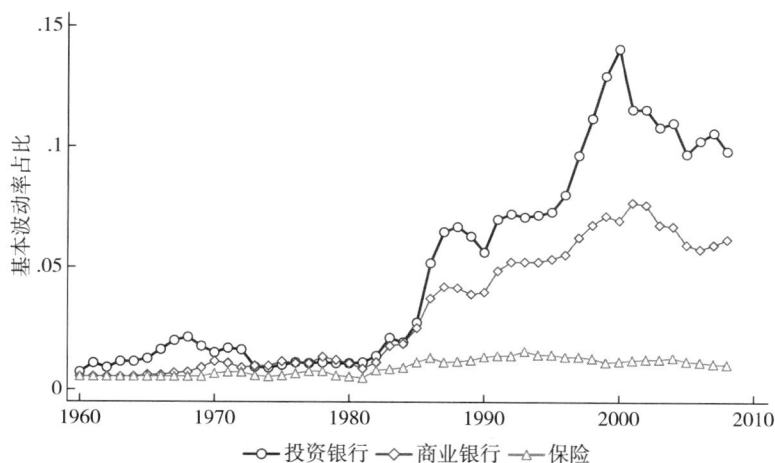

图4　美国1960～2008年美国三大金融部门波动率占GDP波动率之比

资料来源：Bobtcheff, Chaney and Gollier（2016）。

然而，国际金融危机之后，越来越多人开始认同一个新的观点，即与过去相比，保险业正变得越来越不稳定，与系统性风险的相关性显著提升。

其一，保险业与银行、证券等金融部门的同质性增强。20世纪八九十年代开始的金融自由化浪潮导致综合经营大行其道，保险业与其他金融部门的业务边界逐渐模糊，经营模式越来越像，传统的保险公司开始从事许多非传统业务。最典型的是AIG，大量介入CDS、证券出借等类银行活动，导致整个行业经营的波动性显著增加。在2008年国际金融危机后，同质性增强的趋势并没有

停止，反倒有增强态势。特别是危机后的低利率对寿险公司的运营形成巨大挑战，导致寿险公司不得不通过改变产品组合和资产配置等方式，不断适应新的业务环境。例如，面对投资收益的压缩，欧洲地区的寿险公司不得不出售更多地投资联结保险，以便将市场风险向保单持有人转移，而投连险本质上就是一种相互基金业务。此外，保险公司更多地介入基础设施融资等领域，而这类投资传统上主要由银行提供融资。同质性的增加意味着保险公司不可避免地成为系统性风险的重要来源之一。

二是保险投资组合蕴含地风险显著增加。2008年国际金融危机后，主要经济体普遍采用超常规的量化宽松货币政策以应对危机。宽松货币政策以及持续的低利率环境对寿险公司形成了严重的挑战。为了追求回报率，美国和欧洲的寿险公司偏离了其原有的投资习惯，已经更多地投资低评级债券。2008~2016年，美国和欧洲寿险公司投资A级以上债券的比例分别下降了8个和18个百分点；投资BBB级债券的比例分别提高了6个和19个百分点（见表6）。保险公司通过调整资产组合向更高收益债券和更低流动性资产来应对低利率，同时也意味着将承担更多的信用风险、市场风险、流动性风险。

表6   欧洲和美国寿险公司的债券资产配置

	美国		欧洲	
	2008	2016	2008	2016
AAA /AA/A	75	67	83	65
BBB	18	24	4	23
非投资级别	3	3	2	4
没有评级及其他	4	5	11	8

资料来源：IMF，2017。

四、小结

首先，投资是寿险业服务实体经济发展的重要方式，能够产生提供长期融资来源、深化资本市场发展等积极作用。不过，寿险投资活动并非必然会带来正面效果，如果缺乏政策引导和有效监管，寿险投资的正面作用不但无法充分发挥，还可能产生许多负面效果。

其次，政府引导和政策支持对保险投资作用的发挥至关重要。政府的作用在于为保险投资服务实体经济给予明确的方向指引，并适当赋能，包括允许保险公司为基础设施、工业化发展等提供资金；通过税收优惠等手段鼓励保险资金更多投资实体经济等。

再次，有效的监管确保保险投资在创新和稳定之间达成平衡。通过更多介入基础设施等另类投资渠道的方式，保险投资在服务实体经济方面将会发挥更加直接和重要的作用。与此同时，保险业与系统性风险的相关性正在明显上升。如何在风险和收益、创新和稳定之间保持平衡，对保险监管提出了很大挑战。必须以更加系统地理念看待保险业在经济和金融中扮演的作用，并采取宏观审慎和微观审慎相结合的方式认真对待风险防控问题。

第五章　促进中国寿险资金支持实体经济的政策建议

　　寿险资金支持实体经济的前提是推动寿险业转型和高质量发展。只有寿险业通过转型实现高质量发展，才能积聚期限长、规模大的寿险资金，满足实体经济的融资需求。为了促进寿险资金支持实体经济发展，要坚持市场化运作，秉持寿险资金运用的基本原则，促进负债端与资产端投资业务的融合，加强科技在资产管理领域的应用。为了防范寿险资金支持实体经济中的风险，要进一步引导寿险业调整负债结构，提升保险机构以资产负债管理为核心的风险管理能力，完善以防风险为中心的寿险资金运用监管体系，加强对关键领域风险的监控与防范，加强金融监管部门之间的协调与配合，以合作改善投资环境，提升地方政府的整改精神，强化行业风险管理。同时，要完善寿险资金支持实体经济的政策环境，包括深化保险资金运用市场化改革，明确不动产抵押登记政策，消除投资养老健康产业的政策障碍，完善PPP领域的相关配套政策，优化寿险资金参与"一带一路"建设与不良资产处置的政策环境，探索寿险资金开展贷款业务，积极培育保险资产管理市场。

一、推动寿险业转型与高质量发展

　　寿险资金支持实体经济的前提是推动寿险业转型和高质量发展。只有寿险业通过转型实现高质量发展，才能积聚期限长、规模大的寿险资金，满足实体经济的融资需求。

（一）促进寿险业转型

寿险投资活动主要基于负债活动展开，以资产负债匹配为根本指导原则。因此，要推动寿险资金支持实体经济发展，就要推动寿险业转型，以风险保障功能为核心，以负债业务为根基。因此，寿险业要向"以保障功能为基础，兼顾财富管理"转型。即要以健康险和养老险等保障性业务为主导，在税收递延和税前抵扣政策支持下发展，建立可持续的资产负债管理模式，为客户和社会创造价值，成为养老和健康保障体系的重要组成部分。

1. 实现保费增长模式从趸交推动向续期拉动的转型

保费收入趸交和期交增长模式最大的区别是可持续发展能力与业务发展的稳定性不同。期交保费在短期内难以迅速提升保费收入规模，但积累一定时间后保费增长速度会加速。而且期交保费收入占比高的公司业务经营的稳定性也高。因此，行业的转型需要在保费收入增长模式逐步实现从趸交推动增长模式向续期拉动增长模式转型，以增强保费收入增长的可持续性与业务发展的稳定性。

2. 产品结构调整

行业和公司要创新产品体系，**一是要着力发展为死亡风险提供财务保障人寿保险**。根据此前瑞士再保险公司的研究，2015、2016、2017年中国死亡保障缺口为37万亿、43万亿、50万亿美元，并且还有不断扩大的趋势。发展人寿保险，特别是定期寿险，可以为死亡风险提供财务保障，缩小死亡保障缺口。发展以定期寿险为代表的人寿保险也是保险业发达国家的经验。以美国为例，美国寿险市场2016年个人业务渠道共销售了近1000万张寿险保单，其中约400万张是定期寿险保单，这40%的保单只占了20%的总寿险保费，就提供了美国70%的死亡风险保障，平均每张定期寿险保单的保险金额为43万美元、约280万人民币，平均每张定期寿险保单的保费为948美元、约6000人民币；美国有8700万、近70%的家庭拥有人寿保险保障。

二是要发展为病残风险提供财务保障的健康保险。随着我国人口老龄化程度的加深，对医疗保险、重大疾病保险、失能收入保险、长期护理保险等健康保险的需求日益增加。为此，要结合税优健康险试点中存在的问题，夯实商业健康保险发展的制度基础。首先，放松产品的管制，促进竞争。目前税优健康险对产品设计做了很多的要求，有利于保护消费者利益，提升税优健康险对于被保险人的价值。但也带来了逆选择与道德风险难以控制、交易成本较高等问题，在一定程度上弱化了对市场主体的经济激励。因此，要适时放松产品管制，维护市场行动者的自由选择，通过竞争保护消费者利益，在市场主体对利润的追逐和竞争过程中实现"消费者主权"。

其次，提高免税额度，提升需求。目前税优健康险按照2400元/年的限额标准在个人所得税前予以扣除。由于税前扣除的额度有限，节税效果不明显，难以实质性提升健康险的需求。国际经验表明，商业健康保险的发展与其税前抵扣的力度息息相关。为了更加充分地发挥市场机制在我国医疗保障体系中的作用，要大幅提高个人购买商业健康险的税前扣除的额度，以税收优惠杠杆激发需求，促进商业健康保险的发展。同时，要简化税收扣除的程序，方便实践中操作。

再次，推动医疗服务领域的竞争。商业健康保险发展需要竞争性的医疗服务市场。竞争相对充分的医疗服务市场，有助于商业健康保险控制医疗费用成本以及介入医疗服务过程。我国商业健康保险发展的重要障碍是，由于行政管制和公立医院的垄断，造成医疗服务市场供求失衡，保险机构难以控制医疗费用，更难以介入医疗服务过程，管理医疗和支付方式改革难以推动。行政体制管制与垄断使得市场准入受到严格限制，大量的市场资源、民间资源与国际资源难以进入医疗服务市场，无法形成多元化、竞争充分的医疗服务供给格局，造成公立医院事实上的垄断地位。因此，需要打破医疗服务领域的垄断，为商业健康保险的发展奠定良好的制度基础。为此，要实现医疗服务领域对内对外的双向开放，同时推动公立医院体制改革，推动医疗服务和药品价格的市场化。政府应平等对待公立医院与民营医院，为各种所有制医院之间的竞争创造公平的环境。

最后，促进社会医疗保险经办的竞争。要实现社会医疗保险经办从政府到市场与社会的多元部门的转型，建立多中心的治理结构，从而为商业健康保险参与竞争，提升和优化社会医疗保险的运行效率提供制度基础。

三是要发展为长寿风险提供财务保障的养老年金险。自2018年5月1日起，上海市、福建省（含厦门市）和苏州工业园区实施个人税收递延型商业养老保险试点。要在发展定位、完善税收优惠政策以及提高行业供给效率等方面推动税收递延商业养老保险的试点，促进养老年金保险的发展。

首先，要明确商业养老保险的发展定位。要充分发挥市场机制在养老金体系中的作用，真正将商业养老保险作为我国养老金体系的"第三支柱"，以矫正养老金体系存在的结构性失衡。在养老金体系改革和政策调整中，要充分考虑商业养老保险作为第三支柱与基本养老保险之间的互动关系。要有效降低基本养老保险的缴费比例，减轻企业和居民的缴费负担，为商业养老保险的发展提供空间。

其次，完善税收优惠政策，提升商业养老保险需求。目前试点方案实行EET的税收优惠模式，即缴费和投资环节不缴税，领取环节缴税，发挥税收递延的激励作用。由于我国工资、薪金所得的纳税人规模较小，实际享受税收优惠的人群很有限。我国非正规部门就业人数较多，未来可以考虑同时实施TEE的税收优惠模式，即税后缴费，投资和领取环节均不缴税。这将有助于增加养老金账户持有人的选择，扩大其覆盖面，提高税收优惠政策的惠及范围，提升商业养老保险的需求。

最后，提高商业养老保险的供给效率。寿险业要转变发展理念，以保障功能为基础，风险管理与财富管理相结合，推动行业的转型升级。要以养老险为主导性业务，在税收优惠政策的支持下发展，为客户和社会创造价值，成为养老金体系的重要组成部分。寿险公司要加强产品创新，满足与适应多样化的养老保障需求。同时，以市场化为导向，拓宽保险资产运用渠道，提高资产管理的能力和效率，增强商业养老保险的竞争力。

3. 提升渠道价值

对于银保渠道，要利用监管融合的契机，推动银行和保险公司在业务领域的深度融合，促进银保合作的深化，促进银保模式的升级，向期交、保障性业务转型，增加新单业务价值，提升银保渠道的价值。

对于个险渠道，要提高代理人人均产能与销售效率，规范销售行为，保护消费者利益。致力于培育高效高质人力，实现从数量扩张到质量提升的飞跃，配合产品价值转型，从单纯追求保费规模逐步转向追求质量保费。

4. 防范化解行业转型中的流动性风险

2017年以来，由于监管导向的改变以及行业转型，寿险行业原来隐藏的流动性风险逐步显性化，部分寿险公司的现金流风险隐患较为突出。一是保费流入面临压力。在监管趋严的形势下，部分公司的趸交业务规模快速下降，而期交业务增长尚不能弥补趸交业务的规模收缩，从而造成新单保费流入大幅减少。同时，部分公司续期保费收入的稳定性较差，当外部环境出现变化时，续期保费流入可能低于预期，保费流入压力较大。二是现金流出增多。中短存续期存量业务规模较大的公司面临退保和满期给付压力，短期内流动性承压。三是流动性管理难度加大。随着利率走高和负债端久期拉长，人身险公司此前配置了更多长期资产，当出现流动性危机时，长期资产变现周期较长，从而加大了流动性管理的难度。

因此，为了平稳推进寿险业转型，要避免短期内保费收入大幅下滑，尽可能使续期保费的增量与趸交保费的减少量相匹配，实现转"大弯"，避免转

"急弯"衍生出新的风险。为此，要把握好监管的力度以及行业转型的节奏，给公司留下结构调整的时间与空间。

值得指出的是，2018年1～3月，寿险公司未计入保险合同核算的保户投资款和独立账户本年新增交费3387.01亿元，同比增长40.51%，远高于寿险公司原保险保费收入的增速。这有助于缓解一些公司的现金流缺口，为转型发展提供更大的空间。当然，在此过程中，寿险公司要注意资产负债的匹配，避免高负债成本有可能造成利差损以及倒逼资产端作激进投资。

5. 高度关注行业转型中可能出现的新的利差损与费差损风险

在竞争与转型的双重压力之下，部分中小寿险公司有可能被动提高渠道手续费、降低产品定价，由趸交低价值产品转向期交低价值产品，或利用高预定利率的长期年金产品获取保费收入，从而有可能造成利差损和费差损风险。同时由于长期保障和养老年金产品的复杂性和长期性使高承诺利率和高费用率变得更为隐性，进一步容易掩盖利差损和费差损风险。因此，要防范和化解转型过程中短期行为造成的利差损与费差损风险。

（二）推动寿险业高质量发展

推动寿险业高质量发展，是寿险资金支持实体经济的基础。为了推动寿险业高质量发展，提升保险资产在金融业总资产中的比重以及寿险业的发展水平，要深化行业的供给侧结构性改革，不断深化保险要素市场化配置改革，提高供给质量，强化科技创新，推动行业优化升级。为此，要推动行业实现质量变革、效率变革、动力变革，不断提高保险业全要素生产率。

推动寿险业实现高质量发展，要求充分发挥保险机制在经济转型过程中的作用，促进寿险业发挥长期稳健风险管理和保障的功能，重塑寿险市场良序运行的制度基础。

1. 充分发挥寿险在经济转型过程中的作用

一是经济转型过程中的潜在风险要求更好地发挥寿险业的作用。我国经济由高速增长阶段转向高质量发展阶段，在此过程中，国际、国内发展环境和条件深刻变化，转型与改革的时间空间约束不断增强，围绕市场、资源、人才、技术、标准等的竞争更加激烈，气候变化以及能源资源安全等全球性问题更加突出，尚面临一些不确定性与潜在风险。通过商业保险市场化手段解决转型过程中可能出现的风险问题，既可以坚持市场化改革，更好发挥市场配置资源的决定性作用，又可以有效促进社会和谐稳定。

二是转型过程中社会主要矛盾的变化需要更好发挥寿险的作用。目前，我国社会主要矛盾已经转化为"人民日益增长的美好生活需要和不平衡不充分的发展之间的矛盾"。经过改革开放40年的发展，我国社会生产力水平明显提高，社会需求升级，在生老病死、衣食住行、体育文娱等各个领域的保险服务成为保障人民群众美好生活的必需品。在养老、医疗等领域的巨大保障缺口，为保险业提供了广阔的发展空间。

三是转型过程中的重大发展战略实施需要更好发挥寿险的作用。为了促进我国经济由高速增长阶段转向高质量发展阶段，十九大提出了加快建设创新型国家、乡村振兴、区域协调发展等一系列重大战略，为保险业发展提供了新的机遇。保险作为市场化的风险管理、社会管理和灾害救助机制，可以通过服务国家重大战略实现行业价值的提升。

2. 促进寿险业发挥长期稳健风险管理和保障的功能

高质量发展要求促进寿险业发挥长期稳健风险管理和保障的功能，拓展保险市场的风险保障功能。寿险业高质量发展的关键在于充分发挥保险经济给付、风险管理与资金融通的核心功能，分散和转移各种人身风险，并参与风险管理，利用专业的风险管理技术有效管控疾病风险、长寿风险。同时，要发挥寿险资金的长期性优势，促进资金融通，矫正间接融资和直接融资的失衡，优化金融结构。

一是提升保险渗透率，发挥经济给付功能。寿险的首要功能是经济给付，即集合与分散各种人身风险，使个人、家庭在遭遇人身风险时能够得到及时充分的给付。目前寿险业的经济给付功能尚有待进一步发挥。目前人身保险长期保单的投保率不高。2016年，我国购买长期寿险保单的只有四千多万人，投保率不足3%，与保险业发达的国家与地区存在很大的差距。比如，2015年，日本个人人寿保险有效保单件数为1.6011亿，个人年金保险有效保单件数为2075万，团体人寿保险覆盖3875万人，累计有效保单件数为2.1961亿张，当年日本户籍登记人口为1.2711亿人，投保率为172.77%，相当于每人都有1.73张人寿与年金保险保单。又比如，2015年，台湾地区个人人寿保险有效保单件数为4793.4628万，个人年金保险有效保单件数为115.0246万，团体人寿保险覆盖592.3496万人，累计有效保单件数为5500.837万，当年台湾地区户籍登记人口为2349.2万人，投保率为234.16%，相当于每人都有2.34张人寿与年金保险保单。

因此，寿险业要继续立足于保障的根本属性，通过产品与商业模式创新，提升保险的渗透率，提高保险对各种人身风险事故造成经济损失的补偿比例，从而更好地发挥经济给付的功能，分散和转移风险。

二是加强风险管理功能。由经济给付功能衍生出保险的风险管理功能。保险机制是损失补偿与风险控制的统一。保险除了保障以外,还要充分发挥风险管理的功能，向家庭和社会提供专业的风险管理服务。

寿险业要充分发挥自身集合与分散各种人身风险以及对风险进行专业化管理的优势，提升风险管理的水平。以健康保险为例，我国的医疗卫生费用近年来呈现出快速增长的趋势，社会医保体系运行压力随之加大。越来越多的地方，基本医保基金出现入不敷出的情况。与社会保险机构相比，商业保险机构一项突出的优势就在于拥有包括"病前健康管理、病中诊疗监控、病后赔付核查"的全流程医疗风险管控技术，从而对医疗费用上涨和医疗资源浪费起到一定遏制作用。因此，通过商业保险机构参与经办基本医保，将商业保险的风险管控技术应用于基本医疗保险的费用审核，减少不合理医疗费用支出，放大资金使用效率，减轻了参保群众的医疗费用负担，从而有助于抑制医疗费用持续上涨、保持社保基金收支平衡。比如，保险公司将智能监控系统部署到医院端，开展事前提醒、事中监控、事后监督全过程风险控制，建立了优质的医保管理服务平台。另外，商业健康保险经营机构具有与医疗服务提供者深入合作的动力和利益驱动机制，能够在市场竞争中促进医疗服务与医疗保险的一体化经营，从而有效地提高人群健康水平。

三是发挥资金融通功能，优化金融结构。寿险具有资金融通功能，通过资金运用和投资支持实体经济发展。寿险业发挥资金融通功能，可以优化金融结构，从而促进经济发展。

首先，寿险业的发展有助于矫正间接融资和直接融资的失衡。发展寿险业，可以通过投资促进债券和股票市场的发展，并通过股权投资直接进入实体经济，从而有助于矫正我国金融领域直接融资与间接融资的结构性失衡。

其次，可以促进资本市场结构的优化。目前我国资本市场发育相对滞后，资本市场上急需长期有效的机构投资资金，发展寿险业是促进资本市场结构优化的重要途径。寿险公司作为机构投资者，具有专业化程度高、投资计划性强、重视长期投资、投资渠道多元等特点。注重长期投资，关注长期收益，可以增强资本市场的稳定性，促进资本市场良性、健康发展。可见，寿险市场与资本市场发展是一种相互促进，互为前提的关系，寿险基金可以成为促进资本市场发展的重要力量。

3. 重塑寿险市场良序运行的制度基础

目前影响寿险业高质量发展的因素包括：监管定位存在偏差、监管政策差异化不够、股东"贪大求快"、经营层沿袭既有经验与惯性等。从根本上说，这些问题源于寿险市场良序运行的制度基础比较薄弱。为了促进寿险业高质量发展，要重塑寿险市场运行的制度基础，即要推动产权改革、促进市场分工的深化以及彰显企业家精神。

一是推动产权改革。 寿险市场发展最重要的制度基础就是合理的产权制度。只有产权制度合理，险企才能够学会"长大长强"，而不是"做大做强"。目前市场充斥的是一些所谓"做大做强"的逻辑，而不是尊重生命体规律的"长大长强"的逻辑，其问题的根源在于产权制度。因此，必须高度重视保险市场的产权制度改革。只有建立合理的产权制度，寿险市场才真正具备市场化的制度基础，"规模至上"追求短期收益的状况才能从根本上得到遏制。**二是促进市场分工的深化。** 制约市场主体深化分工、提升专业化经营水平的重要原因是保险的市场化机制未得到充分重视。要进一步发挥人寿保险、养老保险、健康保险在社会保障体系中的作用，扩大市场的范围，加强法治，消解与限制政府的权力，形成符合市场逻辑的分工，为各种形式的"专业化经营"的涌现奠定基础。**三是彰显企业家精神。** 寿险市场发展的根本动力是充分彰显企业家精神。为了释放企业家的创新活力，要坚持市场化改革、减少政府控制和干预、保护产权以及实现法治。唯有如此，以彰显企业家精神为基本取向的改革才能成为寿险业高质量发展的制度红利。

二、促进寿险资金支持实体经济的发展思路

（一）坚持市场化运作

寿险资金收益性和安全性的要求决定其应秉持市场化原则，主要投资有良好发展预期的优质实体经济项目，以实现可持续发展。相反，投资收益率偏

低、投资安全挑战大的实体经济项目不适合寿险资金投资。在市场化运作的基础上，寿险资金可以发挥规模大、期限长、稳定性高的优势，支持实体经济发展。

坚持市场化运作，除了以市场的方式支持国家重大战略发展外，需要积极探索寿险资金支持民营经济发展，使市场在寿险资金运用中起决定性作用，从而促进经济发展方式转型。

（二）秉持寿险资金运用的基本原则

一是稳健审慎。寿险产品往往有最低投资回报的要求，这使得寿险资金注重安全性。树立稳健审慎的投资理念，是寿险资金运用安身立命的根基。

二要服务主业。当前，寿险业正在向"以保障功能为基础，兼顾财富管理"转型，寿险资金运用要服务寿险主业的发展。值得指出的是，不能将回归保障与"保险姓保"与财富管理对立起来。面对巨大的保险保障缺口，增加保险的长期保障与风险管理功能非常必要，"保险姓保"不意味着保险不可以介入财富管理。尽管当前"保险姓保"强调回归保障与风险管理职能既必要又迫切，但在发展方向上必须清楚，保险业在有效提高保险资金运作能力的基础上，结合风险保障优势，参与财富管理，特别是为长寿风险提供保障，是"保险姓保"和回归保障的应有之义。为此，寿险业要以保障功能为基础，风险管理与财富管理相结合，推动行业的转型升级。同时，为夯实参与财富管理的基础，保险业需要有效提升保险资金运用能力，实现资产负债管理的匹配。

三是长期投资、价值投资、多元化投资。寿险资金是长期资金、是负债资金，其追求安全、稳定的特性，决定了保险资金运用必须坚持长期投资、价值投资和多元化分散投资。因此，寿险资金要做长期资金的提供者、市场价值的发现者、善意的投资者以及多元化、多层次资产配置的风险管理者。

四是资产负债匹配管理。资产负债匹配管理是寿险公司稳健经营的重要基础，是风险管理的核心内容。寿险公司的资产负债管理需要考虑利率风险、流动性风险、市场风险、信用风险、声誉风险等多种因素。

五是依法合规。一方面，要严格遵守保险资金运用监管规则。另一方面，要持续加强机构自身制度、规则建设，有效防范和化解风险。

（三）支持寿险资金运用服务实体经济发展

在坚持市场化运作，秉持资金运用的基本原则的基础上，要支持寿险资金服务实体经济发展。

金融的本质是服务实体经济。国际上看，尤其是在美日欧等发达经济体中，保险资金在服务实体经济发展、促进产业转型升级、改善经济金融体系效率等方面具有天然优势，发挥了非常积极且关键的作用。主要表现在：一是成为基础设施、城镇化等建设资金的重要提供者。二是成为经济转型升级和新经济发展的重要助推器。保险资金成为支持新兴产业发展、兼并重组、淘汰落后产能的关键。三是成为服务小微企业，创新金融产品的重要参与者。保险资金扮演了与传统的重资产、短久期、低风险偏好的银行体系截然不同的角色，可以更好地服务中小微企业、产业创新和经济转型升级。

结合我国国情，保险资金在服务实体经济中具有明显优势，一是保险资金是长期稳定的资金来源，投资形式丰富多样，能够较好地适应不同经济发展周期下实体经济发展融资需求。二是保险资金可以成为银行资金的有效补充，形成差异化优势，更好弥补并促进经济转型升级的融资需求。三是充分利用健全的资本市场和丰富的金融产品媒介和桥梁作用，来实现保险资金服务实体经济发展。四是保险机构不仅仅是资金的提供方，还可以成立专门机构，发起设立金融工具，如并购基金、杠杆基金、夹层基金等，以弥补资本市场和金融工具等方面的不足和缺陷，改善金融市场效率。

（四）促进负债端保险业务与资产端投资业务的融合

资产与负债的匹配不仅仅体现为期限匹配、收益率匹配，还体现为资产与负债属性的匹配。随着转型的深入，寿险公司越来越致力于健康保险和养老保险领域的挖掘和拓展。随着负债业务中健康保险和养老保险的占比不断提高，为了实现资产与负债有效配置，资产配置领域应增加对于养老、健康产业的投资，实现负债业务与养老、健康产业的协同发展。

寿险公司投资养老、健康产业具有良好的产业协同效应。向上连接养老保险、健康保险、护理保险等产品，向下连接老年医疗、老年护理等产业，使保险产品设计、研发、销售协同发展，并整合相关产业，构建全生命产业链，实现保险主业与养老、健康产业相互促进。保险行业拥有大量的客户群体和强大的服务网络，在保险中引入健康管理和养老保障，为客户提供全方位的服务，可以实现保险机构、投保人、相关产业等多方共赢。

寿险资金具有规模大、期限长的属性，与养老、健康产业的发展需求高度契合。寿险资金投资养老、健康产业能够缓解保险资金错配压力，规避经济周期性风险，弱化因资本市场的不稳定对保险公司投资收益的影响，为寿险公司带来稳定现金流收益，使资产负债匹配趋于合理，从而提升保险公司的抗风险能力和可持续发展能力。

因此，要进一步发挥寿险资金优势，推动健康和养老产业发展。支持保险资金参与医疗、养老和健康产业投资，支持保险资金以投资新建、参股、并购等方式兴办养老社区，增加社会养老资源供给，促进保险业和养老产业共同发展。

（五）加强科技在资产管理领域的运用

在支持实体经济的过程中，寿险资金中另类投资的占比不断提高，这使得保险资产组合构建的方式更为复杂，迫切需要加强科技在资产管理领域的运用。同时，为了防范金融风险，监管部门实施底层资产的"穿透"监管，需要保险公司提供最底层投资的基础资料。这也要求保险公司采用更加动态的方式进行资产负债匹配管理，需要更及时、准确的数据以及快速、高效的资产组合构建能力。科技的应用可以帮助保险公司更好地开展投资管理，适应监管以及新形势发展的需要。

近年来保险资产管理行业积极探索应用新科技，已经从早期的应用互联网技术、各种分析模型和信息技术系统，逐渐向应用大数据、云计算和人工智能等新技术转变。目前，金融科技在保险资产管理业的应用主要包括如下几个方面：[1]一是将人工智能技术应用于智能投研、智能投资、智能投顾等方面。例如，通过综合利用人工智能，深度挖掘历史数据，实时跟踪市场行情，辅助专业人员进行价值判断和风险判断，敏锐地捕捉市场机会。[2]二是将大数据分析应用于信用评级与风险控制、舆情分析、精准营销等方面。比如，在风控方面，通过大数据收集投资企业、交易对手的各类有用信息，从而实现对投资对象或交易对象的信用风险监控。[3]三是利用区块链技术驱动金融创新，区块链在资管行业的应用主要体现在中后台运营、支付转账、金融智能合约等。[4]

科技与资管业务相结合，将有效提升资管市场的内在活力和创造力。金融科技在保险资管投研业务中的应用可以逐步实现自动报告生成、金融搜索引

---

①　中国保险资产管理业协会：《中国保险资产管理业发展报告2018》，中国财政经济出版社，2018年。

②　国寿资产管理公司和泰康资产管理公司先后推出各具特色的人工智能投顾平台，标志着保险资管科技应用进入新的阶段。

③　2018年1月，人保资产发起成立"人工智能发展与应用小组"，旨在"智能风控"领域实现突破。团队从发债主体信用资质变化等大数据入手，着手开发具有人保资产特色的"机器学习算法"：通过精准程序设定，让计算机根据市场内企业公开的财务指标"研判"和"学会"信用资质变化的一般规律，并自主应用此规律开展智能化信用评估。同时，依托大数据和人工智能技术，人保资管开发了"信用舆情智能分析系统"，利用机器学习和自然语言处理加工，通过对市场上广泛传播的报告、新闻、消息等进行快速过滤，让计算机能够对文本的倾向性进行判断，从而提前预警发债主体舆情变化的蛛丝马迹，并作为动态调整其信用评级的依据之一，及时让投资操作提前布局。

④　上海保交所就已在利用区块链服务资管业务方面展开了一些有益的尝试。针对在保险资管业务中存在的存续期不透明、合同信息造假及业务相关参与方信息不对称等问题，保交所通过将产品底层信息"上链"，增加数据流转效率，实时监控资产真实情况，为管理者、投资者及监管机构提供透明、真实的资产信息，提高交易链条各方机构对底层资产的信任程度。

擎、智能辅助投资决策和量化投资等功能；在销售和客户服务环节，可以逐步实现客户分群、客户留存、投资组合拓展、销售提升、销售团队维护以及业务优化等功能；在风险管理环节，可以逐步实现信用风险预警、市场风险预警和操作风险预警的功能；在日常管理环节，可以逐步在科技化办公、人力资源管理、知识管理和企业服务支持等方面提升保险资管机构运营能力。

为了进一步促进科技在资产管理领域的应用，**第一，保险企业加大在科技领域的探索和投资**。为了提升保险资产管理行业的效率，保险公司要加大与科技融合的力度，探索以机器深度学习、知识图谱、大数据、云计算、区块链等前沿技术为基础开发的投融资信息、多平台集成、电子化交易、大数据交互等系统。

第二，完善适应保险科技发展的监管体系。监管部门要以开放包容的心态对待保险科技的发展，为市场主体提供创新的空间。同时，要积极探索"保险科技沙盒"机制，以风险可控的方式在有限范围内开展科技创新业务。另外，要发展监管科技，全面提升风险管理水平。

第三，推动行业数据基础设施建设和共享。推动建立统一的保险资管产品基础业务数据规范，提升数据标准化水平；在实现产品注册系统与中保登登记交易系统对接的基础上，逐步推动与保险资管机构、业内投资人、托管银行等更多市场参与机构系统的互联互通，加强与业外机构系统的联动，形成业内外、场内外交易生态圈。

三、防范寿险资金支持实体经济中的风险

（一）要进一步引导寿险业调整负债结构

保险资产负债错配是为了解决负债成本过高的问题。将负债成本控制在合理范围内，有利于降低错配压力，逐步实现资产负债匹配的长期目标。因此，

需要从负债端出发，解决负债端成本高企倒逼投资端提升风险偏好的问题。保险业需要在负债端把握好风险保障功能与理财功能的主次关系，形成与其他金融机构差异化的竞争力。寿险业要以保障功能为基础，风险管理与财富管理相结合，以养老险和健康险为主导，建立可持续的资产负债管理模式，并成为国家养老和健康保障体系的重要组成部分。

（二）提升保险机构以资产负债管理为核心的风险管理能力

保险公司要以《保险资产负债管理监管规则 1–5 号》的颁布为契机，提升以资产负债管理为核心的风险管理能力，实现资产端和负债端的良性互动，建立可持续的资产负债管理模式。为此，要将资产负债管理前置到战略规划中，把整个资产负债管理的重要性提升到保险公司最显著的位置，促进保险公司内部分散的工作协调集中至统一的平台。一是保险机构不断提升资产负债管理意识和能力，加强组织体系和机制建设，建立资产负债管理的决策体系，建立起公司内部各部门尤其是负债管理部门与资产管理部门之间的横向沟通和协调机制，加强各部门之间的信息交流与反馈。二是优化保险公司团队建设。资产负债管理和保险大类资产配置是保险公司长期最核心最基础的能力，需要有足够的人才储备。保险公司要建立资产负债管理与资本配置的专业化团队，推动保险投资的全面化发展。三是转变保险高管理念。经营层要全面充分了解资产负债情况，建立起整个资产配置理念。四是全面提升投资资产和负债的流动性。投资团队要深入到负债端了解负债的特点和背后的逻辑，在此基础上指导负债端业务，形成投资端和负债端的良好互动机制。五是优化考核体系，推动资产负债管理的有效实施。

对于新兴的业务，比如，参与不良产处置，保险机构在投资过程中应以市场化地方式选择专业的中介服务机构、投资顾问或投资管理人，以利用外部资源提高风险防范与管理能力，以应对不良资产处置中的各种投资、法律、信用等风险。

（三）完善以防风险为中心的寿险资金运用监管体系

一是加快推进资产负债管理监管，实现资产端和负债端的良性互动。为此，要建立定量评估、定性评估和压力测试等规则，综合评估保险公司资产负债匹配状况和资产配置能力，差别化实施偿付能力政策和资金运用政策。进一步科学划分和调整大类资产种类和比例，校准偿二代风险因子，优化对不同资产品种和投资行为的资本约束。二是推进通过外部审计、资本监管、信息披露、分类监管、内部控制、社会监督等多种方式，全面严格保险资金运用监管。三是推动保险统计信息系统和保险资产管理监管信息系统建设，进一步加强保险资金托管银行系统与监管信息系统对接。四是研究探索保险资金投资黄金及相关金融产品，运用股指期货、国债期货、利率互换等更多金融衍生产品来对冲和管理风险。五是加强保险业务监管、资金运用监管、偿付能力监管的协调联动，形成监管合力。

（四）加强对关键领域风险的监控与防范

一是加强对保险债权投资计划前后端的管理和风险防控，防范信用风险。二是进行资产配置压力测试，评估资产配置计划对现金流的影响，并做好现金流风险的应急计划，防范资产负债错配风险与流动性风险。三是规范股权投资计划，避免增加地方政府隐性债务。为此，要回归"股权投资"本源，杜绝"明股实债"。同时，要加强主动管理，消除通道业务和多层嵌套，防控金融风险。

（五）加强金融监管部门之间的协调与配合

银行保险、证券监管部门要加强监管协调和合作，防范监管套利，消除金融跨界所带来的监管空白地带。

密切监测货币、财税、外贸、外汇、利率、房地产、股票、社会保障等宏观因素的变化可能给寿险资金运用带来的影响，分析评估风险传导机制与传递通道，有效防范跨市场跨领域风险。

（六）以合作改善投资环境

对于寿险资金参与"一带一路"建设，挖掘与培育域内基础设施投资的优质项目是提升对寿险资金吸引力的关键，为此应加强合作，大力改善域内基础设施投资环境。合作的重点包括四个方面：一是加强沿线国家多边、双边沟通与协商，构建致力于改善整个区域基础设施投资环境的合作和对话机制。二是在寿险资金与基础设施项目之间搭建起信息互通、风险共担、利益共享的平台，在条件允许的领域率先形成制度化合作机制。建立开放共享的项目融资信息平台，可以缓解各类项目参与主体的信息不对称，有助于引导寿险资金与世界银行、亚洲基础设施投资银行、金砖国家开发银行、丝路基金等多边国际机构加强沟通与协调，形成资金支持的合力，及时对接"一带一路"投融资需求，提升寿险资金支持"一带一路"的运行效率。三是在域内基础设施投资风险的识别、防范与应对方面加强合作。在基础设施建设过程中，任何风吹草动，如政府换届、汇率大升大降、他国干预、民众抗议、宗教运动等，都会造成项目的停滞甚至终止，风险的暴露使得企业、金融机构和国家利益遭受严重损失。对此，沿线国家应就风险考察指标设计、风险因素跟踪、重大风险防范与应对等展开积极合作。四是加快推进投融资条件较好的项目建设，将其打造成为早期收获项目，发挥示范引领作用，推动域内外投资者对"一带一路"项目的信心。

（七）提升地方政府的契约精神

目前在保险资金另类投资中，很大一部分是以基础设施投资计划等保险资产管理产品的形式，投资于地方政府及其所属企业。因此，地方政府的契约精神直接影响到投资的风险和收益。债权投资计划一般回报率不太高，要求风险较为平稳。但在项目执行中，如果政府不遵守契约，风险就会显著加大。目前一些保险资金投资遇到了部分地方政府没有按照原计划的用途使用资金或单方面要求修改收益率条款等情况，不同程度地反映出政府契约精神的缺失问题。另外，基础设施投资计划投资期限较长，往往要经历两届或两届以上的政府，如果政府缺乏契约精神，必然造成政府换届换人所带来的违约风险，给保险投资带来损失。

在政府与企业的合作中，政府由于掌握了政策、规则的制定权而处于强势地位，企业则处于相对的弱势地位。在市场经济中，只有地位平等，才能进行公平的交易。由于政府和企业存在着天然的不平等，就需要用契约规定双方的权利与义务，以确保双方能够以平等关系进行公平交易。因此，为了促进寿险资金支持实体经济，要完善合作契约，提升地方政府的契约精神。保险企业与政府之间要平等地订立契约，建立利益与风险分担机制；同时，双方要尊重并共同信守契约，政府不能滥用权力。短期来看，要尽量制定严密的合同文本，对政府形成难以随便毁约的实质性约束。长远而言，则要提高法治化水平，用健全的制度规范和约束政府的行为。

（八）强化行业风险管理

要加强相关部门的协调，强化行业风险管理。[①]保险业相关行业组织应当切实发挥平台作用，在基础设施投资计划等保险资产管理产品注册、登记相关工作中，依法加强对保险资金运用涉及的地方债务风险的监测，严格查验投资合规性。同时，加快探索建立行业性的区域信用风险评估框架，逐步健全行业性

---

① 　原中国保监会、财政部印发的《关于加强保险资金运用管理 支持防范化解地方债务风险的指导意见》（保监发〔2018〕6号）。

风险预警机制，及时向保险机构提示风险。各省（自治区、直辖市、计划单列市）政府性债务管理领导小组办公室要加快建立跨部门联合监测和防控机制，统计监测涉及保险机构的政府中长期支出事项以及向融资平台公司提供的债权投资情况，加强信息共享和数据校验，定期通报监测结果，支持保险机构完善风险管理体系。

四、完善寿险资金支持实体经济的政策环境

（一）深化保险资金运用市场化改革

要拓展投资领域，把更多选择空间和选择权交给市场主体，将支持实体经济发展作为创新资金运用方式的出发点和落脚点。

第一，扩大保险资金的投资范围。目前险资另类投资主要有三种方式：一是直接开展重大股权投资、不动产投资等；二是投资于债权投资计划、股权投资计划、资产支持计划等保险资管产品；三是投资于集合信托计划。重大股权投资与不动产投资对于保险机构的资金、资源、专业能力要求很高，受制于风险防范与保险机构自身的能力，目前仍主要集中于少数龙头企业，短期内难以成为保险业普遍推行的投资模式。而债权投资计划则主要限定于不动产和基础设施投资领域。这些投资领域的资金需求较大、周期长，和保险资金的期限特征匹配度较高，但在目前的经济结构调整和监管态势下，资金投向和交易对手受政策影响较大，使得保险资金可投资的中长期资产较为缺乏。在这种背景下，对投资领域作严格限定，难以满足保险资金对于非标投资的需求。因此，为了更好地服务实体经济的需求，要逐步放开能够有效匹配保险资金运用需求的投资领域。为此，监管部门要推动保险资金参与长租市场等政策尽快落地，并适时扩大投资范围，增加优质债权投资计划和股权投资计划供给，扩大资产

支持计划业务，逐步允许保险资金对流动性较好、有长期增值潜力资产的投资，如资产支持证券（ABS）、房地产信托投资基金（REITs）、非公开定向债务融资工具（PPN）、黄金、大宗商品等，从而赋予市场更大的资产配置选择空间。[①]

第二，出台保险资管产品业务细则。出台细则可以进一步明确监管要求和业务规范，便于市场主体在实际操作层面更好落实。[②]细则应着眼于长远，兼顾保险资管产品的特点，从而有利于支持资管产品创新，维护业务平稳过渡，促进市场公平竞争，发挥保险资金支持实体经济的作用。在保险资管产品细则中，要基于服务保险主业、加大服务实体经济力度的定位，积极推进多层次的保险资管产品体系建设，更加充分有效地满足保险资金资产配置的多元化需求。[③]为此，一是在推进现有的债权投资计划、资产支持计划等产品转为标准化产品的过程中，适当增加弹性，赋予投融资双方更多的选择权。因为一旦纳入到标准化产品范围内，虽然产品的流动性与公开程度有所提升，但流动性风险与市场风险溢价将相应摊薄，收益率将呈下行趋势，将加大险资收益率提升的难度。因此，要根据市场交易主体的需求，增加转为标准化产品的弹性。如果交易主体更加关注流动性、信息透明度，则可选择公开挂牌转让并满足相应的标准化产品监管要求；如果融资方、投资者或管理人更加看重非流动性溢价，均无公开挂牌的需求，应允许其选择以私募产品形式完成相应的注册或备案程序。二是在债权投资计划、资产支持计划等现有产品体系基础上，逐步增设规范化的非标产品序列。允许保险资管根据资金的特点，在做好风险管理的前提下有针对性地开发与保险资金投资风格和风险偏好相契合的非标产品，发

---

①　曹德云：应尽快出台保险资管产品业务细则，http://www.cs.com.cn/xwzx/hg/201807/t20180728_5849197.html

②　曹德云：应尽快出台保险资管产品业务细则，http://www.cs.com.cn/xwzx/hg/201807/t20180728_5849197.html

③　韩向荣、胡学文：《保险资管非标投资反思与展望》，《中国保险资产管理》，2018年第3期。

挥保险资金专业优势，满足保险资金运用需求，并更好地满足实体经济的融资需求。

第三，完善相关监管规定。一是根据现实情况和市场需要，调整现行法规制度中操作性和适用性不强的条款，适当扩大投资运作空间。比如，现行保险资管产品发行主要从融资主体、资金投向、增信措施、信用评级、风险管理等方面做了较为严格的规定。[①]其中，关于增信措施的规定采用了列举式方式，对于各类增信方式要求较为严格。上述规定有助于提升保险资金运用的安全性，但也导致了现有保险资管产品的交易结构较为单一，使得保险资管产品既难以适应融资方的个性化需求，又难以提升保险资管的专业投资能力和产品设计能力，在资产端竞争中较为被动。因此，要坚持"放开前端、管住后端"的监管理念，优化产品发行相关规定。可以在产品发行条件、增信措施方面予以适当放松及优化，将监管重点集中于信息披露方面，更多地将产品设计能力、风险控制方法等回归市场主体，从而提升保险资金运用的专业能力。二是要完善基础设施债权计划相关的管理规则。要完善融资主体免于增信的条件；适时拓宽投资计划资金用途。三是适时放开保险资金投资股权的范围，包括适时放开间接投资股权的范围；适时放开直接投资股权的范围；适时将保险股权投资审批制改为备案制。四是依据保险机构投资能力水平等实行分级分类的差异化监管，更好引导保险资金运用稳健运行。五是引导保险机构拉长考核期限，优化绩效考核体制，倡导长期投资理念。

（二）明确不动产抵押登记政策

建议明确保险机构在资金融出方面享有与银行等金融机构同等的主体地位，推动国土等部门出台规范土地抵质押登记的政策，允许保险机构依法办理

---

①　韩向荣、胡学文：《保险资管非标投资反思与展望》，《中国保险资产管理》，2018年第3期。

土地抵质押登记手续。

依据我国物权法、担保法的相关规定，"建设用地使用权/国有土地使用权"属于法律规定的"抵押财产"范围，只要债务人或第三人同意为债务人履行债务提供土地使用权抵押担保，对债务人拥有合法债权的"债权人"就可以作为"抵押权人"。我国物权法、担保法对于"债权人"作为土地使用权抵押权人并无其他限制性规定，保险资产管理公司作为其发起设立的不动产投资计划的合法债权人，当然可以作为土地使用权抵押权人。作为土地使用权抵押权人，保险资产管理公司必须与抵押人一起至相关国土部门申请土地抵押登记，否则土地使用权抵押权不能依法设立。

正因为作为上位法的我国物权法、担保法规定"债权人为抵押权人"，且并未对土地使用权抵押权人作其他限制性规定，国土资源部于 2012 年 9 月 6 日下发国土部 134 号文第五条只是规定放贷人可以申请土地抵押登记（未规定只有放贷人方能申请土地抵押登记），并采用不完全列举的方式列举了持有中国银监会颁发的《金融许可证》的银行业金融机构、经营小额贷款业务的小额贷款公司可以作为放贷人。因为，我国物权法、担保法所称的"债权人"并不仅仅包含"放贷人"，还包括其他因借贷、买卖等民事活动产生合法债权的其他企业或自然人。

因此，国土部 134 号文的本意并非是限定只有持有中国银监会颁发的《金融许可证》的银行业金融机构、小额贷款公司等放贷人才能作为土地使用权抵押权人，而保险资产管理公司等其他企业或自然人就无法作为土地使用权抵押权人申请土地抵押登记，只是很多地方国土部门对于国土部 134 号文的相关规定进行了"缩小解释"，导致实践操作中保险资产管理公司作为"保险资产管理公司不动产投资计划"的合法债权人，不能作为土地使用权抵押权人申请土地抵押登记。

为了解决实践中的问题，建议有关部门明确保险资产管理公司可以申请土地抵押登记。2017年6月，中国银监会、国土资源部联合下发《关于金融资产管理公司等机构业务经营中不动产抵押权登记若干问题的通知》，明确金融资产管理公司及其分支机构在法定经营范围内开展经营活动，需要以不动产抵押担保方式保障其债权实现的，可依法申请办理不动产抵押权登记。

建议有关部门明确保险机构在资金融出方面享有与银行等金融机构同等的主体地位，推动国土等部门出台规范土地抵质押登记的政策，允许保险机构依法办理土地抵质押登记手续。即只要债务人或第三人同意提供土地使用权抵押担保，保险资产管理公司作为不动产相关项目的合法债权人，就可以作为土地使用权抵押权人申请土地抵押登记，有关地方国土部门应当为保险资产管理公司相应办理土地使用权抵押登记手续。

（三）消除投资养老健康产业的政策障碍

消除保险机构投资养老健康产业面临的市场准入、土地和财税政策等方面障碍。为此，要明确养老健康服务产业的进入标准、配套设施和专业服务等行业标准，明确养老健康服务产业的用地性质以及营利性的养老健康服务行业税收优惠政策等。

（四）完善PPP领域的相关配套政策

一是进一步完善政府和社会资本合作领域的立法，加大对保险机构参与投资的土地、财税政策等方面的支持。

二是对保险资金投资股权金融产品获得的收益，明确予以免征企业所得税。对于股息收入，《企业所得税法》第二十六条将"股息、红利等权益性投资收益"界定为企业的"免税收入"，免征企业所得税。企业股权投资转让所得则应并入企业的应纳税所得，依法缴纳企业所得税。但由于《企业所得税法》并没有明确资管机构发行的股权投资计划等股权金融产品股息的纳税政策，造成在税收征收的实践层面，保险资金投资保险资产管理机构发行的股权投资计划等股权金融产品，面临双重征税问题，即：被投资企业以股息形式向股权计划支付的收益，来源为其税后利润，已由被投资企业缴纳企业所得税，此为第一次征税；股权计划运用收到的股息向保险资金投资者分配收益，这部分收益被纳入保险公司税前利润，被再次征收企业所得税，此为第二次征税。现行企业所得税法关于股权投资计划项目相关的税务处理没有清晰规定，执行中也出现各方理解和认识角度不同的情况，造成实务操作困难。因此，建议对保险资金投资股权金融产品获得的收益，明确予以免征企业所得税。

三是加强投资者权益保护。保险资金投资的一些重大项目，面临着投资者权益难以保障的局面。因此，要加快央企市场化改革，提高央企的透明度，保护保险机构投资者合法权益。

四是完善国有保险公司项目投资绩效评估机制，明确与民营企业合作政策。由于体制和机制不完善，国有保险公司投资风险偏好相对保守，难以接受投资损失和风险，和民营企业合作有顾虑，对中小微企业和新兴产业的投资力度不大。因此，要完善国有保险公司项目投资绩效评估机制，为其投资以及与民营企业合作创造良好的政策环境。

（五）优化寿险资金参与"一带一路"建设的政策环境

政府的责任是通过优化政策环境，为寿险资金参与"一带一路"建设提供良好的制度环境和有力支持。寿险资金参与"一带一路"建设涉及寿险资金的境外投资及其直接对接实体经济项目，需要完善相关政策的配套。目前寿险公司的保费收入基本都以本币为单位，如果境外投资比例过高会产生货币错配风险。而且，由于境外投资市场的不确定性及险资的安全性，保监监管部门在审核境外投资时仍比较谨慎，外汇监管部门对于险资的流出也比较审慎。开展境外投资，把更多风险判断权和投资选择权交给市场主体，势必增加一些风险的来源和种类，但通过强化事中事后监管，建立现代化的监管体系，能够有效应对上述风险隐患。因此，建议保险与外汇监管部门在有效监管的基础上支持寿险资金审慎开展境外投资。为此，要适时将更多的"一带一路"沿线国家纳入寿险资金可投资国家或地区的范围。同时，鼓励和支持寿险资金管理机构开发"一带一路"相关投资产品。寿险资金管理机构可以根据客户需求，围绕"一带一路"沿线国家的优质资产开发各类投资产品，帮助客户分享投资"一带一路"优质资产带来的收益。

（六）完善寿险资金参与不良资产处置的政策环境

首先，适时放开保险机构参与不良资产证券化投资。资产证券化是依靠市场力量处置不良资产的主要工具，市场发展潜力巨大。为支持保险资金投资不良资产证券化，相关部门要适时放开保险机构参与不良资产证券化，并对不良资产的评级、风险管控等作出明确的规定，完善相关的法律法规。

其次，完善市场化债转股的配套政策。一是将债转股和国有企业混合所有制改革相结合。推动债转股企业的国企改制、员工持股、股权激励等改革，真正转变企业经营机制，从而激发企业和社会投资者参与债转股的热情。

二是建立健全股权退出机制。只有具备通畅的退出渠道，机构投资者才能积极参与债转股，从而避免明股实债。可以通过完善IPO、上市公司资产注入、定向增发等方面的配套政策，支持市场化债转股的退出机制。

三是完善国有股权交易进场和评估方面的政策，推动债转股项目按照市场化和法治化原则实施。

四是完善债转股相关的税收政策，对金融机构通过金融产品实施债转股，研究讨论取消双重征收所得税。

五是通过完善锁价非公开发行、非公开发行规模、募集资金用途及发行股份购买资产范围等相关政策，促进上市公司市场化债转股的实施。

（七）探索寿险资金开展贷款业务

《保险资金运用管理办法》（保监会令〔2018〕1号）规定，除个人保单质押贷款外，不得将保险资金运用形成的投资资产用于向他人提供担保或者发放贷款。这就意味着目前寿险资金不能直接开展贷款业务。

目前探索寿险资金开展贷款业务非常必要。一是有利于缓解寿险资金"长钱短配"的问题，更好地实现资产负债匹配。寿险资金的期限较长，大都在7年以上。随着我国寿险业的转型，10年期以上的寿险资金占比将继续提高。但由于我国目前国债、金融债等固定收益类产品的期限较短，保险资金在配置时很难找到优质长久期固定收益类产品。一些期限较长、利率固定的贷款业务可以满足这类资产的配置需求。二是可以补充银行贷款的不足，满足对长期性贷款的需求。银行由于存款期间一般都较短（5年以上存款占比较少），开展期限较长的贷款容易造成"短债长配"。而与银行相比，寿险资金的期限更长，更有利于从事期限较长的贷款业务。因此，与银行相比，寿险资金的期限结构与期限较长的贷款业务更匹配，可以更好地满足长期性贷款需求。三是寿险资金直接开展贷款业务有助于突破债权投资计划的不足。目前债权投资产品过于强调增信措施，实质上是更加注重交易对手的信用风险防范，而非产品与基础资产风险，导致了这类业务与银行授信的同质化程度较高，但相应的融资成本、产品发行效率等却缺乏优势。[①]可见，债权投资计划等保险资产管理产品在基础资产、交易结构和增信措施等方面的灵活性不足，与银行贷款相比，竞争力有所下降。同时，在货币政策宽松或是放松银行放贷规模限制时，由于保险资金与银行贷款之间存在竞争关系，保险资金就难以从银行渠道获取项目资源和增信支持。因此，寿险资金直接开展贷款业务，将有助于突破债权计划的不足，增强相对于银行贷款的竞争力。四是寿险资金开展贷款业务是很多国家与地区寿

---

① 韩向荣、胡学文：《保险资管非标投资反思与展望》，《中国保险资产管理》，2018年第3期。

险资金运用的经验。保险资金开展贷款业务一直是欧美等发达国家重要投资渠道之一。[①]美国于20世纪初就开始允许保险资金投资抵押贷款，日本在20世纪60年代后期为促进中小企业发展允许寿险公司向中小企业贷款，韩国和中国台湾地区在20世纪七八十年代允许保险资金用于抵押贷款。此外，美国、中国台湾等国家与地区允许保险资金通过认购 MBS 等证券化产品间接流向信贷市场。允许寿险资金开展贷款业务，不仅支持了实体经济对于长期资金的需求，而且获取了较好的收益，从而支持了承保业务的发展。

当前探索寿险资金开展贷款业务也具有较强的现实基础。一是寿险资金通过债权计划等另类投资对接实体经济项目，很大程度上带有贷款的属性。保险公司与保险资产管理公司已经通过另类投资积累了投资实体经济项目的经验，为开展贷款业务奠定了良好的基础。二是一些贷款业务可以为寿险资金提供风险相对较低的投资领域。比如，我国个人住房抵押贷款目前审查较为严格，除了要求较高的首付比率和购买抵押贷款保证保险外，还需贷款人有稳定收入，故业务风险相对较低。这些低风险领域可以成为寿险资金开展贷款业务很好的切入点。

为了积极稳妥地推动寿险资金开展贷款业务，要适时放宽政策限制、选择合适的开展贷款业务的方式、加强组织管理与风险控制。

一是适时放宽对于寿险资金直接发放贷款的限制。要加强银保监会与中国人民银行等部门的沟通和协调，允许寿险资金在一定范围针对特定对象进行直接放贷。另外，寿险资金不能直接发放贷款根本上受制于目前分业经营的金融体制，因此，放开寿险资金直接放贷的限制，还需要逐步修订和完善现行金融法律法规，改革现行金融体制。

二是不同类型的保险公司应根据资源禀赋的差异，选择不同的开展贷款

---

① 　吴杰：《保险资金开展贷款业务的路径选择与风险防范》，《上海保险》，2016年第10期。

业务的方式。其中，资产规模较大、金融牌照全覆盖的大型保险集团公司可以选择独立开展贷款业务的方式。其优点是可以节省委托银行所需的中间业务费用。但不足是保险公司或保险资产管理公司需要设立独立从事贷款业务的部门，并配置相应业务人员。经营规模较小的中小保险公司以及银行系保险公司可以选择"银保合作"开展贷款业务的方式，即保险公司与银行合作，委托银行审批和发放贷款。这种方式的优点是保险公司无需成立新业务部门或机构，避免专业人员和经验不足带来的经营风险。但不足是需要支付银行的中间费用，利润被摊薄。保险公司还可以通过持有MBS等证券化产品间接开展贷款业务。由于MBS产品经过风险隔离、信用增级后已属于固定收益型债券产品，风险较低而收益相对较高，比较适合没有太多直接贷款经验的寿险资金投资。

三是加强对分支机构的权限管理和稽核，规范贷款业务运作。一旦放开保险资金开展贷款业务，对于独立开展抵押贷款业务的保险机构来说，需要分支机构来运作相关业务。为了防范金融风险，放贷资金的审批权可以归总部统一管理，分支机构和网点负责业务操作，以避免20世纪八九十年代保险资金运用监管较为宽松时期曾经发生基层分支机构"人情"放贷、"关系"放贷等混乱情形。同时，应注重对分支机构的稽查，保证贷款业务的良好运行和健康发展。

四是加强风险管控。要加强对借款人的信用风险评估、贷后抵押品价值的动态评估并及时调整抵押比率，实现风险管控。

（八）积极培育保险资产管理市场

寿险资金支持实体经济发展的重要途径是另类投资。另类投资的重要特征是非标准化投资，因锁定期较长、流动性较差而享有更高的流动性风险与市场风险溢价。同时，寿险公司是金融市场最主要的长期机构投资者之一，更有可能承受更高的流动性风险和市场波动风险来获取更高的风险溢价。因此，流动性不足是另类投资的重要内生属性。保险业可以推进保险非标资产的交易平台建设，建立非标资产可交易机制，为保险公司管理流动性提供支撑，提高保险资金运用效率。同时，增加流动性还可以提高保险资管产品的吸引力，扩大产品规模，从而进一步提升保险资金服务实体经济的能力。另外，通过产品交易还可以形成科学合理的收益率曲线，发挥对中长期资金市场定价的基准作用。

长期以来，保险业缺乏保险非标资产交易平台，导致保险资管公司缺乏流动性对冲机制，非标资产流动性的不足在一定程度上抑制了保险资金的优势。因此，相关政策一直鼓励保险资管行业加强平台建设，提高产品流动性。2012年发布的《国务院关于加快发展现代保险服务业的若干意见》中提出，要积极培育另类投资市场，加强市场基础设施建设，组建全行业的资产托管中心和保险资产交易平台；2016年的政府工作报告中再次提出建立保险资产交易机制；同年，《中华人民共和国国民经济和社会发展第十三个五年规划纲要》进一步提出，探索建立保险资产交易机制；2018年4月1日正式实施的《保险资金运用管理办法》规定，"保险资产管理机构开展保险资产管理产品业务，应当在中国保监会认可的资产登记交易平台进行发行、登记、托管、交易、结算、信息披露以及相关信用增进和抵质押融资等业务"。2017年，上海保险交易所股份有限公司设立了专业子公司，即中保保险资产登记交易系统有限公司，负责建设和运营中保保险资产登记交易系统已于2018年上线运行。保险资产管理产品上市交易，可以通过公开市场交易机制盘活存量资产流动性。[①]

为了培育保险资产管理市场，未来要继续加强平台建设，提高产品流动性。

一是加强平台建设。对类标准化产品，可以依托上海保险交易所与其他场内交易市场对接，实现互联互通，为产品提供更加充足的流动性支持和公允定价的基础。为此，要继续加强上海保险交易所和保险资产交易平台建设，在运

---

①　曾于瑾：《夯基实础，高质量建设保险资产登记交易平台》，《当代金融家》，2018年第5期。

行中不断完善保险资产集中登记系统和保险资产交易系统建设。进一步升级中国保险资产管理业协会的保险资产管理产品注册系统，强化数据统计分析处理功能，并开发产品估值模型，为保险资产交易平台上线提供基础性支持。[①]对于类信托产品而言，交易结构取决于双方的风险预期，个性化较强，更适合在场外市场进行交易信息备案及挂牌转让。[②]中国保险资产管理业协会或保交所可以牵头搭建柜台交易市场，在挂牌条件、信息披露、交易结算、产品设计、投资者约束条件等方面与场内市场予以区分，将类信托产品统一纳入备案管理范畴，更加方便进行市场监测和风险把控，并为此类产品提供挂牌转让的场所，为投资者提供适度的流动性选择权。

二是推进保险资产管理产品标准化。保险资产管理产品在产品治理、交易结构、运作流程等方面较为复杂，从便于上市交易考虑，要逐步推进产品标准化，包括合同文本标准化、要素含义标准化、交易结构标准化等。[③]

三是推进非标资产标准化。在集中登记的基础上，通过构建活跃的场内交易市场，形成科学公允的产品估值体系，将保险非标资产转为标准资产，进一步激发保险资管产品的市场活力。[④]

① 曹德云：《保险资产管理产品创新的现实困难与应对措施》，《清华金融评论》，2016年第6期。
② 韩向荣、胡学文：《保险资管非标投资反思与展望》，《中国保险资产管理》，2018年第3期。
③ 曹德云：《保险资产管理产品创新的现实困难与应对措施》，《清华金融评论》，2016年第6期。
④ 曾于瑾：《夯基实础，高质量建设保险资产登记交易平台》，《当代金融家》，2018年第5期。

后　记

为更好促进金融业服务实体经济，国务院发展研究中心金融研究所与英国保诚集团相关部门组成联合课题组，合作开展了"寿险资金支持实体经济研究"。在近一年的研究中，课题组广泛调研了保险监管部门和相关市场主体，深入了解了我国寿险资金支持实体经济的现状、存在的突出问题、主要政策障碍与风险。课题组还出访新加坡和印度尼西亚，围绕寿险业发展、寿险资金投资基础设施与支持实体经济等议题与国外专家开展了深入交流。在深入调研的基础上，课题组于2018年年中完成研究报告讨论稿，并于2018年9月召开了研究成果发布与专家研讨会。在充分吸引国内外专家反馈意见和建议的基础上，课题组进一步修改完善报告，最终形成本书。

在课题研究和本书出版中，课题组得到了各方面的大力支持。国务院发展研究中心王一鸣副主任始终关心和指导课题的研究工作。国务院发展研究中心国际合作局对课题开展提供了广泛支持。英国保诚集团首席执行官Michael A. Wells、亚太区政府关系总监Paul Lynch、英国保诚保险有限公司北京代表处对研究提供了重要支持。有多位监管机构的领导、研究机构和保险公司的专家对课题组的调研和研讨会的召开提供了帮助，在此一并感谢！

在课题研究中，我们恪守专业研究的精神，对寿险资金支持实体经济的问题、风险和政策障碍进行客观分析，提出相应的政策建议。但受理论水平、经验积累和调研不够充分等因素的影响，有些问题论述可能还不够深入，有些观点和判断可能存在不当之处，恳请各位专家学者和广大读者批评指正。

"寿险资金支持实体经济研究"课题组

2018年10月

RESEARCH ON THE LIFE INSURANCE FUNDS IN SUPPORT OF THE REAL ECONOMY

Research Institute of Finance of the Development
Research Center of the State Council

中国发展出版社
CHINA DEVELOPMENT PRESS

Research Team

From Research Institute of Finance of the Development Research Center of the State Council

Project consultant: Zhang Chenghui and Wu Zhenyu

Project leader: Chen Daofu

Project Coordinator: Zhu Junsheng

Main participants: Zhang Liping, Tian Hui, Liu Xuan, Wang Gang, Zhu Hongming, Wang Yang and Bo Yan

From Prudential plc

Steve Bickell, Paul Lynch, Johnny Chang,

Angela Yin, Stephan Van Vliet, Nadir Maruf

Preface One

As China's socialist market economy continues to develop and improve, the status and role of the financial system in the allocation of funds is deepening day by day. As an important part of the modern financial system, the insurance industry has rapidly increased the amount of funds absorbed and used. In 2107, the available balance of insurance funds was as high as RMB 14.920621 trillion. In the same year, the incremental funds were RMB 1.5295 trillion, accounting for 7.8% of the scale of the social financing and strongly supporting the development of the real economy. Life insurance funds are the main body of insurance funds. They have the features of large size, long maturities and high stability, etc., and have displayed natural advantages in supporting the real economy. With the further ageing of China's population, and the increasing demand for the coverage of residents' healthcare and pension insurances and wealth management, the funds from long-term life insurance will see a steady growth and play an increasingly important role in supporting the development of the real economy. Therefore, it is of important theoretical value and positive practical significance for us to study the problems and policy barriers existing in the support to the real economy by life insurance funds and propose the relevant policy recommendations in order to broaden the channels for the life insurance funds

to support the real economy and promote the insurance sector to deliver sustainable support to the real economy.

In order to expand the theoretical horizon and absorb international advanced experience, the Research Institute of Finance of the Development Research Center of the State Council and the relevant departments of the Prudential Plc of the United Kingdom jointly launched the research on the Life Insurance Funds in Support of the Real Economy from the second half of 2017 to the first half of 2018. This book has been revised based on the research report of the topic. The structure of the book is as follows: Chapter I is the connotations and practices of China's life insurance industry in support of the real economy. On the basis of defining the economic connotations of the service industry of life insurance industry, it evaluates the economic situation of China's life insurance industry and proposes the meaning and direction of life insurance funds to support the real economy. Chapter II is the status quo of life insurance funds supporting the real economy. It surveys the policy environment and main methods for life insurance funds to support the development of the real economy, especially the importance of alternative investment such as infrastructure construction in the synergy of the life insurance funds and the real economy and the positive results of the life insurance fund in supporting the real economy. Chapter III covers the challenges, risks and policy barriers that life insurance funds face in support of the real economy. Based on the feedback from market subjects and policy regulators in the survey, it surveys the main challenges, main risks and policy obstacles faced by life insurance funds in supporting the real economy. Chapter IV covers the international experience, lessons and development trends of life insurance funds in support of the real economy. In combination with the latest developments in the international life insurance funds in supporting the real economy, it examines the

main international experiences, lessons, development trends and their implications for China. Chapter V covers the policy recommendations for promoting the life insurance funds to support the real economy. Combining the problems of China's life insurance funds in supporting the real economy and international experience, it proposes policy recommendations to promote China's life insurance funds to support the real economy.

At present, the core task of financial work is to support the development of the real economy development, promote financing facilitation, reduce the cost of the real economy, and improve the efficiency of resource allocation. The Research Institute of Finance of the Development Research Center of the State Council has been conducting research on important theoretical and policy issues in financial reform and development. I hope that the topic of Life Insurance Funds in support of the Real Economy can summarize the new situations, new explorations and new problems in the life insurance funds supporting the real economy, provide certain enlightenment and references for the insurance industry to innovate the support mechanism for the real economy, for the financial regulatory authorities to adjust the regulatory policies and for the policy-making authorities to improve relevant policies, and help promote China's financial reform and development.

WU Zhenyu

Director

Research Institute of Finance

Development Research Center of the State Council (DRC)

October 2018

Preface Two

Prudential, through its joint venture with CITIC Group, began operations in China in 2000. Over the past 18 years China has gone through an exceptional social and economic transformation, with millions being lifted out of poverty, and a rapidly growing middle class. But social and economic challenges remain, as China seeks to ensure that it does not fall into the middle-income trap. The development of a more socially inclusive and sustainable economy is a crucial focus area in China's current five-year plan. We believe Life insurance funds have a key role to play in support of government's ambitions to be a moderately prosperous society by 2021 and a completely developed country by 2049. Therefore, we are proud to have worked together with the Development Research Center (DRC) of the State Council in China on the important topic of "Life Insurance Funds in support of the Real Economy".

The real economy needs a mix of funding options with different characteristics. The banking system is focused on relatively short-term lending with a higher risk profile and a need for liquidity. Life insurance funds need long-term assets to match their long-term promises, of savings and protection, to their customers. This long-term financing is an important tool to foster sustainable growth and financial stability. The lack of it could lead to serious impediment to the growth prospects of an economy.

To date, life insurance and pension funds have not been a significant source of funding for the real economy in the emerging markets, despite their beneficial characteristics. However, this is about to change.

The accumulation and deployment of life insurance premiums has the potential to transform the dormant capital of vast numbers of policyholders into productive long-term capital to support strong economic growth. Typically, the funds are channelled into the economy through long-term Government or municipal bonds, or investment grade corporate bonds. But where appropriate, life insurance funds can also be significant institutional investors in equity markets, taking a long-term view that acts as a counter-balance to short-term volatility. In addition, Governments across Asia have recognised that sustainable growth needs massive investment in infrastructure projects. Life insurers can play a critical role in productive collaboration with Government to finance strategic long-term projects, such as those foreseen under the Belt and Road Initiative, either through debt or equity, using project finance or capital market finance.

The life insurance sector is important not only as a source of funding to the real economy and its growth, but is a significant contributor to professional employment and talent development. It also encourages entrepreneurship and individual investment, as well as consumption, through wealth protection. A study by the UK think tank Oxford Analytica, sponsored by Prudential, found that the multiplier effects of employment, consumer spending and investment meant that every dollar spent on life insurance premiums added nearly three dollars to GDP.a

A well-established and functional regulatory framework can reinforce and help realise the positive benefits created by the life insurance sector and its funds. The

---

[1]   Oxford Analytica's report of "The Indonesian life insurance sector – an economic impact assessment", 1 July 2013

research team has carefully studied how applying the appropriate policies could benefit the Chinese real economy. With this robust piece of research, DRC in collaboration with Prudential have provided policy recommendations to support sustainable deployment of insurance funds to various types of investments into the real economy. We encourage the government to enter into dialogue with the insurance industry to consider the adoption of these recommendations, and support a life insurance framework that enables life insurance funds to have a greater role in supporting the real economy.

Paul Lynch

Regional Director, Government Relations

Prudential Corporation Asia

November 2018

Contents

Chapter IV: International Experience, lessons and development trends in enabling life insurance funds to support the real economy...................116

Chapter V: Policy Recommendations to Facilitate the Real Economy through Life Insurance Funds in China 133

Executive Summary

By the end of 2017, the balance of utilized insurance funds amounted to RMB 14.920621 trillion and strongly supported the development of the real economy; among which the life insurance funds, with its features of large size, long maturities and high stability, etc., have displayed natural advantages in supporting the real economy. With the further ageing of China's population, and the increasing demand for the coverage of residents' healthcare and pension insurances and wealth management, the funds from long-term life insurance will see a steady growth and play an increasingly important role in supporting the development of the real economy. Therefore, it is of important theoretical value and positive practical significance for us to study the problems and policy barriers existing in the support to the real economy by life insurance funds and propose the relevant policies to improve the life insurance funds in supporting the real economy in order to broaden the channels for the life insurance funds to support the real economy and promote the insurance sector to deliver sustainable support to the real economy.

I. Intention and Practice of China's Life Insurance Industry Serving the Real Economy

(I) Intention of Life Insurance Industry Serving the Real Economy

We must understand the intention of life insurance industry serving the real economy from multiple angles including functions, efficiencies and risks. The intention of life insurance industry serving the real economy include: the precondition for the life insurance industry to serve the real economy is the urgent need to vigorously promote (instead of contain) the high quality development of the life insurance industry; the life insurance

industry serving the real economy shall take the risk coverage function as its core and the liability business as the foundation; the life insurance sector can support the real economy by acting as the shock absorber and long-term investor for the economy and providing such services as wealth management and social security; the life insurance industry serving the real economy can generate positive effects and help to promote economic growth and stabilize the financial market; the evaluation criteria of other financial sectors shall not be inappropriately applied to the life insurance industry serving the real economy. We shall not reach the conclusion that the insurance industry has shifted from the real economy to the virtual economy just because the insurance funds have engaged in indirect investment through such channels as banks and securities market, etc., and shall not regard the insurance funds as serving the real economy just because the insurance funds are directly providing funds to enterprise development through debt investment or equity investment plans, etc.

(II) Status evaluation of China's life insurance industry serving the real economy

With its growing strength, China's life insurance industry has been playing an increasingly important role in serving the real economy, with remarkable performance in job creation and increasing revenues, etc. China's life insurance industry displays special features different from its Western counterparts in terms of serving the real economy and the most distinguishing feature is that it is more strongly government-guided in the operation and development. At the same time, as various functions of China's life insurance industry have not been brought into full play, the methods and efforts in serving the real economy still lags far behind the foreign countries with stronger insurance industries. China's life insurance industry has witnessed the shift from real economy to virtual economy in recent years, which is a classic development feature of the primary stage and a reflection of immature development of China's life insurance industry.

(III) Significance and direction for China's life insurance fund to support the real economy

Currently, actively promoting the life insurance investment to serve the real economy is of special significance in that the current funds supply is not sufficient

to meet the demands of China's economic development for large amounts of long-term fund in the future. Though the aggregate shows that China is not short of funds and the funds supply is in plenty, but structurally, the short-term and debt investment funds might become excessive and the long-term and, equity investment funds are remarkably insufficient under the bank-dominated financial system, which is a strong point of the life insurance funds. Such unique advantages as large size, stable sources of income, long maturities, and relatively low requirements on the return on investment, of the life insurance funds has made them the ideal source of long-term funds. Against this backdrop, the unique advantages of the life insurance funds can cater to the features of funds urgently needed for China's economic development, and help to fill up the gaps for funds, which show that life insurance companies are indispensable as funds providers.

Considering the above fact, the future investment direction of China's life insurance funds shall be focused on meeting the effective demands of the real economy, and the key points are: (1) to assist such national strategies as the Belt & Road Initiative (BRI), integrated Beijing-Tianjin-Hebei regional development and Yangtze River Economic Belt; (2) to assist the supply-side structural reform including the state-owned enterprise reform, transformation of economic structure to greening and innovation; (3) to assist to effectively enhance the sense of fulfillment, happiness, and security of the people, including wealth management and social security, etc.; and (4) to assist to take tough steps to forestall and defuse major risks, carry out targeted poverty alleviation, and prevent and control pollution.

II. Status quo of life insurance funds supporting the real economy in China

(I) The insurance regulatory authority guides the support to the development of the real economy by life insurance funds

Firstly, the insurance regulatory authority enhanced the policy and institutional guidance. Starting from 2006, China Insurance Regulatory Commission (the "CIRC")

has printed and distributed a series of policy documents to continuously expand the investment scope and fields of insurance funds and promote their docking with the real economy. Since 2017, CIRC has printed and distributed a series of documents including the *Guidance on the Insurance Industry to Support the Development of the Real Economy* (《关于保险业支持实体经济发展的指导意见》), and modified the *Measures for the Administration of the Utilization of Insurance Funds* (《保险资金运用管理办法》) in an effort to improve the efficiency and levels of the insurance sector in serving the real economy.

Secondly, the insurance regulatory authority diversified the investment vehicles. The product patterns have become more diversified, and the transaction structures have become more flexible, meeting the different financing demands of different sub-sectors of the real economy.

Thirdly, the insurance regulatory authority strengthened the supervision and prevented various risks, by: (1) establishing the professional centralized and well-regulated operating mechanism; (2) adopting the proportional supervision on major classes of assets; (3) enhancing the supervision on the solvency; (4) implementing the investment capacity-based license management; (5) promoting the supervision on asset-liability matching; and (6) strengthening in-process and ex post supervision through internal control, information disclosure, and five-tier classification of assets, etc.

(II) Three major approaches for life insurance funds to support the real economy

There are three major approaches for the life insurance funds to support the real economy: firstly, they provide indirect financing to the real economy by converting bank deposits into bank loans. By the end of 2017, the savings of the insurers at the banks amounted to RMB 1,927.407 billion, accounting for 12.92% of the total deposits, most of which are long-term negotiated deposits and term deposits, and have become an important source of funds for mid- and long-term loans of commercial banks. Secondly, they provide financing to the real economy by investing in such financial market instruments as bonds and stocks, etc. By the end of 2017, the insurance funds invested RMB 5,161.289 billion in bonds, accounting for 34.59% of

the total, RMB 752,477 billion in securities investment funds, accounting for 5.04%, and RMB 1,082.894 billion in stocks, accounting for 7.26%. The total investment in various bonds, funds and stocks exceeded RMB 6.9 trillion. Thirdly, they provide project financing to real economy by issuing or investing in equity investment plans, debt investment plans and asset management plans, etc. By the end of 2017, the insurance funds invested RMB 5,996.553 billion in such forms as financial assets purchased under resale, long-term equity investments, investment real estate, products of insurance asset management companies, financial derivatives, loans, borrowed funds, and other investments, accounting for 40.19% of the total. Among them, the insurance funds invested over RMB 4.6 trillion in the real economy through debt investment plans, equity investment plans, asset-backed securities, industry investment plans, trust plans, private equity, etc., and the fields of investment included transportation, energy, municipal engineering, environmental protection, water services, renovation of rundown areas, logistics and warehousing, affordable housing, industrial parks, etc.

(III) Alternative investment is increasingly important in the support to the real economy by life insurance funds

In recent years, more and more life insurance funds support the financing for projects of the real economy through alternative investment. As seen from the operation models, six models of the alternative investment of the life insurances funds, i.e. the debt investment plans, equity investment plans, asset-backed securities, trust plans, private equity, and direct equity investment are comprehensively adopted to provide financing to the real economy. Among them, the debt investment plans and equity investment plans lead others in the proportion, and the debt investment plans in particular are the most important approach for the life insurance funds to support the development of the real economy.

The other investments of the insurance funds have increased from RMB 1.3 trillion in 2013 to over RMB 5.9 trillion in 2017, with their share in the utilized insurance funds rising from 16.90% in 2013 to 40.19% in 2017. The rapid growth of the other investments was largely due to the increasing number of various debt

investment plans, equity investment plans and asset-backed securities initiated by insurance asset management institutions. By the end of December 2017, the cumulative number of the debt investment plans and equity investment plans already initiated reached 843, and the total filing (registration) scale amounted to RMB 2,075.414 billion.

The major reasons for the rapid increase of alternative investments are: (1) the pursuit of higher returns on investment. The recent years have witnessed the ferocious competition on the financial market and the gradual increase of the liability-side costs of the life insurance sector, which has forced the insurers to find new investment fields; (2) the control on the channels to become alternative loans. As they are not allowed to enter the loan market, insurance funds have turned to invest in financial products that share the characteristics of loans, including trust plans, asset-backed securities, infrastructure investment plans, etc.; (3) demonstration of the value of long-term funds; and (4) the increasing removal of policy restriction on the investment of insurance funds. Since the second-half of 2012, the CIRC has promulgated over 20 new policies concerning the fund utilization, which broadened the channels for investment, promoted the growth of alternative investment from the institutional and mechanism perspectives and better supported the development of the real economy.

(IV) Developments of alternative investments in the infrastructure sector

The investments in infrastructure through debt and equity investment plans are the major channels for insurance funds to support the development of the real economy. By the end of 2016, the cumulative number of infrastructure projects invested by insurance funds reached 437 and the total investments reached RMB 1285 billion, which averaged to the investment of about RMB 3 billion for each project.

The alternative investments in the infrastructure field display the following features: firstly, the areas for investment are concentrated in such key areas of transportation and energy, which accounted for two-thirds of the total in terms of the number of project and the amount of investment. Secondly, the regions for investment are mainly centered in the Eastern China and gradually tilted towards Central and Western China in recent years. The share of investments in Central and Western

China in all regions has increased from 36% in 2013 to 57% in 2016, and the share of investments in the Eastern China has dropped from 60% to 30% during the same period. Thirdly, the debt investment plans prevail. By the end of 2016, the cumulative number of debt investment projects reached 417 and the total investments amounted to RMB 1109.8 billion, accounting for 95.4% of the total number of investment projects and 86.4% of the investments respectively. Fourthly, Type A and Type B credit enhancements (in the form of bank-offered guarantees or enterprise-offered guarantees respectively) for debt investment plans prevail, and enterprise-offered guarantees have become the most important form of credit enhancement in recent years, with the number of credit enhancement-free projects on the rise. Due to the comparatively higher thresholds, the share of Type C credit enhancements (mortgage/pledge-based guarantee) is relatively smaller. Fifthly, the financing subjects are mainly government financing platforms, state-owned enterprises and their subsidiaries, and the share of enterprise-type financing subjects has been increasing. By the end of 2016, the share of the debt investment projects with the governmental agencies, government financing platforms, state-owned enterprises and their subsidiaries, and the private enterprises the debt-paying subjects accounted for 4.1%, 60.2%, 35.3% and 0.5% respectively. The share of the debt investment projects with local investment and financing platforms as the debt-paying subjects has dropped from 72.5% in 2014 to 58.1% at the end of 2016, and the share of the debt investment projects with enterprise-type financing subjects as the debt-paying subjects has increased from 27.5% in 2014 to 41.9% in 2016. Sixthly, the sources of investment have become diversified, and the market concentration is very high. By the end of 2016, a total of 26 insurance asset management subjects invested in infrastructure projects. The top 8 subjects invested RMB 1,024.3 billion in a total of 349 projects, with the number of projects and investments accounting for 80% and 80% respectively of the total. Seventhly, the size of single investments is comparatively large. By the end of 2016, the average single investments of cumulative investment projects amounted to RMB 2.94 billion. Eighthly, the investment horizons are longer and the returns on investment are comparatively higher. By the end of 2016, the average investment horizon of the debt investment projects was 7.3 years and the average return on investment was 6.48%.

(V) Life insurance funds are expected to become the substantial provider of funds for the infrastructure development for the Belt & Road Initiative

Infrastructure connectivity is the priority area in the development of the Belt & Road Initiative (BRI). The development of the physical and social infrastructure in many countries and regions along the BRI route lags behind the needs for development and faces the financing difficulties to different degrees, resulting in the urgent need for financial support. As the life insurance funds have long maturities, they can become the important fund providers for the infrastructure development along the BRI route. The recent years have witnessed the active participation of insurance funds in long-cycle and large-scale BRI infrastructure development. By the end of 2017, insurance funds invested a total of RMB 856.826 billion in BRI development in the form of debt and equity investment plans. The practices in China has proved that insurance funds, life insurance funds in particular, are the key subject to support the infrastructure development of the emerging markets.

(VI) Life insurance funds continuously expand the support to new fields of the real economy

The recent years has witnessed the life insurance funds continuously expand the support to emerging fields of the real economy, including the involvement in the disposal of non-performing assets. As an important provider of long-term funds, the insurers may assume a prudential role in the market-based disposal of non-performing assets under the precondition of effective control of risks, which can alleviate the pressure from the allocation of long-term insurance funds and promote the life insurance funds to better serve the real economy.

(VII) Life insurance funds have achieved positive results in serving the real economy

The life insurance funds in China have supported the development of the real economy by such means as investing in key national projects, supporting the local

economic development and assisting the development of projects for people's wellbeing, and have achieved positive results by: firstly, actively serving the national supply-side structural reform; secondly, actively supporting the Belt & Road initiative; thirdly, actively supporting the national regional development strategy; fourthly, actively participating in the public-private partnership (PPP) projects and major engineering projects; and fifthly, supporting the integrated military and civilian development and the transformation and upgrading of the manufacturing industry.

III. Problems, risks and policy barriers for life insurance funds to support the real economy in China

(I) Problems in the support to the development of the real economy by life insurance funds

The first challenge for life insurance funds to support the real economy lies in the need for the life insurance industry to advance major transformation of the industry.

Firstly, the underdevelopment of the life insurance industry hinders the support of life insurance funds to the real economy. Life insurance funds are the foundation for the life insurance industry to support the real economy development. The underdeveloped life insurance industry goes against the accumulation of funds with long maturities and high stability, and restricts the scope and depth of life insurance funds in supporting the real economy.

Secondly, the inadequate transformation of the development mode of life insurance industry goes against the support of life insurance funds to the real economy. As the life insurance investment activities are mainly based on debt activities, the inadequate transformation of the development mode of life insurance industry will result in irrational debt structure and be detrimental to life insurance funds' support to the real economy.

Thirdly, irregularities weaken the effects of the support to the development of the real economy by life insurance funds. In recent years, due to such reasons as the alienation in the development of universal life insurance, the to-be-improved rules

of the capital market and certain regulatory gaps resulting from cross-sector and coordinated financial development, such problems as irrational acquisitions, unfriendly investment with persons acting in concert, irrational cross-border or cross-sector large-scale investment and M&As, radical operations and radical investments, multi-layer nesting of products and regulatory arbitrage, etc., have occurred to life insurance funds in their support to the real economy, which have to a certain degree weakened their support to the real economy.

Fourthly, the structural problems of life insurance investments are not favorable to the transformation of the pattern of economic development. For example, a majority of the alternative investments by life insurance funds flows to local governments and related state-owned enterprises and offers comparatively weak support to private enterprises; and life insurance funds are mainly invested debt investment plans with much less investment in equity investment plans. All these are not conducive to the transformation of the pattern of China's economic development.

(II) Major existing risks in the support to the development of the real economy by life insurance funds

Firstly, asset-liability mismatch risks. The first risk is that the high liability-side costs have forced the investment-side to increase the appetite for risk. The second risk is the mismatch of maturities. On the one hand, there are the phenomena of long-maturity funds matched to short-term assets. Due to the lack of long-term investment products, the long-maturity life insurance funds have to be passively matched to short-term assets, which not only reduced the returns on investment, but also increased the short-term volatility. On the other hand, there are also phenomena of short-maturity funds matched to long-term assets. Some short-maturity funds are invested in high-yield, low-liquidity and long-maturity immovable assets, such as infrastructure, trusts and other alternative assets, resulting in the highlighted phenomena of short-maturity funds matched to long-term assets. The third risk is the liquidity risk. The structural adjustments of the liability-side business or repayment upon maturity might trigger liquidity risks, while as the non-standard assets, the alternative investments have low liquidity, inactive trading and long cash conversion cycles, and have increased the

risks of inadequate cash flow faced by some companies.

Secondly, credit risks. Against the backdrop of the transformation of the pattern of economic development, deleveraging, removal of stipulation on implicitly guaranteed repayment, the credit risks faced by life insurance in the support to the real economy have increased. In particular, with the mounting debt burden of the local governments, the potential local credit risks might be released.

Thirdly, cross-market and cross-sector risks. With the expansion of the scope and depth of life insurance funds in participating in the financial market and serving the real economy, the risks arising from the utilization of life insurance funds have been deeply interwoven with economic and financial risks, resulting in convoluted risks. With the cross-product, cross-sector and cross-regulator infection and overlapping of risks has increased the difficulties in identifying and dealing with risks.

Fourthly, risks of increasing the implicit debts of local governments. Such irregularities as debt investments in fake equity in some equity investment plans have to a certain degree become the incremental debts of the local governments.

Fifthly, the risks of overseas investment. Take the life insurance funds' participation in BRI development as an example, such challenges as the huge differences in development environment of the countries and regions along the BRI route, the lack of reliable and stable profit models in the investment in infrastructure development and considerable geopolitical risks have increased the investment risks of life insurance funds in participating in BRI development.

Sixthly, the risks in expanding in the emerging fields. Taking the disposal of non-performing assets as an example, the potential risks faced by the insurers include: (1) potential risks brought by the disposal methods of non-performing assets; (2) risks triggered by problems existing in non-performing assets disposal market; and (3) the risks resulting from insufficient risk prevention and control capabilities of the insurers.

(III) Major existing policy barriers in the support to the development of the real economy by life insurance funds

Firstly, the capital utilization policies need to be further optimized. The first is that the relevant management rules and regulations concerning infrastructure-based

debt investment plans need to be improved. In the first place, the conditions for the financing subjects to be exempted from credit enhancement need improvements. The current credit enhancement requirements of debt investment plans set high standards and strict approaches. In the second place, the scope for the fund utilization of investment plans needs to be expanded. The current control on the scope of fund utilization of infrastructure-based debt investment plans not only restricts the development of the debt investment plans but also increases the costs of the financing subjects. The second is that the scope for the insurance funds to invest in equity shall be further expanded. In the first place, the scope for indirect investment on equity shall be expanded to adapt to the multiple investment modes of private equity. In the second place, the scope for direct investment on equity shall be further expanded. Lastly, the examination and approval system on the equity investments by insurance funds shall be relaxed at appropriate time.

Secondly, the registration policies on immovable property for mortgage need to be further improved. The life insurance funds fail to realize their creditor's rights through the mortgage or pledge of immovable property when investing directly or indirectly in immovable property-related projects through debt or equity investment plans, which restricts the means and space for life insurance funds to serve the real economy.

Thirdly, the policies on the investment of life insurance funds in the senior care/ health care industry need to be further improved. For example, there are no well-established and unified industry standards for the access standards, supporting facilities and professional services, etc. for the senior care/health care industry; the relevant regulatory institutions are not complete; and there are no definite preferential policies concerning the type of acquired land and profitability.

Fourthly, there are restrictive factors for life insurance funds to participate in public–private partnership (PPP) projects. The equal contractual relationship and risk coverage mechanism etc. calls for legal safeguards, and the relevant policy environment needs to be further improved, which all influence the motivation of the insurers.

Fifthly, the policy environment for life insurance funds to participate in the disposal of non-performing assets should be further improved. Firstly, the policies on participation in the securitization of non-performing assets shall be further improved.

Competent authorities are expected to open up the policies for insurers to participate in the securitization of non-performing assets, make specific provisions on the ratings and risk control, etc. of non-performing assets and improve relevant laws, rules and regulations. Secondly, there is a lack of supporting policies for insurers to participate in debt-to-equity swap, which includes: the risks of market-oriented debt-to-equity swap do not match well with the returns; the relevant rules concerning the floor trading and appraisal of state-owned equity need to be improved; the existence of double taxation has increased the comprehensive costs of enterprises involved in debt-to-equity swap; and there is certain tension between the market-oriented debt-to-equity swap of listed companies and the current rules and regulations, for example, the size and stock price of the offering being subject to the restrictions from the new rules on refinancing, strict monitoring on repayment of loans by raised funds, and the failure of creditor's rights to be included in the issue of shares to purchase underlying assets.

IV. International Experience, lessons and development trends in enabling life insurance funds to support the real economy

(I) International experience

Firstly, the life insurance companies have played an important role in the field of real economy investment with their outstanding features of large sizes and long maturities, etc. The insurance companies, life insurance companies in particular, have often grown to be an important driving force of economic growth in the developed countries and provided indispensable sources of funds of large sizes and long investment period for various financing activities.

Secondly, investment activities shall be centered on liability activities, and take the asset-liability matching as the fundamental guiding principle. Life insurance companies are engaged in classic liability-driven assets investment. To a large degree, the type of insurance portfolio determines the type of asset allocation portfolio. Ensuring the asset-liability matching is the overarching principle for the investment of

life insurance funds.

Thirdly, the investment of life insurance funds shall remain sensitive to the macro-economic trends and policies changes and make timely adjustments to the investment orientation and portfolio allocation. Both the pursuit of returns on investment and the efforts to ensure that investment business effectively support the liability operations all require that insurance investment must follow the macroeconomic trends and actively respond to the various demands posed by the real economy.

Fourthly, the investment of life insurance funds shall keep close interaction with the capital market and make positive contribution of the deepening of the capital market. The symbiosis and co-incidence and mutual promotion between the capital market and the investment of life insurance funds indicates that the investment of life insurance funds is inseparable from a well-established capital market and varied line of financial products. Similarly, the deepening of the capital market has to rely on the drive of such long-term institutional investors as life insurance companies.

(II) International lessons

Firstly, insurance asset and liability business shall maintain stable operations and avoid overaggressive moves. Due to the special features of insurance business, stable operations are very important for both the individual insurers and the whole sector. Stable operations include both the liability business and asset business. If the whole business model deviates from the stability principle and remains excessively radical, even the good asset-liability matching will drag the companies into dangerous situations and even create impacts on the stability of the whole industry and even the financial system.

Secondly, the investment of life insurance funds is not independent from effective supervision, the lack of which would easily result in serious problems. The life insurance industry needs strict regulation and is highly dependent on market innovations. How to maintain the equilibrium between risk control and encouraging innovation has remained a difficult issue for all regulatory authorities. Without the effective supervision and against the backdrop of large regulatory gaps and regulatory arbitrage, the market competition would easily deviate from the normal tracks, generate various problems and even trigger the outbreak of systematic risks.

(III) International development trends

Firstly, life insurance companies are making more positive moves into the long-term investments in infrastructure and new ventures and the share of alternative investments has witnessed a remarkable increase. Due to the long-term low-rate environment and the growing uncertainty of investment in the open stock and bond markets since the global financial crisis of 2008, a remarkable move of the global investment of life insurance funds is the significant increase of allocation ratio of investment in alternative assets in pursuit of higher returns on investment and the improvement of diversification of investment to flatten the short-term fluctuations and reduce the risks.

Secondly, more and more life insurance companies are investing in insurance technologies in the hope of improving the risk management and increase the returns on investment from portfolios. Insurance technologies have bright prospects in investing activities, mainly because insurance investment activities are growing more complicated. Firstly, the conventional approaches of portfolio creation have become increasingly obsolete against the backdrop of sustained low rates and continuously rising capital market volatility. Secondly, the rising proportion of alternative assets is a symbol that the approaches of asset portfolio have become more complicated. Thirdly, new regulatory rules including the Solvency II Directive have raised new requirements on the development of information infrastructure in insurance companies. In response to the above new changes, insurance companies need to take more dynamic and complicated approaches than before to arrange asset-liability matching, and need more timely and accurate data and rapid and highly efficient capabilities in asset portfolio creation to support such matching. The development of insurance technologies will help to place insurance companies in a better position to conduct investment management and adapt to the requirements of the new trends and developments.

Thirdly, the correlation between the insurance industry and the systematic risks is on the rise and how to prevent and control risks of the asset and liability business and maintain the stability of the industry has become a huge challenge. When compared to the past, the homogeneity between the insurance industry and the financial sectors of banking and securities, etc. have increased, the risks contained in insurance portfolios

have dramatically increased, and the insurance industry have become more and more instable with the correlation with the systematic risks remarkably increased.

V. Policy recommendations to facilitate the real economy through life insurance funds in China

(I) Efforts shall be made to promote the transformation and high-quality development of the life insurance industry

Firstly, efforts shall be made to promote the transformation of the life insurance industry. (1) Efforts shall be made to achieve the transformation of the mode of premium increase from lump-sum payment–driven to renewal-driven in the hope of increasing the sustainability of premium income increase and stability of business development. (2) Adjustments of product structures. The insurance industry and insurance companies need to innovate the product system and concentrate on providing life insurance which offers financial security against death risks, health insurance which offers financial security against illness and disability risks, and endowment and annuities insurance which offer financial security against longevity risks. (3) Efforts shall be made to increase the values of channels. The insurance industry shall promote the in-depth integration of banks and insurance companies in the business field, facilitate the deepening of the bank-insurance cooperation and the upgrading of bank-insurance mode; increase the per capita capacity of the insurance agents, regulate the marketing practices, protect the consumers' interests and realize the leap forward from quantitative expansion to quality enhancement. (4) Efforts shall be made to forestall and defuse liquidity risks in the transformation of the life insurance industry. In order to advance the transformation of the life insurance industry in a stable way, it is necessary to avoid the sharp decrease of premium income within a short period of time and try best to match the increment of the renewal premium income with the decrease of lump-sum premium, make a huge but not sharp turn and avoid triggering new risks. Therefore, attention shall be paid to maintain balance between the regulation and the transformation of the insurance industry and leave the time and space for the

companies to advance structural adjustment. (5) Efforts shall be made to forestall and defuse the risks of new interest spread loss and fee loss caused by the middle- and short-term practices during the transformation process.

Secondly, efforts shall be made to promote the high-quality development of the life insurance industry. In order to promote the high-quality development of the life insurance industry, enhance the proportion of insurance assets in the total assets of the financial industry and the development of the life insurance industry, it is needed to deepen the commitment to the supply-side structural reform of the industry, continuously deepen the market-based reform of the allocation of insurance factors, increase the supply quality, enhance technological innovation and promote the optimized upgrading of the industry. To this end, efforts shall be made to promote the life insurance industry to realize the reform of quality, efficiency and driving forces, and continuously improve the total factor productivity of the insurance industry. The promotion of the high-quality development of the life insurance industry necessitates bringing into full play the role of insurance mechanism in the economic transformation, promoting the life insurance industry to play the roles of long-term stable risk management and security, and reshaping the institutional foundation for the well-ordered operation of the life insurance market.

(II) Ideas on promoting the life insurance fund to support the development of the real economy

Firstly, we should follow the market-oriented principles. The requirements on the profitability and security of the life insurance funds make it necessary for the funds to adhere to the market-oriented principles and the funds shall be invested in quality projects of the real economy with promising development expectations to achieve sustainable development. Apart from market-based approaches to support the major national strategic development, to adhere to the market-based operation requires that we explore how to use life insurance funds to support the development of private sectors, enable the market to play a decisive role in the utilization of life insurance funds and promote the transformation of the pattern of economic development.

Secondly, efforts are needed to adhere to the basic principles for the utilization of life insurance funds. (1) principle of stability and prudence, which is the foundation for the utilization of life insurance funds; (2) serving the core business, i.e. the utilization of life insurance funds shall provide support to bringing into play the risk coverage function; (3) long-term investment, value investing, and diversified investments; (4) asset-liability matching management, which is an important foundation for the stable operation of life insurers; and (5) compliance with laws and regulations.

Thirdly, efforts are needed to support the utilization of life insurance funds to serve the development of the real economy. On the basis of following the market-oriented principles and adhering to the basic principles for the utilization of life insurance funds, we should support the life insurance funds to serve the development of the real economy and bring into full play the obvious advantages of life insurance fund in serving the real economy.

Fourthly, Trromote the integration of liability-side insurance business and asset-side investment business.

Fifthly, strengthen the application of science and technology in the field of asset management.

(III) Efforts shall be made to prevent the risks in the support to the development of the real economy by life insurance funds.

Firstly, efforts are needed to further adjust the asset-liability structure of the life insurance sector, and solve the problem of high liability-side costs forcing the investment-side to raise the appetite to risks. The life insurance sector shall establish the sustainable asset-liability management modes with the coverage function as the basis and pension and healthcare insurance as the top priorities and combining the risk management and wealth management, and become an important component of the national senior care/health care system.

Secondly, efforts are needed to strengthen the risk management capabilities of the insurance institutions with the asset-liability management at the core. Insurance companies shall achieve the sound interaction between the asset side and liability side, and establish the sustainable mode of asset-liability management. Firstly,

insurance institutions shall continue to improve the awareness and capability of asset-liability management, strengthen the development of the organizational system and mechanism, establish the decision-making system for the asset-liability management, set up the horizontal communication and coordination mechanism between the various intra-company departments, especially the liabilities management office and assets management office, and enhance the information communication and feedback between various intra-company departments. Secondly, the team building of insurance companies shall be optimized. Thirdly, we should change the ideas of the executives of the insurance industry. Fourthly, we should fully improve the liquidity of the invested assets and liabilities. Fifthly, efforts shall be made to optimize the evaluation system and promote the effective implementation of the asset-liability management.

Thirdly, efforts are needed to accelerate to create the risk prevention-centered regulatory system on the utilization of life insurance funds, by: (1) making a quick move to promote the supervision on asset-liability management, and realizing the positive interaction between the asset side and the liability side, for which efforts are needed to establish such rules as quantitative evaluation, qualitative evaluation and pressure test, etc., comprehensively evaluate the asset-liability matching situations and assets allocation capability of the insurers, implement the differentiated solvency policies and fund utilization policies, further classify and adjust the type and proportion of major classes of assets, correct the risk factors of the China Risk Oriented Solvency System (C-ROSS) and optimize the capital constraints on different types of assets and investing behaviors; (2) comprehensively and strictly enhance the supervision on the utilization of insurance funds by various means including promoting external auditing, capital supervision, information disclosure, classified regulation, internal control and public supervision, etc; (3) promoting the development of the insurance statistical information system and insurance asset management supervision information system, and further enhancing the docking of insurance fund custodian bank system with the regulatory information system; (4) studying and exploring the ways for insurance funds to invest in gold and relevant financial products, and using stock index futures, treasury bond futures, interest rate swaps and more financial derivatives to hedge and manage the risks; (5) strengthening the coordinated and interconnected supervision on

insurance services, fund utilization and solvency, and forming the supervision synergy.

Fourthly, efforts are needed to strengthen the monitoring and prevention of the risks in key areas, by: (1) strengthening the front-end and back-end management and risk prevention and control for debt investment plans of insurance funds, and preventing credit risks; (2) evaluating the impact of asset allocation plans on cash flows by conducting asset allocation pressure tests, and making the contingency plans for the cash flow risks for protection against asset-liability mismatch risks and liquidity risks; and (3) regulating the equity investment plans to avoid increasing the implicit debts of the local governments. Therefore, we should return to the basics of equity investment, and stamp out debt investments in fake equity in some equity investment plans, and strengthen the proactive management, passageway business and multi-layer nesting of products in an effort to prevent financial risks.

Fifthly, efforts are needed to enhance the coordination and cooperation between the financial regulatory authorities. The insurance, securities and banking regulatory authorities shall enhance the coordination and cooperation with each other to guard against regulatory arbitrage, and eliminate the regulatory gaps from cross-sector financial activities; keep a close eye on the possible impacts to the insurance sector by the changes of macro factors including currency, finance and taxation, foreign trade, foreign exchange, interest rate, real estate, stocks, and social security, etc., analyze and evaluate the risk transmission mechanism and transfer channels, and effectively prevent cross-market and cross-sector risks.

Sixthly, efforts are needed to improve the investment environment through cooperation. As far as the participation in the BRI development by life insurance funds, efforts shall be strengthened to significantly improve the environment for infrastructure investment within the region and the focuses of cooperation shall include: firstly, efforts shall be made to strengthen the bilateral and multilateral communication and negotiation between and among the countries along the BRI route and create the cooperation and dialogue mechanism dedicated to improving the infrastructure investment environment of the whole region. Secondly, efforts shall be made to create a platform for information, risk and benefit sharing between the life insurance funds and infrastructure projects, and take the lead to form the

institutionalized cooperation mechanism in the fields with mature conditions. Thirdly, cooperation shall be strengthened to identify, prevent and deal with the infrastructure investment risks within the region.

Seventhly, enhance the spirit of the contract annong local gooernments.

Eighthly, strergthen industry risk management.

(IV) Efforts shall be made to improve the policy environment for life insurance funds to support the real economy

Firstly, efforts are needed to deepen our commitment to the reform of market-oriented utilization of life insurance funds. Efforts shall be made to expand the investment fields, provide the market subjects more choices and rights to choose under the precondition of compliance with the laws, and take the support to the development of the real economy as the starting point and foothold for innovating the ways to utilize the insurance funds.

(1) Weshould expand the investrnent scope of insurance funds.

(2) The cletailed business rules for insurance asset management products should be introduced.

(3) Relevant regulatory requirements shall be improved.

Secondly, efforts are needed to define the registration policies on the mortgage of immovable property. It is recommended to define the equal status of insurance institutions and banks and other financial institutions as subjects in terms of fund provision, and promote the state land administration authorities to issue the policies to regulate the mortgage and pledge registration of land, and allow insurance institutions to handle the procedures of mortgage and pledge registration of land according to the laws.

Thirdly, efforts are needed to eliminate the barriers faced by the insurance institutions in such fields as market access, land and taxation and fiscal policies when investing in the senior care/health care industry. It is recommended to specify the industry standards for the access standards, supporting facilities and professional services, etc. for the senior care/health care industry, and specify the type of acquired land for the senior care/health care industry and preferential taxation policies for the for-profit senior care/health care industry.

Fourthly, we need improve the relevant supporting policies in the PPP field. It is recommended to further improve the legislation in the fields of cooperation between the government and private capital, enhance the support to the insurance institutions in terms of land and taxation and fiscal policies, etc. in their investment, and improve taxation policies on the profits from the investment on equity-related financial products by insurance funds.

Fifthly, efforts are needed to optimize the policy environment for life insurance funds to participate in the BRI development. It is recommended that the insurance regulatory and foreign exchange administrative authorities of various countries shall support the life insurance funds to conduct prudential overseas investments on the basis of effective regulation. To this end, more countries along the BRI route shall be included in the list of countries or regions worth the investment by life insurance funds in due time. At the same time, we should encourage and support the life insurance fund management institutions to development the BRI-related investment products.

Sixthly, efforts are needed to improve the policy environment for life insurance funds to participate in the disposal of non-performing assets. Firstly, efforts shall be made to open up the policies for insurers to participate in the securitization of non-performing assets, make specific provisions on the ratings and risk control, etc. of non-performing assets and improve relevant laws, rules and regulations. Secondly, efforts shall be made to improve the supporting policies on debt-to-equity swap by (1) combining the debt-to-equity swap and mixed ownership reform of SOEs with the focus on transforming the operational mechanism of enterprises; (2) improving relevant rules concerning the floor trading and appraisal of state-owned equity; (3) implementing debt-to-equity swap on the financial institutions through financial products, and canceling the double taxation on income taxes; (4) exploring the consent to private offering at locked price, appropriately relax the restrictions on the scale of private offering, use of raised funds and the scope of assets to be purchased through issued shares, in order to encourage the life insurance funds to explore the investment in the market-oriented debt-to-equity swap of listed companies.

Seventhly, explore life insurance funds to carry out loan business.

Eighthly, actively cultivate the insurance asset management market.

Chapter I: Intention and Practice of China's Life Insurance Industry Serving the Real Economy

I. Intention of Life Insurance Industry Serving the Real Economy

China's life insurance industry has become an important force on the financial market both in China and globally: By premium sizes, China's life insurance industry ranked third of the globe and contributed the largest share of the new incremental income of global life insurance premiums; China's life insurance industry has one of the largest insurance companies of the world, which is one of the largest institutional investors of China's capital market. Considering the fact that China's life insurance industry only resumed the domestic business in early 1980s and started nearly from scratch, it is an amazing achievement for the industry to develop so fast and grow so strong within less than 40 years.

China's life insurance industry never escaped the ups and downs in its development. The latest setback came from the criticism on the shift from real economy to virtual economy by the life insurance industry. The criticism emerged against the macroeconomic background that the public opinions, competent governmental organs and regulatory authorities have since 2015 generally started to perform deep introspection on the failure of China's financial system, including the life insurance industry, to well serve the real economy and its shift from the shift from real economy to virtual economy. As far as the life insurance industry is concerned, the shift from real economy to virtual economy manifests not only as the deviation from the basic function of risk coverage, which means that the insurance industry has shifted its focus from insurance to other business, but also as continued accumulation and superposition of the liquidity risks, asset-liability mismatch

risks and reputational risks, etc. associated with the fermentation of such phenomena as the private capital making significant inroads into the insurance industry, the rising development model of asset-enabled liability, frequent acquisition of listed companies by insurance companies, the ultra-convention development of short-term universal life insurance products with high yields, and engagement in multi-layer nesting/channel businesses by insurance funds, etc., which finally transformed the life insurance industry into a particularly important link of China's chain of rapidly rising financial risks. Against this backdrop, how to promote the life insurance industry to shift from virtual economy to real economy, restore its basic functions and better serve the real economy has become a pressing and critical topic, both for preventing and defusing financial risks and for promoting the transformation of the industry.

So, how should we understand the life insurance industry serving the real economy? As a matter of fact, "the life insurance industry serving the real economy" has the following specific meanings when we take into consideration the international experience and the national situations of China:

Firstly, the precondition for the life insurance industry to serve the real economy is the urgent need to vigorously promote (instead of containing) the high quality development of the life insurance industry.

The recent years have witnessed the added value of China's financial sector as a percentage of GDP rising year by year, rising rapidly from 4% in 2005 to 8.44% in 2015 and exceeding 9% at certain time-point. Despite slight slumps in the two years of 2016 and 2017, the percentage still remained top and even exceeded the levels of countries including the U.K. and the USA that have highly developed financial markets[1]. The rapid risisng of the financial added value within a short period of time and the growth rate of the financial sector remarkably higher than that of the industry[2]. indicates the over-development of the current financial market of China and

---

[1]　When compared with such developed countries as the USA, UK and Japan, the added value of China v financial sector as a percentage of GDP overtook that of the USAin 2013 and that of the UK in 2015. The added values of the financial industry as a percentage of GDP in the four countries of China, the USA, Japan and the UK reached 8.4%, 7.2%, 4.4% and 7.2% respectively in 2015, indicating that China had exceeded the other three countries.

[2]　The growth rates of the added value of China'of the added value of ChinaApto 2016 were 9.4%, 10.6%, 9.9%, 16% and 5.7%, while the growth rates of the industrial added value were 8.1%, 7.7%, 7%, 6% and 6%. Except for Year 2016, the growth rates of the added value of the financial sector were all higher than that of the industry.

its crowding-out or plunder effect on the real economy. The emphasis on the financial industry's serving the real economy was proposed against this backdrop, suggesting that the financial industry shall scale down to match with the development of the real economy. However, it is may be right that the banking industry is over-developed, but it is never the case that the insurance industry is over-developed. Currently, China's insurance industry accounts for less than 1% of the GDP, which is far lower than the level of the developed countries of the Europe and the USA. The aggregate might not be an issue for the future development of the banking industry, but the key issue lies in the structure; however, the insurance industry is faced with both the issue of structural adjustment but also the issue of inadequate development of the aggregate. Given that, one of the implied preconditions for the insurance industry to serve the real economy is to vigorously promote the development of the insurance industry and boost the expansion of the business scale instead of containing the development and scaling down. Of course, the development of the life insuanrce industry must be high quality-oriented and shall promote the continued expansion of the business volume on the basis of the focus on quality and efficiency instead of simply pursuing fast scaling up and disregarding the quality.

Secondly, the life insurance industry serving the real economy shall take the risk coverage function as its core and the liability business as the foundation

In general, the functions of the financial industry are not unitary[1]. For different financial sectors, their functions often overlap and superpose each other. However, the core functions of different financial sectors are often unique. For example, clearing and payments are core functions of the banking industry, but they are not the core functions

---

[1]   According to the summary of Merton Miller, a financial system has the following six basic functions: Function 1: clearing and payments function, i.e. a financial system provides a payments and clearing system for the exchange of goods and labor services and transaction of assets. Function 2: financing and equity division function, i.e. a financial system provides a mechanism for the pooling of funds to undertake large-scale indivisible enterprise. Function 3: provision of channels for transfer of economic resources through time and space, i.e. a financial system provides a way or mechanism to transfer economic resources through time and across geographic regions and industries. Function 4: risk management function, i.e. a financial system provides a way or approach to manage uncertainty and control risk. Function 5: information provision function, i.e. a financial system provides price information (interest rates, yield rates and exchange rates, etc.) that helps coordinate decentralized decision-making in various sectors of the economy. Function 6: solution to incentive problems, i.e. a financial system provides a way to deal with the asymmetric-information problems when one party to a financial transaction has information that the other party does not and incentive problems in principal-agent actions.

of the life insurance industry. The difference in core functions not only helps ensure that the real economy obtains comprehensive of the financial services industry, but also increases the diversified returns of the entire financial system, which is conducive to the realization of financial stability.

The core function of the life insurance industry is to provide financial stability and protection to customers in different life cycles and help them manage risks such as death, illness, survival, and longevity. In other words, risk protection is the core function of the life insurance industry. The liability business that carries out the guarantee function is the foundation of the life insurance industry. Although many other functions have been derived from the continuous development of the life insurance industry, it is impossible to disregard the core function of "risk protection"; otherwise the existence of the life insurance industry will lose its significance. Correspondingly, the foundation for the vigorous expansion of insurance business is to promote the expansion of insurance protection business.

Thirdly, the life insurance sector can support the development of the real economy in various ways

A variety of ways for the life insurance industry to serve the real economy have been derived by starting from the core function of risk protection. Specifically, it mainly includes: 1. Economic shock absorbers: the life insurance industry creates an environment with redduced uncertainty through the sharing of accidental losses and the provision of loss/income compensation, making the social and economic life more stable; 2. Long-term investors: life insurance companies are important institutional investors with a long-term investment perspectives, and they can not only provide capital financing for long-term projects such as infrastructure development, but also make positive contributions to the growth and deepening of the financial market; 3. Wealth Management: Life insurance contracts generally maintain the organic combination of protection and investment elements and effectively manage wealth through the unique functions of compulsory saving, tax deferral, and asset preservation; 4. Social security: The life insurance industry is an important component of the multi-level social security system; especially in the areas of retirement and medical care, the active cooperation between the commercial insurance sector and

the social insurance sector can effectively ease the pressures on public finances and increase the efficiency of the social security system. These methods cooperate with each other to promote life insurance industry to ultimately become a globally accepted and indispensable financial service after a long period of development.

Table 1 not only analyzes the various ways the life insurance industry serves the real economy, but also compares it with other financial sectors, which has revealed some unique functions of the life insurance industry. For example, while both insurance and bank loans can intervene in the face of the risks of personal injuries or loss of income after an accident, the advantage of insurance is not only that it is an ex ante mechanism, but also that after the accident, the customers can obtain compensation and have no need to repay the funds. As another example, although bank savings can also bear the function of the protection of retirement life, insurance still has the unique functions of tax deferral, compulsory savings, and periodic payments. In terms of long-term investment and asset preservation, the unique advantages of life insurance are beyond any doubt.

Table 1: Analysis on the Ways for Life Insurance Industry to Serve the Real Economy

Ways	Intention	Social and economic effects	Uniqueness compared to other financial sectors such as banks
Economic shock absorber	Economic compensation after the occurrence of insurance accidents	Reduce uncertainty, promote consumption, and cultivate investments and innovations	As an ex-ante mechanism with no need to repay the compensation funds
fund mobilization and financing	Insurance reserves provide funds for the real economy through investment channels such as capital markets	Promote the development of the capital market as a long-term capital provider	Obvious advantages in the long-term investment and the stability of funding sources, etc.
Wealth management	Wealth preservation and appreciation through the functions of compulsory saving, tax deferral, asset preservation, etc.	Help achieve economic sustainable development	For example, regular payment of premiums tends to create a form of compulsory savings, while bank savings are voluntary and can easily be missed
Social security	Provide supplementary protection beyond government-led basic pension and medical insurance	Improve the overall level and efficiency of security	Life insurance products have such advantages as tax deferral and regular payments, etc.

In addition, from the perspective of the targets, the life insurance services are offered to a wide range of tagets, which include both individuals and families, as well as enterprises, public service organizations, and government departments.

Fourthly, the life insurance industry serving the real economy can generate positive effects and help to promote economic growth and stabilize the financial market

As an important modern service industry, the life insurance industry not only provides support for economic growth through the performance of various functions, but also becomes an integral part of national economic growth by creating jobs and increasing tax revenues, etc.

More importantly, the related activities of the life insurance industry should help to stabilize rather than disrupt financial markets and mitigate rather than amplify the probability of systemic risk outbreaks. Fortunately, both theory and practice show that raditional insurance activities are not the source of systemic risks, and as long as the business model is not distorted, and the insurance industry adheres to its core business of insurance, the life insurance industry can qualify for the role of "stabilizer" for the financial market.

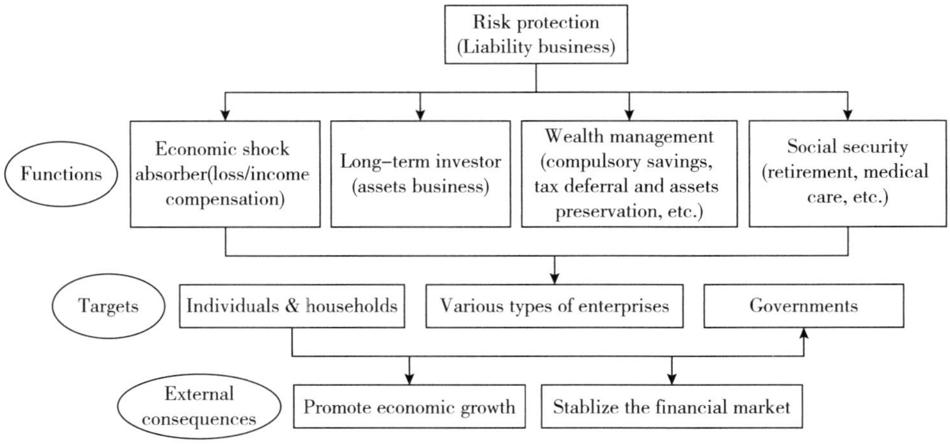

Figure 1   Ways for Life Insurance Industry to Serve the Real Economy

Fifthly, the evaluation criteria of other financial sectors shall not be inappropriately applied to the life insurance industry serving the real economy

In the term of the "shift from the real economy to the virtual economy", "the virtual economy" refers mainly to the financial sector. In short, the so-called "shift from the real economy to the virtual economy" means that the financial sector fails to brinn into full play its functions and is unable to effectively support the development of non-financial sectors.

For different financial sectors with different natures of their respective businesses, the intentions and methods of serving the real economy are also different. When comparing the banking industry with the life insurance industry, an important manifestation of the current banking industry's "shift from the real economy to the virtual economy" is that there has been a large increase in interbank assets and interbank liabilities, which has led to the circulation of funds within the financial system. However, the criterion of "funds circulating within the financial system" cannot be applied to the life insurance industry simply because domestic and international practice shows that insurance funds have always been important investors in bank deposits and securities markets. For example, insurance funds in Germany invest heavily in the banking system. When measured by market value, as of the end of the first quarter of 2014, investment in banks accounted for approximately 41% of the total insurance investments (approximately 474 billion Euros), and in the investment portfolio of life insurers, the proportion of investment in banks was approximately 42% (just over 300 billion Euros)[1]. Obviously, we shall not reach the conclusion that the insurance industry has shifted from the real economy to the virtual economy just because the insurance funds have engaged in indirect investment through such channels as banks and securities market, etc., and shall not regard the insurance funds as serving the real economy just because the insurance funds are directly providing funds to enterprise development through debt investment or equity investment plans, etc.

---

[1] Source: Deutsche Bundesbank, "Analyses of the importance of the insurance industry for financial stability", Monthly Report, July 2014

II. Status evaluation of China's life insurance industry serving the real economy

1. With its growing strength, China's life insurance industry has been playing an increasingly important role in serving the real economy, with remarkable performance in job creation and increasing revenues, etc.

Since the resumption of business in the early 1980s, the domestic life insurance industry has only a short 40-year history of development. However, the growing strength of the industry indicates that the life insurance industry has an increasingly strong foundation for serving the real economy and plays increasingly important roles. The following table shows the changes in the strength of China's life insurance industry from 1997 to 2016. It can be found that both in the scale of premium income and the total assets of the insurance industry, the Chinese life insurance industry has made considerable progress in the past 20 years.

Table 2: Changes in the strength of China' s life insurance industry in the past 20 years

	1997	2016
Life insurance premium income (USD 100 million)	75.6	2626.2
Global ranking of life insurance scale	15	3
Global share of life insurance premium (%)	0.61	10.03
Life insurance premium per capita (USD)	6.1	189.9
Life insurance premiums as a percentage of GDP (%)	0.82	2.3
Total assets of the insurance industry (RMB 100 million)*	2604	167500
Total assets of insurance industry as a percentage of GDP (%)*	3.3	20.3

* The historical data of the total assets of the insurance industry and the total assets of insurance industry as a percentage of GDP are for year 1999 instead of 1997.

Source: Swissre, China Insurance Regulatory Commission

The prosperity and development of the life insurance industry has had an important impact on the China's economy, most prominently in the two major aspects of job creation and increase of tax revenues. Restricted by the access to relevant data, the following uses insurance industry data to replace the life insurance industry data to illustrate the situation.

The first is the outstanding performance in job creation. In 1980, there were

only 3941 Chinese insurance employees, and by the end of October 2015, the number had reached nearly 6 million. According to the main data communique of the third National Economic Census, by the end of 2013, there were 29,000 financial enterprises operating as legal persons across China, with 5.139 million employees, of whom 1.123 million were employed by the insurance industry, accounting for 21.9% of all employees of the financial sectors.

Table 3: Financial enterprises as legal persons and employees grouped by sector

	Enterprises as legal persons (10,000)	Employees (10,000)
Monetary and financial services	1.5	369.5
Capital market services	0.1	26.2
Insurance sector	1.2	112.3
Other financial sectors	0.1	6.0
Total	2.9	513.9

Source: The main data communique of the third National Economic Census (http://www.stats.gov.cn/tjsj/zxfb/201412/t20141216_653701.html)

According to the latest data released by the China Insurance Regulatory Commission, the number of insurance employees reached 9.25 million at the beginning of 2018[1], accounting for 1.2% of the employed population of 776.4 million by the end of 2017. Compared to the contribution of less than 1% of the insurance industry to China's GDP at the end of 2017, the insurance industry's contribution to employment obviously cannot be ignored.

The second is the outstanding performance in increasing tax revenues. Many studies have shown that the actual tax bearing rate of China's insurance industry is not only significantly higher than that of banking, securities, and other financial sectors, but is also significantly higher than the statutory corporate income tax rate of 25%.[2] The fact that the actual tax bearing rate is high indicates that the insurance

---

[1] Source: Speech of Chen Wenhui, Vice Chairman of China Insurance Regulatory Commission (CIRC), at the 2018 National Insurance Regulatory Meeting (全国保险监管工作会议)

[2] For example, some studies take the financial data of 68 financial enterprises on the stock markets of Shanghai and Shenzhen in 2015 as the basis and group them by sectors of banking, securities, insurance and other financial sectors, and obtain the following tax bearin rates of the above sectors: insurance- 39.08%, banking – 31.99%, securities- 31.20% and other financial sectors- 31.17%. When calculated on the sample of 123 insurers that have operated for more than 3 years in the insurance market by 2015, the tax bearing rates of the property insurers and life insurers were 48.98% and 33.38% respectively. http://www.sohu.com/a/128519972_479770

industry's relative contribution to China's tax revenue growth is high. In fact, before the "replacement of business tax with value-added tax (VAT)", the business tax of the financial and insurance industry has become an important source of local government revenues. Take Fujian Province as an example. The local tax revenues of Fujian Province from the financial industry maintained rapid growth from 2010 to 2014 and its average annual growth rate was 3.8 percentage points higher than the growth rate of the local tax revenues over the same period. Among them, the business tax contribution from the financial and insurance industry is outstanding, accounting for over 60% of the local tax revenues from the financial industry of Fujian Province. Correspondingly, the contribution rate of the business tax from the financial and insurance industry to the local public revenues in Fujian Province has continuously increased from 4.4% in 2010 to 5.9% in 2014[1].

2. China's life insurance industry displays special features different from its Western counterparts

The most distinguishing feature is that it is more strongly government-guided in the operation and development.

Undoubtedly, the influence of the government in China is significantly stronger than that of many advanced economies. Accordingly, the ways and efforts of the insurance industry to serve the real economy are also affected more by the macro-control policies and regulatory systems. The liability business and asset business are no exception. The investment activities of life insurance companies in developed countries in Europe and America are also guided by government policies. However, the influence of such guidance is even more pronounced in China.

Take the asset business as an example. The *Several Opinions of the State Council on Accelerating the Development of the Modern Insurance Service Industry* (《国务院关于加快发展现代保险服务业的若干意见》) promulgated in 2014 highlighted the governmental guidance on insurance investment by proposing that" efforts shall be made to encourage insurance funds to support livelihood projects

---

[1]　Source: Research Team of Fujian Local Taxation Bureau. (2015). Impacts of the Replacement of Business Tax with Value-Added Tax in the Financial and Insurance Industry on the Local Tax Revenues and Recommendations on Countermeasures (c金融保险业"营改增"对地方税收收入的影响及对策建议"地. Fujian Finance. Issue 1.

and national key projects including major infrastructure, shantytowns transformation and urbanization development, etc. by such means as debt investment and equity investment plans; encourage insurance companies to provide financial support to the development of technology-oriented enterprises, micro- and nano-enterprises and strategic emerging industries through various approaches including investing in the equity, creditors' rights, funds and asset-backed plans, etc. of enterprises under the precondition of rational management and control of risks; and research and formulate the relevant policies for insurance funds to invest in venture capital funds". Under the guidance of the macroeocnomic policies, the life insurers of China have since 2006 started to participate in infrastructure investment through cebt investment plans, equity investment plans and other plans, providing long-term, low-cost funding for China's urbanization initiatives. In addition, insurance funds also actively support the development of a green economy in China against the background that since the Third Plenary Session of the 18th CPC Central Committee, accelerating the ecological progress and promoting green development have become a strategic task for China's economic and social development. This idea has been further reflected in the 13th Five-Year Development Plan. The 13th Five-Year Development Plan puts forward five development concepts including "Green Development" as the guiding principle for the future development of China's economy. In response to the need for a green transition in China's economy, the green tendency of insurance funds is also quite obvious. According to statistics from the Insurance Asset Management Association of China, as of the end of March 2017, a total of 20 professional management institutions registered 200 debt investment plans to invest in various green industry fields such as clean transportation, clean energy, resource conservation and recycling, and pollution prevention. The total registered capital reached RMB 550.625 billion, accounting for 39.20% of the cumulative registered capital of the debt investment plans. The scale and proportion of China's investment in infrastructure and green economy development by the insurance funds are significantly higher than those of international counterparts, and have become a major highlight of China's insurance industry serving the real economy. This bright spot mainly comes from following the macroeconomic guidance of the government.

3. As various functions of China's life insurance industry have not been brought into full play, the methods and efforts in serving the real economy still lags far behind the foreign countries with stronger insurance industries.

China is undoubtedly a country with a large-scale insurance industry, but it is still not a country with a strong insurance industry. An important demonstration is that the insurance popularity is very low, which is far below the levels of developed countries whether it is based on the insurance policies ownership per capita or the insurance density or insurance depth. For example, according to the data from the China Insurance Regulatory Commission, China's life insurance policy holders only account for 8% of the total population, and the average number of policies held per capita is only 0.13. The low popularity means that the various functions of the life insurance industry are far from being played.

Selecting several key areas for evaluation can also lead to the above conclusions. For example, in the context of the current financing function of the financial system being overemphasized and the risk management function being largely ignored, the risk protection function provided by the life insurance industry is very weak; under the banking-led financial system in China, the life insurance industry plays a limited role in promoting the further development of China's capital market; in the social security system dominated by the first pillar, the security provided by retirement income through commercial insurance is overall negligible.

Table 4: Comparison of strength of life insurance markets of five countries in 2015

	USA	UK	Germany	Japan	China
Life insurance premium income (USD million, 2016)	558847	199369	94661	354053	262616
Life insurance premiums as a percentage of global total	21.36%	7.62%	3.62%	13.53%	10.03%
Global rankings of life insurance premiums	1	4	8	2	3
Life insurance premium depth (life insurance premium income/GDP)	3.02%	7.58%	2.75%	7.15%	2.34%
Life insurance premium density (life insurance premium per capita, 2016, USD)	1724.9	3033.2	1150.6	2803.4	189.9

Table 5: Comparison of various functions of life insurance industry

	China	Developed countries in Europe and America
Risk protection function	China's life insurance policyholders only account for 8% of the total population. The average number of insurance policies per capita is only 0.13, which is far below the levels of more than 1.5 policies in developed countries. At present, China's life insurance industry plays a very low role in risk protection. Taking death protection as an example, the research report released by Swiss Re in 2011 shows that in 2010, there is only USD12 savings and insurance coverage for every USD100 protection needs in China. The protection gap is as high as $88. From 2000 to 2010, China's death protection gap expanded from USD3.7 trillion to USD18.7 trillion.	The developed countries also have a certain guarantee gap, but compared with China, the gap is much smaller, and its life insurance penetration rate is much higher than China.
Deepening the development of the capital market	Investors in China's stock market are still dominated by retail investors. In recent years, institutional investors' shareholdings have risen rapidly. However, the shareholding ratio of all the institutional investors is about 20%, accounting for about one-third of the value of the A-share stock market. Among them, the proportion of insurance fund holdings in the total market value of A shares is less than 3%. In the bond market, insurance companies entered the interbank bond market in 1998 as the first non-bank institutional investor apart from the commercial banks and special clearing members, and retained the status of the largest non-bank institutional investor and the second largest institutional investor on the bond market in addition to the above two till 2012 when this position was exceeded by the fund investments. In other words, in the bond market, the relative importance of insurance companies as institutional investors has decreased significantly in recent years.	In most developed countries, insurance companies are either the most important institutional investors or the second largest institutional investors second only to pension funds. In specific areas such as corporate bonds, foreign bonds, and stocks, US life insurers are institutional investors with systemic importance. In 2009, US life insurers held approximately 16.7% of US corporate bonds and foreign bonds, 10.3% of commercial mortgages, and 6.2% of company stocks. In the Eurozone, insurance companies are the largest holders of government bonds. In 2014, 40% of the Eurozone government bonds were held by insurance companies.

Continuation

	China	Developed countries in Europe and America
Social Security System	In China, although the three-pillar pension system has been established, the development is not balanced. The first pillar—the basic pension insurance (employee pension insurance and urban and rural residents pension insurance) covers the largest number of people (915 million people insured in 2017) with absolute dominance in the insurance market; the second and third pillars cover a limited number of people, and the substitution rate provided is negligible (for example, at the end of 2017, corporate annuities and professional annuities covered only 23 million people.) Life insurance companies are involved in the development of the social security system mainly through the provision of commercial pension insurance and participation in enterprise annuity trusteeship management, etc. The unbalanced pension insurance system in China means that life insurance companies play a very limited role in the development of the social security system.	At present, public pension plans play an important role in ensuring the security of old-age income in most regions of the world. According to the 2014 data of the International Labour Organization, senior citizens aged 65 and above in OECD countries derive 59% of their family income from public pension income and 17% from the capital income, and the capital income is mainly composed of private pension funds. Insurance companies are important players in the private pension system and play an increasingly important role in increasing the replacement rate of retirement income.
Wealth management for residents	The wealth of Chinese households is dominated by the real estate, which accounts for more than 60% of the total household wealth. Other financing methods are mainly savings, and the insurance coverage is extremely low.	In 2012, the contractual obligations of insurance companies in the Eurozone' to policyholders accounted for an average of 32% of household wealth in the region, of which the German insurance compannies' liabilities corresponded to 36% of the national household financial wealth.

4. China's life insurance industry has witnessed the shift from real economy to virtual economy in recent years, which is a classic development feature of the primary stage and a reflection of immature development of China's life insurance industry.

The survival and catch-up pressure and motivation, relatively narrow

development space for insurance business plus the characteristics of the primary development stage have led to the alienation of behaviors of some life insurance companies in China, especially the small and medium-sized and newly established life insurance companies, which has quickly pushed up the industry risks. Among them, there have been many manifestations of the shift from the real economy to the virtual economy in the life insurance industry, which are closely related to the fact that the current insurance industry is still in the primary development stage. Because the history of China's insurance industry has not yet exceeded 40 years, it is still in the initial stage of development. The inherent immaturity at this stage is further amplified in the process of innovation of small and medium-sized companies, leading to the alienation of behaviors, which are manifested in the following aspects:

The first is the alienation of shareholders' business objectives. The understanding of insurance in the entire society is still superficial. It can be said that it is at the beginning of the learning curve. Many new forms of capital are no exception. For example, although insurance is a dual-wheel industry driven by both liabilities and assets, and the liability business is the foundation, new capitalists tend to hightlight the asset business. They neither understand nor value the liability business, or even ignore some basic rules of the industry's operations, thus becoming the "barbarians and laymen" of the insurance industry.

The second is the alienation of business models. Many small and medium-sized life insurance companies hold high the banner of "asset-driven liability model" and aggressively implement catch-up strategies. In this process, the foundation of liability business is often completely abandoned. Life insurance companies are no longer the institutions that undertake the risks of birth, old age, illness and death, but are completely pure asset management institutions. When the degree of alienation of the insurance business model is measured by the multiples of FYP/ original premium income, the higher multiples indicates the more similar the insurance company is to an "asset management agency" and the more alienated the business model is. Table 6 shows that from 2013 to 2016, the alienation degree of the life insurance industry as a whole has gradually increased. The alienation of small and medium-sized life

insurance companies is much higher than that of the old seven Chinese insurers (i.e. China Life Insurance, Ping An Life Insurance, China Pacific Life Insurance, New China Life Insurance, Taikang Life Insurance, PICC Life Insurance, and Taiping Life Insurance), and the degree of alienation of domestic-funded small and medium-sized life insurance companies is significantly higher than that of foreign-funded companies. In 2017, with the gradual implementation of a series of strong regulatory measures of China Insurance Regulatory Commission, the degree of alienation of the life insurance industry has weakened.

Table 6: Changes of First-Year Premiums (FYP) / Preimiums Income of Chinese Insurers, 2013-2017

Year	Old 7 life insufers	All remaining small- and medium-sized life insurance companies	All remaining doemstic-funded small- and medium-sized life insurance companies	Average Level of the Industry
2013	1.15	1.94	2.22	1.31
2014	1.15	1.82	1.97	1.33
2015	1.17	2.2	2.39	1.52
2016	1.26	2.03	2.53	1.59
2017	1.17	1.35	1.38	1.24

Source: calculated based on the data from China Insurance Regulatory Commission website

The third is the alienation of business operations. In the context of the alienation of goals and models, the alienation of specific business links comes so naturally. For example, in terms of products, many small and medium-sized life insurance companies regard short-term universal life insurance products with high yields as the main tool to promote the rapid expansion of business scale. These products have short deadlines, high costs, and extremely weak protection functions, completely overturning the original image. In terms of investment, in order to cater to the characteristics of short-term universal life insurance products with high yields, a large number of high-risk assets allocations have been made, and the risks from short-maturity funds matched to long-term assets are particularly highlighted.

At present, institutions, markets, and supervision are all in the process of "preventing risks, rectifying chaos, and addressing weak links", and it has become a consensus to enhance the efforts in services to the real economy.

III. Significance and direction for China's life insurance fund to support the real economy

This report focuses on life insurance funds supporting the economic development of the entity under the framework of the life insurance serving the real economy.

Compared with the risk protection function, investment is a derivative function of the life insurance industry, but it is extremely important: on the one hand, insurance investment is a typical debt-driven investment, and how the insurance asset business supports the real economy to a large extent reflects how the liability business supports the real economy; on the other hand, the full play of protection, financial management and other functions of the life insurance industry is inseparable from the contribution of investment activities.

Currently, actively promoting the life insurance investment to serve the real economy is of special significance in that the current funds supply is not sufficient to meet the demands of China's economic development for large amounts of long-term fund in the future. The Report delivered at the 19th National Congress of the Communist Party of China for the first time proposed to build a modern economic system. In this process, whether it is urbanization or industrialization or the transition from economic development to green and innovation, long-term funding is needed. The fact that the leverage is excessively high also determines that equity funds are more popular. However, the existing funding supply has failed to satisfy the demand. Though the aggregate shows that China is not short of funds and the funds supply is in plenty, but structurally, the short-term and debt investment funds might become excessive and the long-term, equity investment funds are remarkably insufficient under the bank-dominated financial system, which is a strong point of the life insurance funds. Such unique advantages as large size, stable sources, long maturities, and relatively low requirements on the return on investment, of the life insurance funds has made them the ideal source of long-term funds. Against this backdrop, the unique advantages of the life insurance funds can cater to the features of funds urgently needed for China's economic development, and help to fill up the gaps for funds, which show that life insurance companies are indispensable as funds providers.

Considering the above fact, the future investment direction of China's life insurance funds shall be focused on meeting the effective demands of the real economy, and the key points are: (1) to assist such national strategies as the Belt & Road Initiative (BRI), integrated Beijing-Tianjin-Hebei regional development and Yangtze River Economic Belt; (2) to assist the supply-side structural reform including the state-owned enterprise reform, transformation of economic structure to greening and innovation; (3) to assist to effectively enhance the sense of fulfillment, happiness, and security of the people, including wealth management and social security, etc.; and (4) to assist to take tough steps to forestall and defuse major risks, carry out targeted poverty alleviation, and prevent and control pollution.

The above demands of the real economy all contain huge investment opportunities, and it also poses a great challenge to the life insurance industry. The Chinese life insurance industry must actively respond by establishing more effective government-market partnerships, flexible use of multiple investment modes, and strengthening risk management capabilities.

Chapter II: Status quo of life insurance funds supporting the real economy in China

The life insurance funds, with its features of large size, long maturities and high stability, etc., caters to the capital needs by the development of the real economy; therefore, life insurance funds have unqiue advantages in supporting the real economy. In recent years, the policy environment for life insurance funds to support the real economy has been continuously optimized, and alternative investments have become the main method for life insurance funds to dock with the real economy projects. Life insurance funds actively participate in infrastructure projects through alternative investments and continue to expand to support new realities in the real economy. The major achievements from the support of life insurance funds to the real economy include: actively serving the national supply-side structural reform, actively supporting the Belt & Road initiative, actively supporting the national regional development strategy, actively participating in the public-private partnership (PPP) projects and major engineering projects and supporting the integrated military and civilian development and the transformation and upgrading of the manufacturing industry.

I. Features of Life Insurance Funds and Their Potential Advantages in Supporting the Real Economy

(I) Features of life insurance funds cater to the capital needs by the development of the real economy

By the end of 2017, the balance of utilized insurance funds amounted to RMB 14.920621 trillion, of which about 85% were life insurance funds. Life insurance

companies have a long period of liabilities, which makes life insurance funds characterized by large scale, long maturities and high stability, and makes it possible for life insurance funds to actively participate in long-term, large-scale real economy projects.

With the change of China's insurance regulatory guidance and the environment, the transformation of the life insurance industry is being enhanced, the proportion of long-term insurance policies will continue to increase, and the long-term nature of life insurance funds will be further reflected. Taking Year 2017 as an example, in the original regular premium income on new business, the income from policies with three-year less maturities was RMB 15.413 billion, accounting for 2.60%; the income from policies with 3- to 5-year maturities was RMB 177.695 billion, accounting for 29.93%; the income from policies with 5- to 10-year maturities was RMB 918.90 billion, accounting for 15.48%; and the income from policies with 10-year and above maturities was RMB 308.704 billion, accounting for 52.00%. It can be seen that with the transformation of the life insurance industry, new insurance policies with the maturities of more than 5 years, especially 10 years or more, have increased rapidly. The funds with the long-term attribute formed by long-term liabilities need to be docked with long-term investment projects. They are perfectly suitable for real economy projects with large capital requirements, long construction periods, and stable returns anc can provide long-term, stable funding for the real economy. With the further ageing of China's population, and the increasing demand for the coverage of residents' healthcare and pension insurances and wealth management, the funds from long-term life insurance will see a steady growth and play an increasingly important role in supporting the development of the real economy.

(II) Distinctive advantages of life insurance funds in supporting the real economy

The advantages of life insurance funds in serving the real economy are demonstrated in the following three aspects:

Firstly, they can provide the long-term stable capital protection through the cycles. Life insurance funds are mainly focused on long-term investments, adhere to

the investment philosophy of long-term investment, value investment, and sound and stable investment, and can become an important fund provider for the real economy. As for funds supply, the life insurance sector can provide lots of mid- and long-term funds and complement the short-term and liquid funds of other financial sectors; and as for capital price, the life insurance sector mainly adopts fixed interest rates in pursuit of asset-liability match and reasonable returns on investment, and maintains relatively stable costs.

Secondly, the life insurance sector has made remarkable achievements in supporting the development of major engineering projects for public benefits. Such properties as large size, long maturities, and stable sources, etc., of the life insurance funds can naturally cater to the capital demands of the real estate projects.

Thirdly, there are fairly diversified ways and approaches for life insurance funds to support the real economy. Life insurance funds can directly or indirectly invest in major investment projects in the real economy through debt, equity, debt+equity, equity investment plans, asset-backed plans and private equity funds, etc. In addition, life insurance companies can simultaneously provide such services as financial intermediation and loss protection etc. to reduce the project financing costs and risk management costs.

II. The policy environment for life insurance funds to support the real economy continue to be optimized

In recent years, the insurance regulatory authority has promoted the life insurance funds to support the development of the real economy mainly through policy and institutional guidance, diversifying investment vehicles, and strengthening supervision and risk prevention.

(I) The insurance regulatory authority enhanced the policy and institutional guidance

Starting from 2006, China Insurance Regulatory Commission (the "CIRC") has printed and distributed a series of policies and regulations including the *Measures*

for the Administration of the Pilot Program of the Indirect Investment of Insurance Funds in Infrastructure Projects (保险资金间接投资基础设施项目试点管理办法) and the *Interim Provisions on the Administration of Infrastructure Debt Investment Plans* (《基础设施债权投资计划管理暂行规定》) etc. to allow insurance fund to invest in infrastructure projects through debt or equity investment plans. Since 2010, the CIRC has printed and circulated a series of policies and regulations including the *Interim Measures for Equity Investment with Insurance Funds* (《保险资金投资股权暂行办法》), the *Interim Measures for the Investment of Insurance Funds in Real Estate* (《保险资金投资不动产暂行办法》), and the *Circular on Certain Issues Concerning the Equity Investment and Real Estate Investment with Insurance Funds* (《关于保险资金投资股权和不动产有关问题的通知》) etc., to continuously expand the investment scope and fields of insurance funds and promote their docking with the real economy, gradually open the channels for insurance funds to invest in Growth Enterprises Market (GEM), preferred stock, venture capital funds, private equity funds and asset-backed investment plans, etc., and basically achieve the full integration with the real economy.

In May 2017, the CIRC printed and distributed the *Guidance on the Insurance Industry to Support the Development of the Real Economy* (《关于保险业支持实体经济发展的指导意见》), and proposed to target at the key areas and weak links of economic and social development, innovate insurance services, and improve the efficiency and levels of the insurance sector in serving the real economy. Later on, the CIRC printed and distributed a seires of supporting documents including the *Circular on Matters Relating to the Investment in Public-Private-Partnership Projects with Insurance Funds* (《关于保险资金投资政府和社会资本合作项目有关事项的通知》) and the *Circular of China Insurance Regulatory Commission on Matters Relating to the Investment in Key Projects with Debt Investment Plans* (《关于债权计划投资重大工程有关事项的通知》) etc. to clarify specific support policies from technical details.

The CIRC promulgated the the revised *Measures for the Administration of the Utilization of Insurance Funds* (《保险资金运用管理办法》) which was implemented from April 1, 2018. The *Measures for the Administration of the*

Utilization of Insurance Funds has upgraded the useful practical experience and relevant normative documents in the past few years on how to use insurance funds to support the real economy to departmental regulations to better enhance the legal effectiveness, which mainly include: clarifying that insurance funds can invest in private equity funds such as venture capital funds and establish the real estate, infrastructure, pension and other professional insurance asset management institutions, further supporting the development of small and micro enterprises, and improving the breadth And depth of insurance funds in supporting infrastructure, pension and other key areas, in order to help promote insurance funds to support the development of the real economy.

(II) The insurance regulatory authority diversified investment vehicles

In terms of product patterns, in addition to infrastructure debt investment plans, the equity investment plans, asset-backed plans, portfolio asset management products, and insurance private equity investment funds are gradually evolving. In terms of transaction structure, life insurance funds have gradually evolved from a relatively single transaction structure such as debt and equity investments to a more flexible trading structure consisting of equity+debt integration and preferred stocks to meet the different financing needs of different sub-sectors of the real economy. In 2015, the China Insurance Investment Fund was formed with an initial scale of RMB 300 billion.

In terms of product issuance mechanism, the CIRC changeed the issuance mechanism of insurance asset management products, such as infrastructure investment plans, from record filing system to registration system, and changed the case-by-case record filing and approval system in 2013. The CIRC continuously improved the registration standards and registration procedures, etc., and authorized the Insurance Asset Management Association of China to be responsible for the specific registration procedures. As of the end of 2017, a total of 843 debt investment plans and equity investment plans have been initiated, with a total record (registration) scale of RMB 2,075.414 billion.

(III) The insurance regulatory authority strengthened the supervision and prevented various risks

(1) The CIRC established the professional centralized and well-regulated operating mechanism, and promoted the headquarters of the insurance companies to centralize the management of insurance funds. The insurance companies exercise professional management by establishing an asset management department and insurance asset management companies. (2) The CIRC adopted the proportional supervision on major classes of assets. It set the upper limits of investment ratio for equity, real estate and financial products, etc., and set an upper limit of concentration for a single investment type to prevent systematic risks. (3) The CIRC enhanced the supervision on the solvency. (4) The CIRC implemented the investment capacity-based license management. It specified the persons responsible for the treatment of risks, strengthen the supervision of investment capabilities and license management in seven high-risk areas such as stocks and equity, and require the establishment of relevant systems, personnel, and operational mechanisms. (5) The CIRC promoted the supervision on asset-liability matching; and (6) The CIRC strengthened in-process and ex post supervision through internal control, information disclosure, and five-tier classification of assets, etc.

In addition, the newly revised *Measures for the Administration of the Utilization of Insurance Funds* emphasizes that the use of insurance funds must be based on serving the insurance industry; made it clear that the use of insurance funds should be clearly and independently operated, and shareholders of insurance companies must not interfere with the use of insurance funds in violation of laws and regulations. It strengthened supervision of overseas investment and specified that overseas investments by insurance funds should comply with the relevant regulations of the China Insurance Regulatory Commission, the People's Bank of China, and the State Administration of Foreign Exchange, and specified that the insurance asset management institutions should, when carrying out insurance asset management products business, should conduct issuance registration and information disclosure, etc. on the asset registration and trading platforms approved by China Insurance

Regulatory Commission, develop the data analysis and risk warning systems, and further strengthen the supervision on asset management products. It strengthened the commissioned trusteeship management, required that the investment managers, when entrusted with the management of insurance funds, shall not sub-entrust trust funds or provide channel services for entrusting institutions, and strengthened de-nesting, de-leverage and de-channeling work. It specified the administrative penalties that can be applied to the illegal use of insurance funds, emphasize the "double penalty" mechanism for insurance institutions and related persons, and strengthened internal accountability; strengthened the regulatory constraint on securities and investment business conducted by insurance institutions, and further clarified the securities industry should comply with the relevant laws and regulations. These newly added regulations will be very conducive to advancing the use of insurance funds to establish a risk prevention mechanism that covers pre-and post-event and in-process events, foster a prudent and stable investment culture, and promote insurance funds to better serve the insurance industry and the development of the real economy.

III. Alternative investment is an important way for life insurance funds to support the real economy

Guided by the policies of the regulatory authorities, insurance institutions are constantly exploring ways and means of life insurance funds to support the real economy.

(I) Three major approaches for life insurance funds to support the real economy

There are three major approaches for the life insurance funds to support the real economy under the guidance of the regulatory authority:

Firstly, they provide indirect financing to the real economy by converting bank deposits into bank loans. By the end of 2017, the savings of the insurers at the banks amounted to RMB 1,927.407 billion, accounting for 12.92% of the total deposits, most of which are long-term negotiated deposits and term deposits, and have become an important source of funds for mid- and long-term loans of commercial banks.

Secondly, they provide financing to the real economy by investing in such financial market instruments as bonds and stocks, etc. By the end of 2017, the insurance funds invested RMB 5,161.289 billion in bonds, accounting for 34.59% of the total, RMB 752,477 billion in securities investment funds, accounting for 5.04%, and RMB 1,082.894 billion in stocks, accounting for 7.26%. The total investment in various bonds, funds and stocks exceeded RMB 6.9 trillion.

Thirdly, they provide project financing to real economy by issuing or investing in equity investment plans, debt investment plans and asset management plans, etc. By the end of 2017, the insurance funds invested RMB 5,996.553 billion in such forms as financial assets purchased under resale, long-term equity investments, investment real estate, products of insurance asset management companies, financial derivatives, loans, borrowed funds, and other investments, accounting for 40.19% of the total. Among them, the insurance funds invested in the real economy through debt investment plans, equity investment plans, asset-backed securities, industry investment plans, trust plans, private equity, etc., and the fields of investment included transportation, energy, municipal engineering, environmental protection, water services, renovation of rundown areas, logistics and warehousing, affordable housing, industrial parks, etc.

(II) The importance of alternative investment in life insurance funds' docking with the real economy has continuously increased

Life insurance funds are linked to the financing of real economy projects mainly through alternative investments, ie, financial products other than traditional bank credits and standardized financial products such as bonds, stocks and funds that are traded in the interbank markets and the stock exchange markets. Alternative investments have the characteristics of non-standardization, that is, the core elements and main terms of interest rates, deadlines, guarantee measures, repayment arrangements, etc., of the funds are usually negotiated and determined by both parties. At the same time, alternative investments are off-exchange, with poor liquidity and generally higher returns than standardized products.

Seen from the nature of products, alternative investments can be classified

into debts, equity, and asset securitization investments. From the point of view of development institutions, they mainly include financial products of banks, aggregate trust plans and unitrust plans of trust companies, debt investment, equity investment, and asset-backed plans of insurance asset management institutions, special asset management plans of securities companies, and quasi-trust products of fund subsidiaries. As seen from the operation models, six models of the alternative investment of the life insurances funds, i.e. the debt investment plans, equity investment plans, asset-backed securities, trust plans, private equity, and direct equity investment, are comprehensively adopted to provide financing to the real economy.

1. Debt investment plan

Debt investment plans refer to financial products under which insurance asset management companies and other professional management organizations, as trustees, issue certificates of trust receipt to the trustors to raises funds and invest in the real economy projects (infrastructure projects) by means of debt investment in accordance with the *Administrative Measures for the Indirect Investment of Insurance Funds in Infrastructure Projects* (《保险资金间接投资基础设施项目管理办法》) and the *Interim Provisions on the Administration of Infrastructure Debt Investment Plans* (《基础设施债权投资计划管理暂行规定》), pay the expected incomes as agreed and repay the principal.

2. Equity investment plan

Equity investment plans refer to financial products under which insurance asset management companies and other professional management organizations, as trustees, issue certificates of trust receipt to the trustors to raises funds and invest in the real economy projects (infrastructure projects) by means of equity investment in accordance with the Administrative Measures for the Indirect Investment of Insurance Funds in Infrastructure Projects (《保险资金间接投资基础设施项目管理办法》), and obtains the dividends and capital gains from the sale of equity and other benefits for the beneficiary. At the same time, the equity investment plans as a means of indirect investment in equity by insurance funds must also comply with the relevant stipulations of the Administrative Measures for the Indirect Investment of Insurance Funds in Infrastructure Projects (《保险资金间接投资基础设施项目管理办法》)

and the *Interim Provisions on the Administration of Infrastructure Debt Investment Plans* (《基础设施债权投资计划管理暂行规定》), etc. According to the investment target, the equity investment plans can be divided into enterprise type and fund type. Among them, the corporate type equity investment plans refer to the cases where the trustees, upon the intention of the trustors, take the capital raised for the equity investment plans as the equity of the relevant real economy projects in their own name; and the fund type equity investment plans refer to the cases where the trustees, upon the intention of the trustors, invest the capital raised for the equity investment plans in some specific equity investment funds in their own name and then invest in the relevant real economy projects through the equity investment funds.

3. Asset-backed plans

Asset-backed plans refer to the business activities where insurance asset management companies and other professional management organizations, as trustees, set up support plans with the cash flows generated by underlying assets as the repayment support, and issue certificates of trust receipt to qualified investors such as insurance institutions. According to the *Interim Measures for the Management of Asset-Backed Plan Business* (《资产支持计划业务管理暂行办法》) (No.85 [2015] of the China Insurance Regulatory Commission), underlying assets refer to property, property rights or asset portfolio composed of property and property rights that can directly generate independent and sustainable cash flow in compliance with laws and regulations.

4. Trust plans

The trust plan refers to the aggregate fund trust plans investged in by professional fund management institutions such as insurance asset management companies. According to the stipulations of the *Notice on Using Insurance Funds to Invest in the Relevant Financial Products* (《关于保险资金投资有关金融产品的通知》) (No.91 [2012] of the China Insurance Regulatory Commission) and the *Notice of the China Insurance Regulatory Commission on Matters concerning the Investments in Collective Fund Trust Plans with Insurance Funds* (《关于保险资金投资集合资金信托计划有关事项的通知》) (No.38 [2014] of the China Insurance Regulatory Commission), in the aggregate fund trust plans invested in by the insurance funds,

the underlying assets are limited to financing assets and non-listed equity assets with controllable risks. Among them, the credit ratings for the fixed-income aggregate fund trust plans shall not be lower than the A rating or credit rating equivalent to A rating assessed by the domestic credit rating agencies. Life insurance funds are not allowed to invest in unitrust plans or invest in trust plans whose underlying assets belong to the industries or sectors explicitly prohibited by the state.

5. private equity funds

Insurance funds can establish private equity funds ranging from growth funds, buyout funds, emerging strategic industry funds, mezzanine funds, real estate funds, venture capital funds, and fund of funds that takes the above funds as their main investment targets. According to stipulations of the *Circular of China Insurance Regulatory Commission on Certain Issues Concerning Establishing Private Equity Funds with Insurance Funds* (《中国保监会关于设立保险私募基金有关事项的通知》) (No.89 [2015] of the China Insurance Regulatory Commission), the direction of investment of the private equity funds set up by the insurance funds should be the industries and sectors supported by the state, including but not limited to major infrastructure projects, shanty town transformation, new urbanization projects, and other people's livelihood projects and national major projects; science and technology enterprises, small and micro enterprises, strategic emerging industries, and other enterprises or industries supported by the state; retirement services, health and medical services, security services, and the Internet financial services and other industries or business forms that conform to the extended directions of the insurance industry chain.

6. Direct equity investment

Direct investment equity refers to the act of an insurance company (including an insurance group (controlling company)) investing and holding equity in the name of a contributor. The direct investment equity shall comply with the relevant provisions of the *Interim Measures for Equity Investment with Insurance Funds* (《保险资金投资股权暂行办法》) (No.79 [2010] of the China Insurance Regulatory Commission) and the *Circular on Certain Issues Concerning the Equity Investment and Real Estate Investment with Insurance Funds* (《关于保险资金投资股权和不动产有

关问题的通知》) (No.59 [2012] of the China Insurance Regulatory Commission). According to the newly revised *Measures for the Administration of the Utilization of Insurance Funds* (Ordinance No.1 [2018] of the China Insurance Regulatory Commission), insurance group (holding) companies and insurance companies shall use its own funds to purchase real estate for self use, conduct acquisitions of listed companies, or engage in equity investments with the purpose of achieving holdings in other companies. The equity investment that an insurance group (holding) companies or insurance companies hold in order to have holdings over other enterprises shall meet the solvency regulations. If the insurance branch companies of the insurance group (controlling) companies do not meet the regulatory requirements for solvency of the China Insurance Regulatory Commission, the insurance group (controlling) companies may not invest in non-insurance financial companies. The equity investment for the purpose of achieving holdings shall be limited to the following enterprises: (1) insurance enterprises, including insurance companies, insurance asset management institutions, insurance professional agencies, insurance brokerage agencies, and insurance assessment agencies; (2) non-insurance financial enterprises; and (3) enterprises related to insurance business.

Among the above six models, the largest ones are the debt investment plans and equity investment plans, especially the debt investment plans. This is currently the leading model for life insurance funds to support the development of the real economy, and is also the focus of the following analysis of this report.

IV. Development of alternative investment by life insurance funds

(I) Overall development of alternative investment and the causes

1. Overall development of alternative investment

By the end of 2017, the insurance funds invested RMB 5,996.553 billion in such forms as financial assets purchased under resale, long-term equity investments, investment real estate, products of insurance asset management companies, financial derivatives, loans, borrowed funds, and other investments,.The other investments of

the insurance funds have increased from RMB 1.3 trillion in 2013 to over RMB 5.9 trillion in 2017, with their share in the utilized insurance funds rising from 16.90% in 2013 to 40.19% by the end of 2017, with the proportion continuously increasing (see Figure 1). Among them, the insurance funds invested over RMB 4.6 trillion in the real economy through debt investment plans, equity investment plans, asset-backed securities, industry investment plans, trust plans, private equity, etc., and the fields of investment included transportation, energy, municipal engineering, environmental protection, water services, renovation of rundown areas, logistics and warehousing, affordable housing, industrial parks, etc.

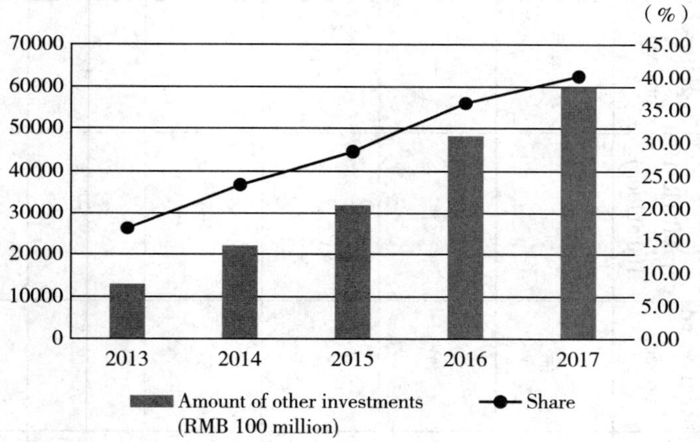

Figure 1: Amount and share of alternative investments in China' s insurance funds in recent years
Source: China Insurance Regulatory Commission, Insurance Asset Management Association of China

The rapid growth of the alternative investments was largely due to the increasing number of various debt investment plans, equity investment plans and asset-backed securities initiated by insurance asset management institutions. From 2013 to 2017, 103, 175, 121, 152, and 216 items of various asset management products were registered respectively (see Table 1 and Figure 2) and the registered amounts were RMB 368.827, 380.102, 270.613, 317.439, and 507.547 billion respectively (see Table 1 and Figure 3). By the end of December 2017, the cumulative number of the debt investment plans and equity investment plans already initiated reached 843, and the total filing (registration) scale amounted to RMB 2,075.414 billion.

Table 1 : The number of registered projects and registrered scale of various types of insurance

assets management products

	Infrastructure debt investment plans		Real estate debt investment plans		Equity investment plans		Project asset-backed plans		Total of registered projects	Total registered capital (RMB 100 million)
	Registered projects	registered capital (RMB 100 million)	Registered projects	registered capital (RMB 100 million)	Registered projects	registered capital (RMB 100 million)	Registered projects	registered capital (RMB 100 million)		
2007-2012	—	—	—	—	—	—	—	—	—	2941
2013	—	—	—	—	—	—	—	—	103	3688.27
2014	—	—	—	—	—	—	—	—	175	3801.02
2015	42	1027.45	69	1019.68	5	465	5	194	121	2706.13
2016	57	1477.53	77	1001.86	18	695	0	0	152	3174.39
2017	81	2466.45	123	2113.52	11	488.5	0	0	216	5075.47

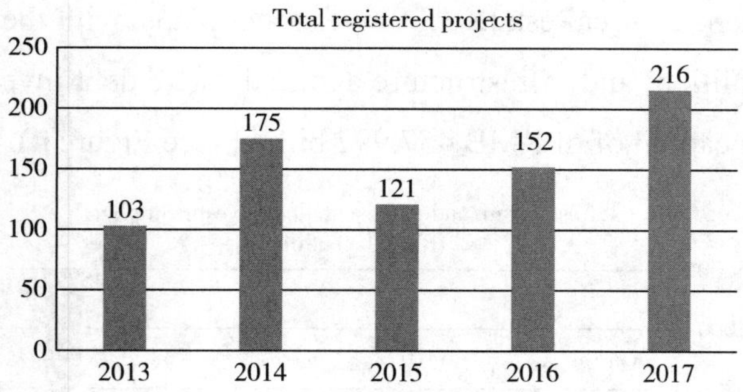

Total registered projects

Figure 2: Number of registered projects of various types of insurance assets management products of China in recent years

Source: Insurance Asset Management Association of China, the same below

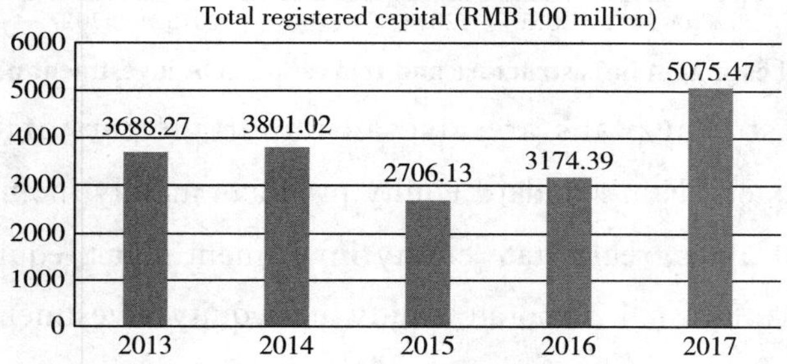

Total registered capital (RMB 100 million)

Figure 3: Registered capital of various types of insurance assets management products of China in recent years

Among the various insurance asset management products, the infrastructure and real estate debt investment plans have the largest number of registered projects and scale. Infrastructure and real estate debt investment plans are mainly based on a loan interest rate of over 5 years as the benchmark interest rate, and are divided into fixed interest rates and floating interest rates. Such plans are mainly for municipal engineering development, highways, railways, electricity projects, public rental housing, and shanty town transformation.

From 2007 to 2012, the cumulative registered capital of insurance debt investment plan products was RMB 294.1 billion, and the registered capital of the new debt investment plans in 2013 was equal to the total registered capital of the previous 6 years, reaching RMB 287.76 billion. In 2014-2016, the registered capital of the new debt investment plans reached RMB 310.96 billion, RMB 204.713 billion and RMB 247.939 billion respectively. In 2017, 24 insurance asset management companies registered 81 infrastructure debt investment plans, with the registered capital of RMB

246.645 billion yuan; 123 real estate debt investment plans, with the registered capital of RMB 211.352 billion; and infrastructure and real estate debt investment plans with the total registered capital of of RMB 457.997 billion (see Figure 4).

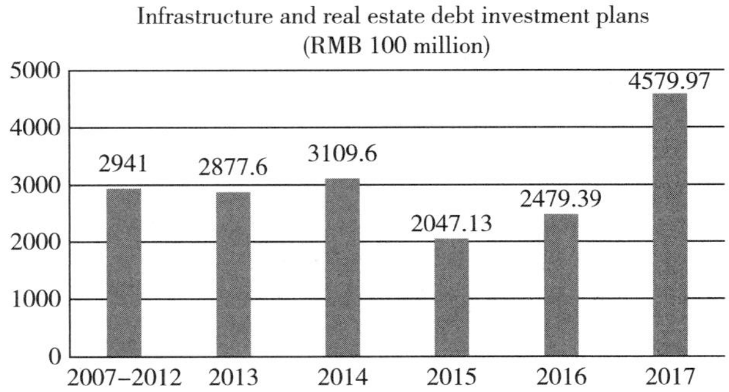

Figure 4: Registered capital of infrastructure and real estate debt investment plans in recent years

Equity investment plans are also an important part of insurance asset management products. Non-standard equity products mainly include infrastructure equity investment plans, real estate equity investment plans, equity-based project asset-backed plans, unlisted corporate equity and equity investment funds, etc. The alternative products of the debt investment plan are mostly the integrated equity+debt plans with debt investments in fake equity, and as the substitute products of debt investment plans, are largely complementary to the supply of debt investment plans. In 2015, 2016 and 2017, the registered capital of equity investment plans was RMB 46.5 billion, RMB 69.5 billion and RMB 49.550 billion respectively.

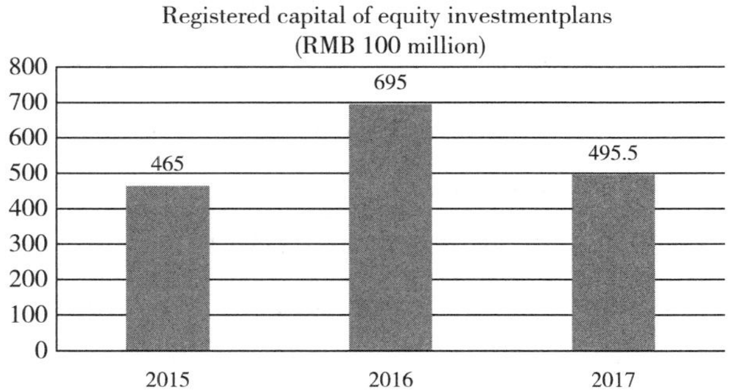

Figure 5: Registered capital of equity investment plans in recent years

Insurance asset management products also include project asset-backed plans, which mainly invest in assets or portfolios (underlying assets) that lack liquidity but have predictable cash flows, and financial product that use the cash flows generated by

the underlying assets as repayment support. In 2015, the insurance asset management institutions registered a total of 5 project asset-backed plans, with the registered capital of RMB 19.4 billion. In 2016 and 2017, no project asset-backed plan was registered.

2. The major reasons for the rapid development of alternative investments

The rapid growth of alternative investment in China's insurance industry is mainly due to the following aspects:

Firstly, the pursuit of higher returns on investment. The recent years have witnessed the ferocious competition on the financial market and the gradual increase of the liability-side costs of the life insurance sector. As the traditional investment products of bank deposits and bonds, etc. are no longer meeting the demand of the insurance assets for the rates of return, the insurers are being forced to find new investment fields.

Secondly, the control on the channels to become alternative loans. After several years of market-oriented reforms, China's insurance fund allocation has basically been in line with international standards, but there are also some significant differences. One important manifestation is that the insurers are not allowed to directly issue insurance funds as loans. The insurance funds of the United States, Japan, Germany, and other countries can directly link to the real economy through the form of loans and even issue individual housing mortgage loans. However, in China, insurance funds cannot be used for loan business, and the available investment types are insufficient. In practice, a considerable proportion of insurance funds are deposited in banks. Due to the lack of direct investment channels for loans issued by foreign insurance institutions, insurance funds have to be turned to financial products such as investment trusts, asset-backed plans, infrastructure investment plans and other loans. In a sense, some investment projects such as trusts and asset-backed plans are essentially similar to bank loans.

Fourthly, demonstration of the value of long-term funds. China's capital market lacks long-term investment varieties, and long-term asset allocation is difficult. Insurance funds have to be allocated to short-term assets, resulting in mismatch of assets and terms of the liabilities, both at the expense of investment income and

increasing the short-term volatility.

Fifthly, the increasing removal of policy restriction on the investment of insurance funds. Since the second-half of 2012, the CIRC has promulgated over 20 new policies concerning the fund utilization, which broadened the channels for investment, and improved the policies on proportion regulation, including liberalizing investment in financial products such as trusts and launching pilot projects for asset management products. At the same time, the CIRC advanced the reform of the recording system to become a registration system of infrastructure debt investment plans, which greatly increased the issuance efficiency, promoted the growth of alternative investment from the institutional and mechanism perspectives and better supported the development of the real economy.

It is noteworthy that a large part of the alternative investment in the insurance industry in China has the property of loans, which makes them different from the international alternative investments. Internationally, an important criterion for distinguishing between alternative investments and traditional investments is whether the pricing mechanism is fair and transparent and whether the returns are relatively stable. If the pricing mechanism is not transparent or open, and the income is uncertain, the investment is classified as an alternative investment. According to this standard, some new investment types invested by China's insurance funds, such as infrastructure debt plan, trusts, asset-backed plans, and portfolio asset management products, are quasi-fixed-income products that have the nature of bonds and are not intrinsically classified as alternative investment as defined by the international standards. In fact, only direct real estate investments and long-term equity investments can be considered alternative investments in the true sense. The scale of true alternative investments is not too large.

(II) Infrastructure is an important field of alternative investments of insurance funds

As mentioned above, alternative investments including debt and equity investment plans are important forms for the life isnruance to serve the real economy, where the investments in infrastructure through debt and equity

investment plans are the major channels for insurance funds to support the development of the real economy.

Since 2006, except for the impact of macro-environmental factors in 2015, the number of projects and investment amount of insurance fund invested in infrastructure have generally risen. Especially in 2013 and 2014, the investment amount reached nearly RMB 300 billion respectively. By the end of 2016, the cumulative number of infrastructure projects invested by insurance funds reached 437 and the total investments reached RMB 1285 billion, which averaged to the investment of about RMB 3 billion for each project (see Figure 6).

Table 6: The number of projects and investment amount of insurance fund invested in infrastructure

1. Investment fields

Transportation and energy are the key fields for life insurance funds to invest in the infrastructure, which accounted for two-thirds of the total in terms of the number of projects and the amount of investment. The rest of the insurance funds are invested in municipal engineering, shantytowns transformation, land reserves, water conservancy, affordable housing and other fields concerning people's livelihood. By the end of 2016, the cumulative infrastructure investment in the transportation sector of was RMB 568.3 billion, accounting for 44.22%; the infrastructure investment in the energy sector was RMB 295 billion, accounting for 22.96%; the infrastructure investment in the municipal engineering sector was RMB 120.4 billion, accounting for 9.37%; the infrastructure investment in

the shantytowns transformation sector was RMB 96.8 billion, accounting for 7.53%; the infrastructure investment in land reserve sector was RMB 94 billion, accounting for 7.31%; and infrastructure investment in other areas (including water conservancy, indemnificatory housing, transformation of old cities, environmental protection, iron and steel, senior living property etc.) totaled RMB 110.5 billion, accounting for 8.6% (see Figure 7 and Figure 8).

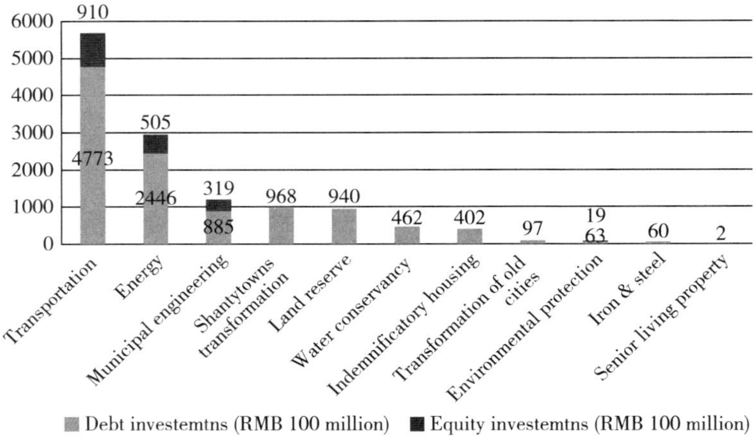

Figure 7: Distribution of investment amount in fields of infrastructure investment by insurance funds

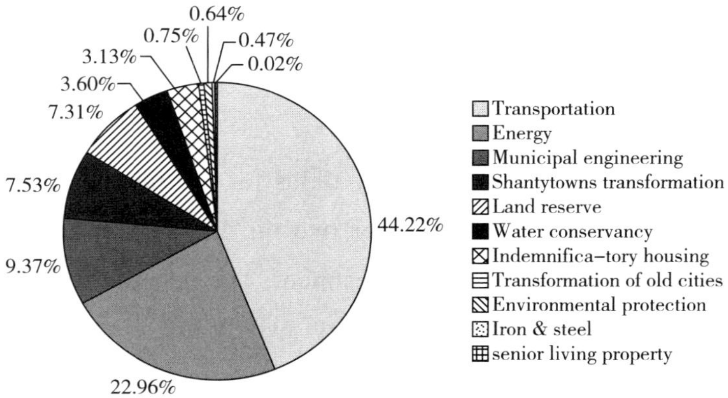

Figure 8: Proportional distribution infrastructure investment by insurance funds, by fields

From the trajectory of changes, the initial stage is mainly concentrated in transportation, and the proportion of transportation investment has dropped from 74% in 2009 to 20% in 2011. Since 2012, it has stopped falling and has kept rising. In 2016, it accounted for 56% of the infrastructure investment. Energy investment accounted

for 39% of the total in 2011 and has gradually declined since 2012, accounting for 14% in 2016. Municipal engineering investment began in 2011, with its share rising moderately, reaching 11% in 2016. The proportion of other investments fluctuated greatly before 2013, and it has stabilized at around 20% since 2014.

From the perspective of the industrial distribution of investment, the largest number of investment projects and investment amounts are in the areas of transportation and energy such as highways, electricity, railways, coal and urban rail transits, etc. The total investment projects of the five industries reached 249, with an investment of RMB 671.4 billion. By the end of 2016, the accumulated investment in the highways was RMB 284.7 billion, accounting for 22.2%; the investment in the electricity field was RMB 150 billion, accounting for 11.7% (including investment of RMB 62.6 billion in clean energy generation, accounting for 4.9%); the investment in the railways was RMB 101.2 billion, accounting for 7.9%; the investment in the coal was RMB 83.8 billion, accounting for 6.5%, and the investment in urban rail transits was RMB 51.7 billion, accounting for 4.0%.

2. Investment regions

In the four major regions, the investment by insurance funds in infrastructure was mainly concentrated in the eastern region. As of the end of 2016, a total of 183 projects were invested in the eastern region, with a total investment of RMB 550.5 billion, accounting for 41.9% of the total investment projects and 42.8% of the investment amount respectively. In the western region, a total of 124 projects were invested, with a total investment of RMB 271.6 billion, accounting for 28.4% of the total investment projects and 21.1% of investment amount respectively. In the central region, a total of 87 projects were invested with a total investment of RMB 193.9 billion, accounting for for 19.9% of the total investment projects and 15.1% of the investment amount respectively. There are few investment projects in the northeast region. In the past 10 years, only 9 projects in total have been invested, and the total amount of investment is only RMB 16.9 billion, accounting for 2.1% of the total investment projects and 1.3% of the investment amount respectively. (See Figures 9 and Figure 10).

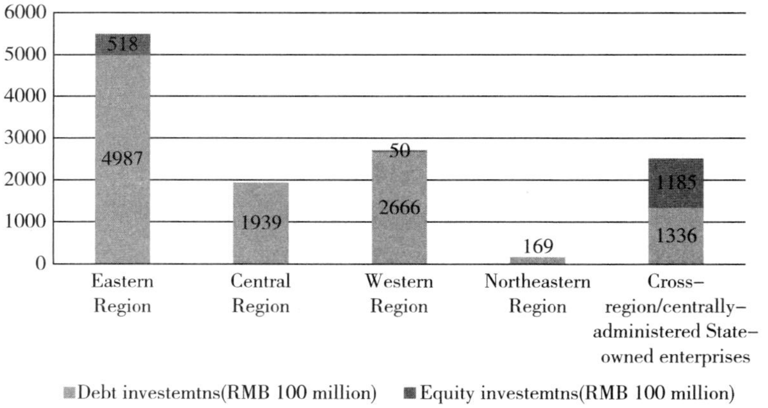

Figure 9: Geographical distribution of infrastructure investment amounts by insurance funds

Note: As for debt investment plans, the cross-region plans includes two forms: First, a single project that crosses regions; second, there are multiple projects distributed in different regions in the same investment plan. As for the equity investment plans, the plans are first of all divided by the central and local enterprises, and then the local enterprises are divided by geographical locations.

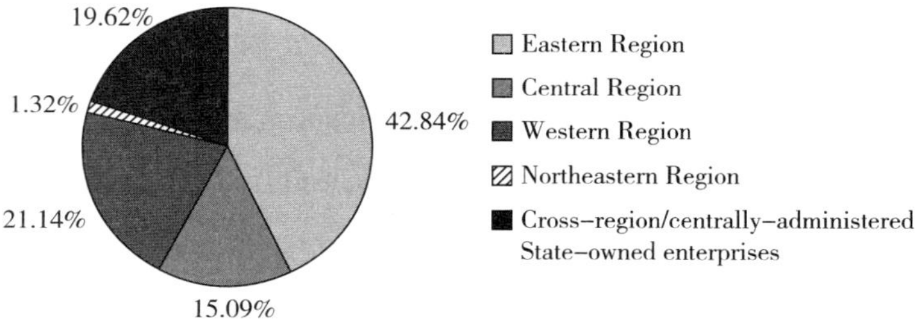

Figure 10: Geographical distribution of infrastructure investment in insurance funds (calculated by investment amount)

By the trend of changes, after Year 2009, the proportion of investment in the eastern region has declined, gradually tilting towards the central and western regions. This trend has become more apparent since 2013: the share of investments in Central and Western China in all regions has increased from 36% in 2013 to 57% in 2016, and the share of investments in the Eastern China has dropped from 60% to 30% during the same period.

In addition, the debt investment plans also include a number of cross-regional projects. By the end of 2016, there were cumulatively 26 cross-regional debt investment projects with an investment amount of RMB 133.6 billion. A large proportion of

the equity investment plans was invested in the centrally-administered State-owned enterprises. As of the end of 2016, there were a total of 8 equity investment projects for the centrally-administered State-owned enterprises with an investment amount of RMB 118.5 billion.

3. Investment methods

The infrastructure investments by insurance funds consist mainly of debt investments and equity investments (see Table 2 and Figure 11).

Table 2: Ways of infrastructure investments by insurance funds

Year	Debt investment projects	Debt investment amount (RMB 100 million)	Equity investment projects	Equity investment amount (RMB 100 million)
2007	6	203		
2008	4	144	1	160
2009	7	230		
2010	10	243		
2011	29	845		
2012	37	1246		
2013	77	2626	1	360
2014	120	2583	7	405
2015	53	1272	2	409
2016	74	1706	9	419
Total	417	11098	20	1753

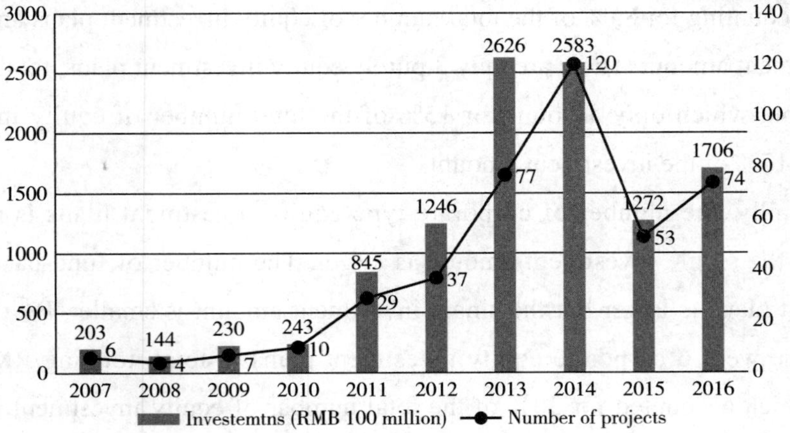

Figure 11: Infrastructure investments by debt investment plans

Among them, the debt investment plans dominate the infrastructure investments by insurance funds. By the end of 2016, the cumulative number of debt investment

projects reached 417 and the total investments amounted to RMB 1109.8 billion, accounting for 95.4% of the total number of investment projects and 86.4% of the investments respectively (see Figure 13 and Figure 14).

As of the end of 2016, the cumulative number of equity investment projects reached 20, and the total investments amounted to RMB 175.3 billion (see Figure 12), accounted for 4.6% of the total investment projects and 13.6% of the investment amount respectively (see Figure 13 and Figure 14). Among them, the vast majority of equity investments are debt investments in fake equity. There are only 3 purely equity investment plans in the true sense[①], and the investment amount is only RMB 30.5 billion, accounting for only 0.7% of the total investment projects and 2.4% of the investment amount respectively.

From the perspective of temporal distribution, there are no other equity investment projects except the Beijing-Shanghai High-Speed Railway before 2013. After 2013, debt investments in fake equity began to rise. In 2016, the project number of debt investments in fake equity reached 9 with an investment of RMB 41.9 billion.

The distribution structure of the equity investment plans shows the following characteristics:

Firstly, the dominance of debt investments in fake equity. By the end of 2016, there were a total of 17 investment projects and a total investment of RMB 144.8 billion, accounting for 85% of the total number of equity investment plans and 83% of the investment amount. There are only 3 purely equity investment plans, totaling RMB 30.5 billion, which only account for 15% of the total number of equity investment plans and 17% of the investment amount.

Secondly, the number of corporate-type equity investment plans is relatively small but the single investment amount is larger. The number of fund-based equity investment plans is larger but the single investment amount is smaller. By the end of 2016, there were 6 corporate equity investment plans in total, totaling RMB 104.9 billion, which accounted for 30% of the total number of equity investment plans and

---

① The 3 purely equity investment plans are: Beijing-Shanghai High-Speed Railway, RMB 16 billion, PICC Asset Management Cmpany Limited investing in Sinopec Marketing Co., Ltd., RMB 9.49 billion, and Changjiang Pension Insurance Co., Ltd. investing in Sinopec Marketing Co., Ltd., RMB 5 billion.

60% of the investment amount, with an average investment of RMB 17.5 billion for each plan. In contrast, the investment amounts in fund-based equity investment plans are relatively low. By the end of 2016, a total of 14 fund-based equity investment plans totalled RMB 70.4 billion, accounting for 70% of the total number of equity investment plans and 40% of the investment amounts, with an average investment of RMB 5 billion for each plan.

Thirdly, equity investment plans are mainly concentrated in transportation, municipal engineering, and energy sectors. Among them, the traffic sector has the most investment plans: a total of 9 plans totaled RMB 97.8 billion, accounting for 45% of the total number of equity investment plans and 56% of the investment amount respectively, with an average investment of RMB 10.9 billion for each plan; a total of 6 municipal enginenering plans totaled RMB 25.1 billion, accounting for 30% of the total number of equity investment plans and 14% of the investment amount respectively, with an average investment of RMB 4.2 billion for each plan; the number of equity investment plans in energy is small, but the single investment amount is relatively large, with 3 plans totaling RMB 50.5 billion, accounting for 15% of the total number of equity investment plans and 29% of the investment amount respectively, with an average investment of RMB 16.8 billion for each plan; and the number of equity investment plans in environmental protection sector is the smallest, with 2 plans totaling RMB 1.9 billion, accounting for 10% of the total number of equity investment plans and 1% of the investment amount respectively, with an average investment of RMB 1 billion for each plan.

Fourthly, almost all of the investment targets are centrally-administered State-owned enterprises or local state-owned enterprises and government-led funds in developed provinces and cities such as Beijing, Shanghai, Guangdong, and Jiangsu in the eastern region. The only exception is the equity investment plan of the Guizhou Railway Development Fund.

Fifthly, there are seven insurance asset management institutions that have issued equity investment plans, of which the largest number comes from enterprises under the PICC (including PICC Asset Management and PICC Capital Investment Management). A total of 8 equity investment plans total RMB 41.5 billion, accounting

for 40% of the total number of equity investment plans and 24% of the investment amount respectively; Taikang Life Insurance has made the largest investment amount of RMB 48 billion, accounting for 10% of the total number of equity investment plans and 27% of the investment amount respectively; and China Insurance Investment only has 1 plan with the investment amount of RMB 40 billion, which is the largest individual investment.

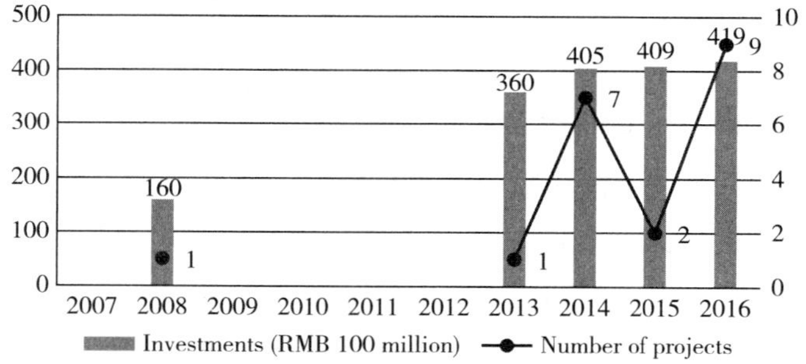

Figure 12: Infrastructure investments by equity investment plans

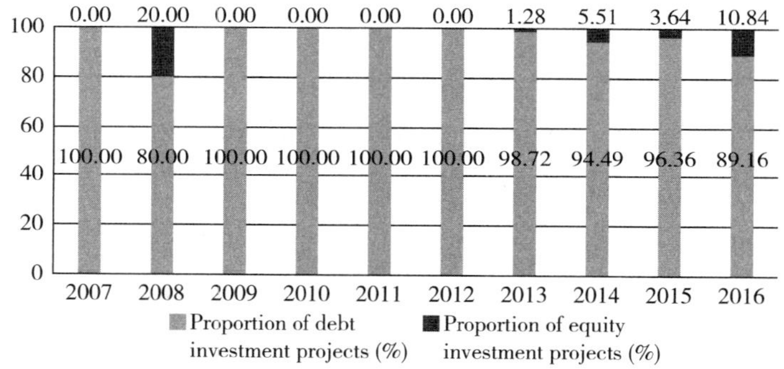

Figure 13: Proportions of different forms of infrastructure investment by insurance funds (calculated by the number of projects)

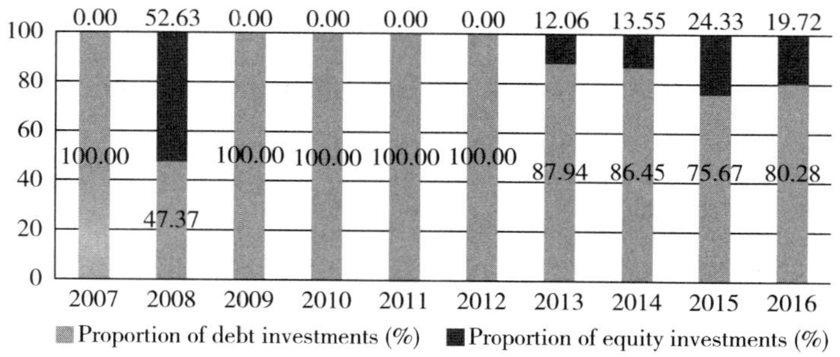

Figure 14: Proportions of different forms of infrastructure investment by insurance funds (calculated by the investment amount)

4. Status of credit enhancement of debt investment plans

According to the *Interim Provisions on the Administration of Infrastructure Debt Investment Plans* (《基础设施债权投资计划管理暂行规定》) (No.92 [2012] of the China Insurance Regulatory Commission), a professional management institution shall determine an effective credit enhancement when establishing a debt investment plan and meet the following requirements: (I) The credit enhancement methods shall be mutually independent from the repayment source of debt-paying entity. (II) The credit enhancement adopts one of the following methods or a combination thereof: Firstly, Type A credit enhancement: State special funds, policy banks, state-owned commercial banks or joint-stock commercial enterprises with a credit rating of AA or above (including AA ratings) in the previous year shall provide the unconditional, irrevocable and joint liability guarantees for the full principal and interests. Where the provincial branches of the above-mentioned banks provide the guarantees, the branches shall provide the legal documents of the head office's guarantee authorization, and explain the guarantee limit and the amount of guarantee already provided.

Secondly, Type B credit enhancement: Enterprises (companies) legally incorporated within the territory of China shall provide the unconditional, irrevocable and joint liability guarantees for the full principal and interests, and meet the following conditions: (1) The guarantor's credit rating is not lower than the credit rating of the debt-paying subject; (2) Where the issuing scale of debt investment plans does not exceed RMB 2 billion, the guarantor's net assets at the end of the previous year shall not be less than RMB 6 billion; where the issuing scale of debt investment plans exceeds RMB 2 billion but less than RMB 3 billion, the guarantor's net assets at the end of the previous year shall not be less than RMB 10 billion; and where the issuing scale of debt investment plans exceeds RMB 3 billion, the guarantor's net assets at the end of the previous year shall not be less than RMB 15 billion; (3) the total amount of guarantees provided by the same guarantor shall not exceed 50% of its net assets. The total amount of guarantees and net assets are determined based on the scope of the assets provided by the guaranteeing entity; (4) Where the parent company or the actual

controller of the debt-paying entity provides guarantees, the net assets of the guarantor shall not be less than 1.5 times the net assets of the debt-paying subject; and (5) The guarantee activity shall fulfill all legal procedures.

Thirdly, Type C credit enhancement: the pledge guarantee is provided with the tradable shares of listed companies with a high liquidity, a fair value not less than 2 times the value of the debts, and of which the guarantor has the full right to dispose; or the pledge guarantee is provided with the transferrable right to charge according to the laws; or the mortgage guarantee is provided with the physical assets of which the guarantor has the full right to dispose and that have the potential of appreciation and are easy to cash in on. Pledged guarantees shall be handled for pledge registration, and mortgage guarantees shall be handled for the registration of collaterals, and the mortgage rights shall be ranked first, with the value of the collaterals no less than 2 times the value of the debts. The fair value of the mortgaged or pledged assets shall be assessed by an appraisal agency with the highest professional qualifications and shall be reviewed no less than once a year. If the value of the mortgage or pledged assets is reduced or the liquidation risk arises, which affects the property security of the debt investment plans, the professional management institutions shall promptly adopt measures such as starting the stop-loss mechanism, increasing the guarantee entity, or adding additional legal value to the mortgaged or pledged product to ensure that the full amount of the guarantee is valid.

A debt investment plan that meets the following conditions simultaneously may also be exempted from credit enhancement: (1) The debt-paying subject's net assets shall not be less than RMB 30 billion, and its annual operating income shall not be less than RMB 50 billion in the two most recent fiscal years, and shall comply with the *Measures for the Administration of the Pilot Program of the Indirect Investment of Insurance Funds in Infrastructure Projects* (保险资金间接投资基础设施项目试点管理办法) and requirements of this regulation; (2) The debt-paying subject has issued unsecured bonds in the last two years, both the entity and the bonds it issued have credit ratings of AAA; and (III) The issuance size does not exceed RMB 3 billion.

In 2017, the China Insurance Regulatory Commission issued the *Circular of*

China Insurance Regulatory Commission on Matters Relating to the Investment in Key Projects with Debt Investment Plans (《中国保监会关于债权投资计划投资重大工程有关事项的通知》) (No.135 [2017] of the China Insurance Regulatory Commission), which proposed that in order to support the investment of insurance funds in major projects which are of great significance to the national economy and people's livelihood, and to further serve the real economy, debt investment plans that invest in major projects that have been approved by the State Council or the investment authorities under the State Council and have the debt-paying subjects that have AAA long-term credit ratings may be exempted from credit enhancement.

It can be seen that except for a few major projects supported by national credit and a few projects whch require high qualifications on the debt-paying subjects, these debt investment plans are required to provide guarantees in one or combinations of three ways of Type A, B, and C credit enhancement. Simply put, Type A credit enhancement is a guarantee provided by the banks, Type B credit enhancement is a guarantee provided by the enterprises, and Type C credit enhancement is a mortgaged or pledged guarantee. Various types of credit enhancements have higher requirements on the subjects or the mortgaged assets that provide the guarantees. As of the end of 2016, the accumulativ debt investment plan included 51 credit enhancement-free projects with an investment amount of RMB 216.9 billion, which accounted for 12.38% of the total number of projects and 20.27% of the total investment amount respectively; 159 Type A credit enhancement projects with an investment amount of RMB 318 billion, which accounted for 38.59% of the total number of projects and 29.71% of the total investment amount respectively ; 174 Type B credit enhancement projects with an investment amount of 406 billion yuan, accounting for 42.23% of the total number of projects and 37.94% of the total investment amount respectively; 28 Type C credit enhancement projects with an investment amount of RMB 129.3 billion, accounting for 6.80% of the total number of projects and 12.08% of the total investment amount respectively. It can be seen that about 80% of the projects adopt Type A and Type B credit enhancement, accounting for about 70% of the investment amount (see Figures 15, 16 and 17).

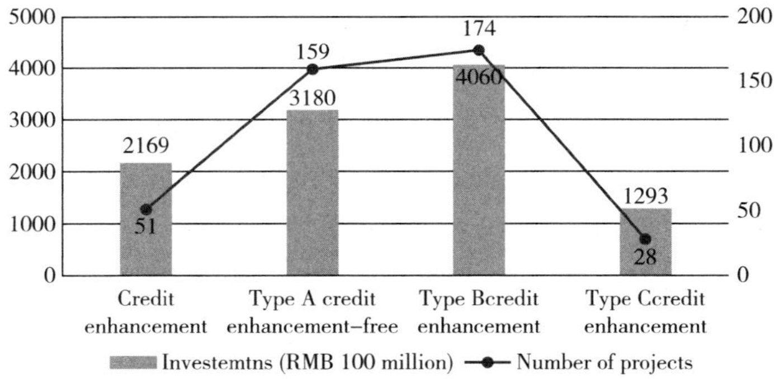

Figure 15: Methods of credit enhancement for infrastructure investment by insurance funds

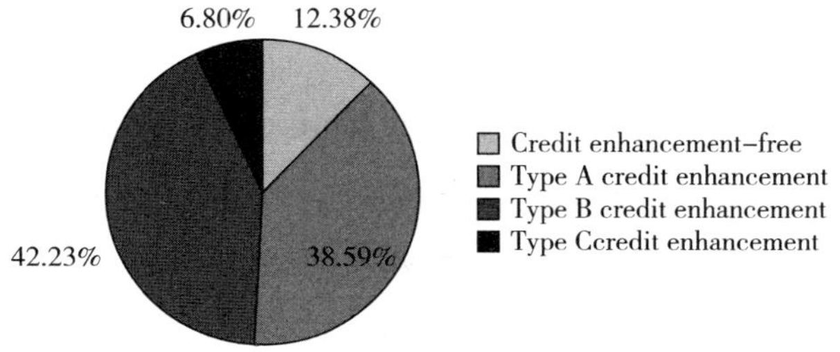

Figure 16: Proportion of different credit enhancement methods in the infrastructure investment projects by insurance funds

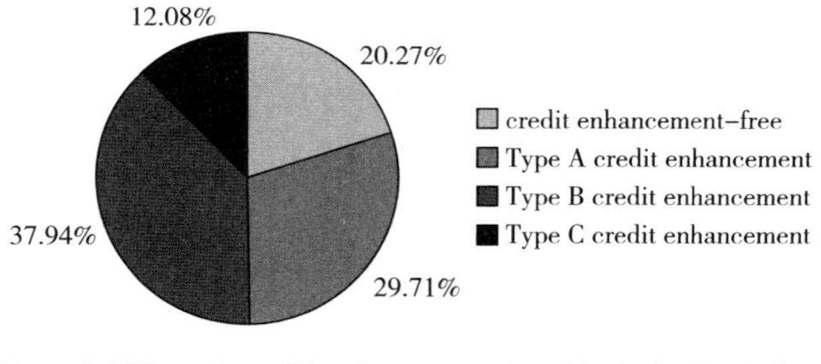

Figure 17: Proportion of different credit enhancement methods in the infrastructure investment amounts by insurance funds

From the perspective of trends, the Type A credit enhancement as a percentage of the total continued to increase, while the proportion of Type B credit enhancement decreased during the period from 2010 to 2014. Since 2015, the situation has reversed. Affected by factors such as intensified interbank competition, it is more and more difficult to expect banks to provide guarantees, which resulted in the subsequent decrease of Type A credit enhancement and the increase of Type B credit enhancements which are based on corporate guarantees. During this period, the proportion of Type A credit enhancement decreased from 51% in 2014 to 23% in 2016 and the proportion

of Type B credit enhancement increased from 28% in 2014 to 55% in 2016, becoming the most important way to enhance credit. In addition, the proportion of Type C credit enhancement is relatively small as it sets higher threshold standards, and it is hard to implement the relevant policies because the insurance assets management institutions are not considered as financial institutions in practice.

In recent years, there has been an upward trend in the credit enhancement-free projects, accounting for 19% of the total in 2016. The *Circular of China Insurance Regulatory Commission on Matters Relating to the Investment in Key Projects with Debt Investment Plans* (《中国保监会关于债权投资计划投资重大工程有关事项的通知》) (No.135 [2017] of the China Insurance Regulatory Commission) issued by the China Insurance Regulatory Commission in 2017 stipulates that debt investment plans that invest in major projects that have been approved by the State Council or the investment authorities under the State Council and have the debt-paying subjects that have AAA long-term credit ratings may be exempted from credit enhancement.. With the implementation of this *Circular*, the number of credit enhancement-free projects have further increased.

5. Financing subjects

By the end of 2016, among the cumulative 417 debt investment projects, there are 17 projects involving governmental agencies as debt-paying subjects (5 projects for the central government, and 12 project for the provincial governments), 251 projects involving government financing platforms as debt-paying subjects (130 projects for provincial platforms, 112 prefecture or municipal level platforms and 9 county-level platforms), 147 projects involving state-owned enterprises and their subsidiaries as debt-paying subjects (85 projects for centrally-administered State-owned enterprises and 62 projects for local state-owned enterprises) and 2 projects involving private enterprises as debt-paying subjects (see Figure 18)[1], accounting for 4.1%, 60.2%, 35.3% and 0.5% of the total respectively. It can be seen that the financing subjects are mainly government financing platforms, state-owned enterprises and their subsidiaries.

---

[1]   Ping'an invested RMB 3 billion in Inner Mongolia Yitai Coal Co., Ltd. in 2013 and Sun Life EverBright Life Insurance Co., Ltd. invested RMB 100 million in Sanpuweite Park Construction Development Co., Ltd. (a subsidiary of China Fortune Land Development CO., LTD.) in 2016

Before 2014, the financing subjects are mainly local financing platforms. After the *Several Opinions of the State Council on Strengthening the Administration of Local Government Debts* (《国务院关于加强地方政府性债务管理的意见》) (No.43 [2014] of the State Council) was promulgated in 2014, the debt investment/financing of local financing platforms were strictly restricted, the proportion of the project with local investment/financing platform as the debt-paing subjects dropped accordingly from 72.5% in 2014 to 58.1% at the end of 2016 (with the number of projects dropping from 81 to 38), and the share of the projects with enterprise-type financing subjects as the debt-paying subjects has increased from 27.5% in 2014 to 41.9% in 2016. Moreover, the ranks of government-type financing subjects (including governmental agencies and government financing platforms) has gradually moved downward: the governmental agencies were all from central government before 2012 and all from provincial governments from 2013; and the government financing platforms were all provincial-level platforms, and the prefecture and municipal level platforms became the main force from 2014 with the county-level financing platforms on the rise.

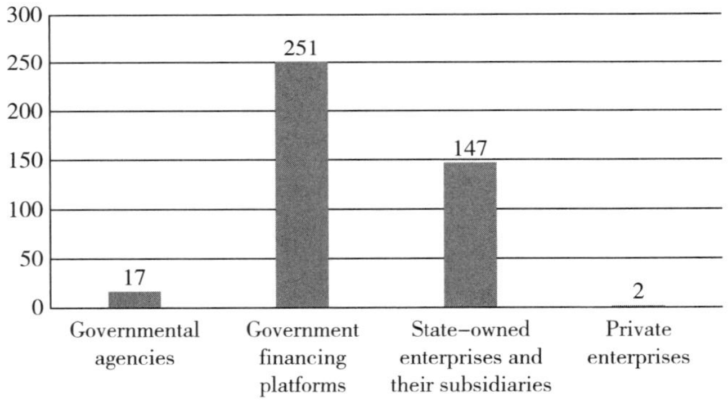

Figure 18: Number of projects with different financing subjects

6. Investment subjects

In recent years, the rapid development of insurance assets management has formed a relatively complete system of insurance asset management subjects. At the end of July 2017, there were more than 200 insurance asset management institutions, including 24 comprehensive insurance asset management institutions, 13 professional asset management institutions, 7 pension management companies, 1 wealth

management company, 11 Hong Kong-based asset management sub-branches,10 insurance private equity funds, 10 insurance-related securities investment fund companies, and 173 internal asset management centers or departments of insurance companies.

By the end of 2016, a total of 26 insurance asset management subjects invested in infrastructure projects. The top 8 subjects invested RMB 1,024.3 billion in a total of 349 projects, with the number of projects and investments accounting for 80% and 80% respectively of the total. Among them, Ping An Asset Management invested RMB 307.8 billion in 92 projects, accounting for 21% of the total number of projects and 24% of the total investment amount respectively. In the equity investments, PICC-related enterprises are the largest subjects and have invested RMB 41.5 billion in a total of 8 projects, accounting for 40% of the total number of projects and 23.7% of the total investment amount respectively (see Figure 19).

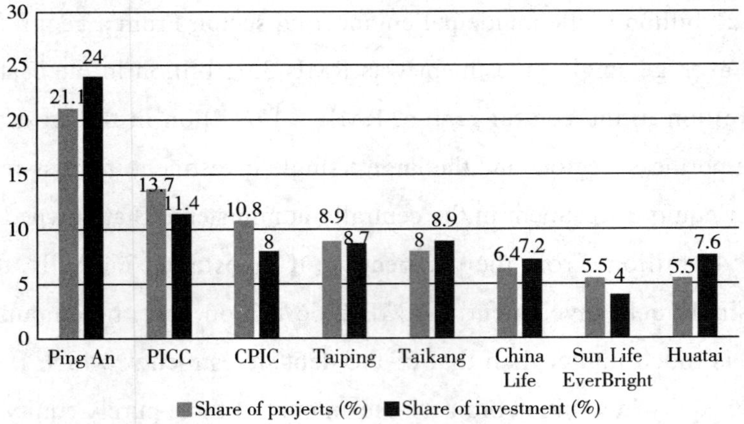

Figure 19: Top 8 investment subjects of infrastructure investment by insurance funds

Note: The data cover investment projects accumulated by the end of 2016. PICC-related enterprises include PICC Asset Management Compnay Limited and PICC Capital Investment Management Company Limited.

7. The size of single investment

By the end of 2016, the average single investments of cumulative investment projects amounted to RMB 2.94 billion. The number of projects increased significantly in 2014, but the amount of investment in 2014 was basically the same as in 2013, and the amount of single investment was reduced accordingly. In 2016, the single investment

was RMB 2.56 billion. Compared with 2015, the number of projects increased by 28, while the single investment decreased by RMB 500 million (see Figure 20).

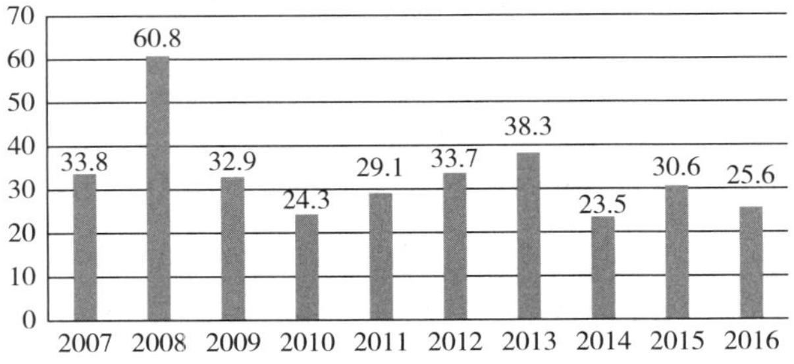

Figure 20: Single investment of infrastructure investment by insurance funds (Unit: RMB 100 million)

The average investment amount of the single investment varies in different investment fields, regions, and by different investment methods. In the cumulative investment projects as of the end of 2016, the average investment amount in the transportation sector was RMB 3.38 billion, RMB 2.48 billion in the energy sector, and RMB 2.27 billion in the municipal engineering sector. From a geographical point of view, the average single investment was RMB 3.01 billion in the eastern region, RMB 2.23 billion in the central region, RMB 2.17 billion in the west, RMB 1.87 billion in the northeast region, and the largest single investment in cross-regional debt investment or equity investment in the centrally-administered State-owned enterprises was RMB 7.41 billion. From the perspective of investment methods, the average amount of single debt investment is RMB 2.66 billion, and the amount of equity investments is much higher than that of the debt investments, which is RMB 8.76 billion. In the equity investment projects, the amount of three purely equity investment amounts to RMB 10.16 billion, and the amount of 17 debt investments in fake equity is RMB 8.52 billion.

8. Investment horizons and returns on investment

By the end of 2016, the average investment horizon of the cumulative 417 debt investment projects was 7.3 years and the average return on investment was 6.48%. Judging from the major investment industries of debt investment plans, the investment horizons and return rates are not much different. Among them, the coal industry has the highest rate of return at 6.68% and the average investment horizon is 7.1 years. The

average rate of return for the railway industry is the lowest at 6.30% and the average investment horizon is 8.3 years (see Figure 21).

In addition, the average investment horizon for the 17 debt investments projects in fake equity is 8.4 years, and the average rate of return is 6.66%. Compared with the debt investment plans, the investment horizon is 1.1 years and the rate of return is 18 bp higher. Except for the investment project of Taikang Asset Management Co., Ltd. in China Petroleum West Pipeline Co., Ltd. which has the horizon of 20 years, other investment projects have the horizons of 5 to 10 years.

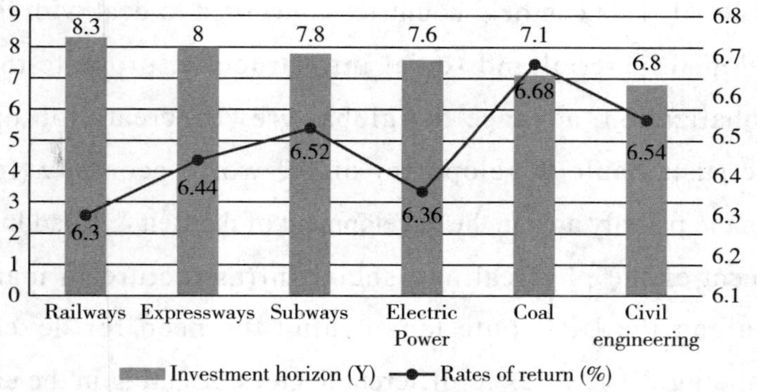

Figure 21: Investment horizons and rates of return major debt investment industries of insurance funds

From 2007 to 2016, the rates of return of infrastructure investments by insurance funds fluctuated slightly between 5.7% to 7.3%, with an average of 6.5% over ten years. Compared with the overall rate of return on the utilization of insurance funds during the same period, the average rate of return level is 0.8% higher and the volatility is much smaller (see Figure 22).

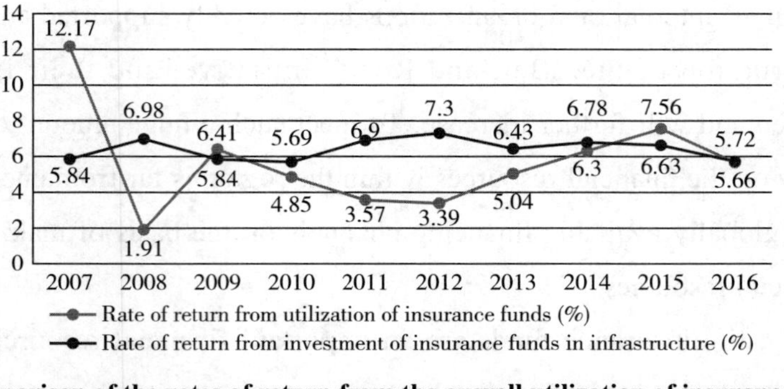

Figure 22: Comparison of the rates of return from the overall utilization of insurance funds and the rates of rate of infrastructure investment by insurance funds

(III) Life insurance funds are expected to become the substantial provider of funds for the infrastructure development for the Belt & Road Initiative

1. The Belt & Road Initiative development brought opportunities to the global allocation of life insurance funds

First of all, there is a huge demand for the financing of the BRI infrastructure development. The BRI development aims to strengthen the connectivity of countries along the Silk Road. This can help countries concerned to deal with the challenges of underdeveloped material and social infrastructure, promote the process of economic globalization, advance the global growth, create job opportunities, and boost the sustainable development of the world economy. Infrastructure connectivity is the priority area in the development of the Belt & Road Initiative (BRI). The development of the physical and social infrastructure in many countries and regions along the BRI route lags behind the need for development and faces the financing difficulties to different degrees, resulting in the urgent need for financial support.

According to the research team of the "One Belt and One Road" facility and Unicom Research of the Development Research Center of the State Council, the demand for infrastructure investment in infrastructure in 64 countries along the "One Belt and One Road" between 2016 and 2020 is at least USD10.6 trillion. In addition, given the open nature of the "One Belt One Road" initiative, more than 140 countries and more than 80 international organizations have actively supported and participated in the construction of the "Belt and Road" initiative, and their infrastructure investment demand will further increase. To meet such a huge amount of investment, relying solely on the financial resources within the region is far from enough. We must integrate the globally available financing channels on the basis of making full use of internal financial resources.

Secondly, life insurance funds are an important financial resource for the BRI infrastructure development. For the BRI infrastructure developmn, the available funds mainly include the financial resources within the countries along the route, the

interflow of financial resources between countries along the route, and international financial resources. Life insurance funds are an important financial resource for the BRI infrastructure development. Firstly, the national life insurance funds of the countries along the BRI route are an important part of the internal financial resources of each country and are an important source of funding for the development of domestic infrastructure. Secondly, the national life insurance funds of the countries along the BRI route are important participants in the interflow of financial resources among countries and provide a good financial basis for the connectivity and integration of financial resources and the realization of facilities connectivity throughout the region. Finally, large life insurance companies, especially multinational life insurance companies, are important providers of international financial resources. These institutional investors can mainly become financial investors of the BRI infrastructure projects and seek to achieve a reasonable return on capital through early participation in the projects.

Finally, the BRI development offers opportunities for the global deployment of life insurance funds. Diversified and international insurance assets allocation is an important direction for the development and utilization of life insurance funds. The BRI development provides a new path for overseas investments of insurance funds in various countries. Life insurance companies can take advantage of the BRI development to expand overseas investment business of insurance funds, and take advantage of the investment opportunities brought by a large amount of infrastructure financing to deploy investment portfolio in a wider space and with more investment opportunities, diversify investment risks, and obtain more stable investment returns.

2. Status quo of China's insurance funds participating in BRI development

Under the policy guidance and support, China's life insurance funds (mainly life insurance funds) have been actively involved in large-scale BRI infrastructure projects covering long periods of time. On the one hand, these funds are utilized to support the construction of key projects in the fields of roads, ports, oil and gas pipelines, adn telecommunications, etc., of the key regions within the territory of China and

the construction of parks in the provinces along the BRI route, including such key infrastructure projects as the mainline of Lianyungang-Horgos Expressway, Nuozhadu Hydropower Station, Guiyang Urban Rail Transit and Xi'an Free Trade Zone, etc. On the other hand, these funds are utilized to actively and safely participate in the overseas infrastructure development including communication and energy pipelines, etc., and explore the possibility of investing in oil and gas industrial park and Sino-foreign industrial cooperation bases located abroad. The insurance funds have actively participated in and taken the initiative to play an its role in such key projects as the energy cooperation in China-Mongolia-Russia Economic Corridor and China–Pakistan Economic Corridor, and China-Kazakstan Capacity and Investment Cooperation, etc.

By the end of 2017, the size of funds utilized to support the investment in BRI development amounted to RMB 856.826 billion (the majority of which were life insurance funds). In addition, the RMB 300 billion-worth China Insurance Investment Fund has been set up with the principal investment in national strategic projects, including the BRI. China Insurance Investment Fund not only helps to innovate the ways to use insurance funds, and improve the operational efficiency of funds, but also better promotes insurance funds to provide orderly and centralized services to the BRI development, and invest in key infrastructure projects.

(IV) Life insurance funds continuously expand the support to new fields of the real economy

The recent years has witnessed the life insurance funds continuously expand the support to emerging fields of the real economy, including the involvement in the disposal of non-performing assets. As an important provider of long-term funds, the insurers may assume a prudential role in the market-based disposal of non-performing assets under the precondition of effective control of risks, which can alleviate the pressure from the allocation of long-term insurance funds and promote the life insurance funds to better serve the real economy.

1. Insurance institutions have the advantages of horizon match in participating in the disposal of non-performing assets

The insurance institutions (especially the life insurance companies) have long horizons for liabilities, which makes the long horizons of insurance funds perfectly matching the longer period of the non-performing assets disposal business. It has the advantage of matching cross-cycle disposal of non-performing assets.

The disposal of non-performing assets has a cross-cycle property, that is, an increase in the supply of non-performing assets during the economic downturn is also the ramp-up period for non-performing assets investments, and as the economy recovers and the valuation of non-performing assets rises, investors can obtain a cross-cycle premium. The funds with the long-term attribute formed by long-term liabilities of insurance companies, especially life insurers, match the long-term business cycle of non-performing assets. Therefore, the long-term advantages of life insurance funds allow them to have considerable potential advantages in the disposal of non-performing assets, and can provide long-term and stable financial guarantees for the cross-cycle disposal of non-performing assets. Life insurance funds are mainly long-term investments and can become one of the important institutional investors in the disposal of non-performing assets, by upholding the investment philosophy of long-term investment, value investment, and sound investment, they have become an important fund provider in the disposal of non-performing assets. At the same time, the cross-cycle feature of the disposal of non-performing assets will also help relieve the pressures on the allocation of long-term insurance funds and help insurance funds to better serve the real economy.

2. The paths for insurance institutions to participate in the disposal of non-performing assets

In recent years, under the guidance of policies, insurance institutions have mainly participated in the disposal of non-performing assets through indirect and direct routes (see Table 2) and are gradually becoming an important subject in the market of non-performing assets disposal.

Table 2: The Paths and Ways for Insurance Institutions to Participate in Disposal of Non-Performing Assets

Participation path	Spcific ways of participation
Indirect	Insurance institutions can invest in non-performing assets securitization products issued by financial institutions such as investment assets management institutions and trust companies
	Insurance institutions can invest in non-performing assets private equity funds in the form of limited partnerships
	Insurance institutions can set up or buy shares in local assets management companies
Direct	Insurance institutions issue debt investment plan packages
	Insurance institutions can set up a debt-to-equity swap implementation institution
	Insurance institutions can set up special debt-to-equity swap funds
	Insurance institutions can directly acquire non-performing assets

Source: Cao, Deyun. Insurance Institutions may Invest in the Field of Non-Performing Assets Disposal (《保险机构可布局不良资产处置领域》), speech at China Financial Forum 2017, June 8, 2017

The insurance funds participate in the disposal of non-performing assets in indirect ways, including three methods:

Firstly, insurance institutions can invest in non-performing asset securitization products issued by financial institutions such as investment assets management institutions and trust companies. Insurance institutions can work with professional asset management institutions to invest in financial products that are based on non-performing assets. The stable returns, adequate mortgaged or pledged assets, and good asset quality of investment in non-performing asset securitization products are conducive to obtaining considerable returns while reducing investment risks. At present, there are certain policy obstacles for insurance institutions to participate in the securitization of non-performing assets as investors. This method has not yet started.

Secondly, insurance institutions can invest in non-performing assets private equity funds in the form of limited partnerships. The disposal of non-performing assets has higher requirements on the professionalism of the investment management teams. The insurance institutions can cooperate with senior asset managers and invest in non-performing asset private equity funds as a limited partner. For example, China Life Insurance (Group)Company invested in Guangzhou Xinhui Industrial Investment Fund Partnership and participated in the acquisition of non-performing assets packages

of China Merchants Bank as a limited partner. Insurance institutions investing in non-performing assets private equity funds can, on the one hand, take advantage of the professional investment managers' comprehensive capabilities in information acquisition, valuation pricing, industry research, and legal application etc. to enable insurance assets to obtain investment income from non-performing assets through external forces; and on the other hand, look for specific investment opportunities in the upstream and downstream industry chains of insurance institutions targeted at industrial chain integration, better integrate resources, and achieve synergies.

Thirdly, insurance institutions can set up or buy shares in local assets management companies. As of the end of 2017, domestic non-performing assets management institutions included four major state-owned asset management companies, local asset management companies, and private non-licensed asset management companies. The number of license–holding institutions exceeded 60, and there were more than 200 non-licensed institutions. In particular, after the CBRC issued a notice in October 2016 to allow the establishment of additional asset management companies at the local levels, the license holding of non-performing assets disposal institutions has received extensive attention. At present, local asset management companies have obtained the most basic asset disposal functions of the four state-owned asset management companies, and they can play an active role and have the comparative advantages of accessing local resources. The establishment or purchasing the shares of local asset management companies by insurance funds is an important way for them to participate in the non-performing assets disposal market. In recent years, Happy Life and China Ping An have successively participated in the investment in several local asset management companies. Insurance institutions cooperating with local governments in setting up or purchasing shares in local asset management companies can access resources of non-performing assets industry more easily, and take advantage of the local asset management companies' professional teams to participate in the disposal of non-performing debts.

The ways for insurance institutions to directly participate in the disposal of non-performing assets include:

Firstly, the insurance asset management institutions can explore asset-backed

plans. Insurance asset management institutions can explore asset-backed plans based on non-performing loans, non-performing assets of non-bank financial institutions, and bad debts of corporate accounts receivable as their underlying assets, and seize the direct opportunities for the disposal of non-performing assets through active asset-backed plans.

Secondly, insurance institutions can explore debt-to-equity swap-related business. The insurance asset management institutions can bring into full play their comparative advantages and explore the entry into the debt-to-equity swap market.

Thirdly, insurance institutions can directly purchase non-performing assets packages for disposal. The direct purchase of non-performing asset packages by insurance institutions for disposal requires an internal professional investment management team and the ability to handle the entire process of disposal of non-performing assets. In comparison, this method is more difficult and sets higher requirements on the company.

The direct participation of insurance funds in the disposal of non-performing assets is mainly reflected in the participation of insurance institutions in debt-to-equity swaps. At present, insurance institutions are generally very cautious about debt-to-equity swaps, mainly because China Life Asset Management Company Limited has implemented five debt-to-equity swap projects. As of the end of 2017, China Life Asset Management Company Limited has implemented five single equity-to-equity swap projects covering Sichuan to East China Gas Transmission Company, Shaanxi Coal Industry Company Limited, China Shipbuilding Industry Company Limited, China Huaneng Group and China Yellow River Foundation, with a total scale of RMB 50 billion.

V. Life insurance funds have achieved positive results in supporting the real economy

The life insurance funds in China have supported the development of the real economy by such means as investing in key national projects, supporting the local economic development and assisting the development of projects for people's

wellbeing, and have achieved positive results by: actively serving the national supply-side structural reform, actively supporting the Belt & Road initiative, actively supporting the national regional development strategy, actively participating in the public-private partnership (PPP) projects and major engineering projects and supporting the integrated military and civilian development and the transformation and upgrading of the manufacturing industry.

(I) actively serving the national supply-side structural reform

In recent years, the insurance regulatory authority has actively guided insurance funds to serve the supply-side structural reforms; surrounding the supply-side structural reforms and the five major tasks of "reducing over-capacity, de-stocking, de-leveraging, reducing cost and addressing weak links", bring into full play the role of financing and guidance of insurance funds; support the insurance asset management institutions to initiate the establishment of funds for reducing over-capacity, M&A and restructuring, promote the accelerated transformation and development of iron and steel, coal, and other industries, become profitable and realize upgrading; support insurance funds to initiate the establishment of debt-to-equity swap institutions and start market-oriented debt-to-equity swaps; support insurance asset management institutions to carry out special situations investment businesses such as disposal of non-performing assets and initiate the establishment of special debt-to-equity swap funds etc. As of the end of August 2017, a total of 14 perpetual bonds had been registered with the bond size of RMB 80.8 billion. At present, the insurance funds have participated in the RMB10 billion-worth debt-to-equity swap project of Shaanxi Coal and Chemical Industry Group Co., Ltd. and the RMB 2 billion-worth debt-to-equity swap project of China Shipbuilding Industry Corporation.

(II) actively supporting the Belt & Road initiative

In recent years, under the guidance of the regulatory authority, insurance institutions have taken advantage of the long-term stability of insurance funds and actively participated in long-term, large-scale BRI infrastructure projects. Insurance funds are an important force in supporting the development of the real economy.

They have long-term and stable characteristics, and are in great harmony with the characteristics of the BRI infrastructure development projects with large capital requirements, long construction periods, and stable returns. Life insurance funds can directly or indirectly invest in major BRI investment projects and promote common development and common prosperity through debt, equity, debt+equity, equity investment plans, asset-backed plans and private equity funds, etc. as well as through investments in financial products launched by AIIB, and other financial institutions. On the one hand, these funds are utilized to support the construction of key projects in the fields of roads, ports, oil and gas pipelines, and telecommunications, etc., of the key regions within the territory of China and the construction of parks in the provinces along the BRI route, including such key infrastructure projects as the mainline of Lianyungang-Horgos Expressway, Nuozhadu Hydropower Station, Guiyang Urban Rail Transit and Xi'an Free Trade Zone, etc. On the other hand, these funds are utilized to actively and safely participate in the overseas infrastructure development including communication and energy pipelines, etc., and explore the possibility of investing in oil and gas industrial park and Sino-foreign industrial cooperation bases located abroad. In order to support the BRI development, insurance regulatory authority urged insurance institutions to continuously increase overseas investment capabilities and support insurance funds to participate in the development of major infrastructure and important resources, key industry cooperation, and financial cooperation in countries and regions along the BRI route; support insurance funds to provide investment and financing support for the economic and trade cooperation and bilateral and multilateral connectivity within the BRI framework, and provide long-term financial support for large-scale investment projects in the form of equity, debt, equity+debt, and funds, etc.; and encourage Chinese insurance institutions to "go global" and deploy their presence in countries or regions along the BRI route and provide insurance protection services for the BRI development.

(III) actively supporting the national regional development strategy

In recent years, the regulatory authority has encouraged insurance funds to serve the coordinated development of Beijing, Tianjin and Hebei, the development of the

Yangtze River Economic Belt and the development of the west, the rejuvenation of the northeast, the rise of central China, and the leading development of the eastern region; support insurance funds to connect with key projects in the development of national free trade zones and development of city clusters such as Guangdong-Hong Kong-Macao Greater Bay Area; actively guide and support insurance funds to participate in the development of Xiong'an New District, explore new investment and financing mechanisms, and provide long-term financial support for major projects such as transportation infrastructure, water conservancy, ecology, energy, and public services in the New District. As of the end of 2017, the scale of strategic investment for supporting the Yangtze River Economic Belt and the coordinated development of Beijing, Tianjin and Hebei, reached RMB 365.248 billion and RMB 156.799 billion respectively; and the scale of investment in green industries including clean energy, resource conservation and pollution prevention and control reached RMB 667.635 billion.

(IV) actively participating in the public-private partnership (PPP) projects and major engineering projects

In recent years, insurance regulatory authority has promoted the participation of insurance funds in PPP projects and major project construction; supported qualified insurance asset management companies and other professional management institutions, as the trustee, to initiate the establishment of infrastructure investment plans, and raises insurance funds to invest in eligible PPP projects; under the premise of controllable risks, adjust regulatory requirements on qualifications and credit enhancements, etc. for PPP project companies to provide financing, and promote innovative models of PPP project financing; encourage the insurance funds to invest in various infrastructure projects and people's livelihood projects of great significance to the national economy and people's livelihood, gradually improve the supervision and control standards for investment plans, relax the requirements for credit enhancements and the scope of the guarantee subjects, expand the number of credit enhancement-free financing subjects, innovate the trading structure, and accurately support the key projects that have an important role to play with the macroeconomic environment and the regional economy.

In recent years, the insurance regulatory authority successively printed and distributed a series of ancillary documents, such as the *Circular on Matters Relating to the Investment in Public-Private-Partnership Projects with Insurance Funds* (《关于保险资金投资政府和社会资本合作项目有关事项的通知》) and the *Circular of China Insurance Regulatory Commission on Matters Relating to the Investment in Key Projects with Debt Investment Plans* (《关于债权计划投资重大工程有关事项的通知》), and defined specific support policies in terms of technical details, such as optimizing regulatory requirements in such areas as investment channels, investment methods, subject qualifications and credit enhancements etc. As of the end of 2017, a total of 843 debt investment plans and equity investment plans have been initiated, with a total record (registration) scale of RMB 2,075.414 billion.

(V) supporting the integrated military and civilian development and the transformation and upgrading of the manufacturing industry

In recent years, the insurance regulatory authority has encouraged insurance funds to serve the integration of military and civilian development, actively explored the participation of insurance funds in the military industrial integration model, and supported insurance institutions and military enterprises in jointly launching an insurance-military-civilia integration development fund. For instance, PICC Asset Management - China Aerospace Military and Civil Integration Development Fund Equity Investment Plan (Phase I) has a scale of RMB 5 billion. At the same time, the insurance asset management institutions are encouraged to initiate the establishment of financial products such as debt investment plans, equity investment plans, and equity investment funds that support the innovation and development, mergers and acquisitions, and transformation and upgrading of manufacturing industries, so as to better serve the transformation and upgrading of the manufacturing industry. For example, Huatai-COMAC debt investment scheme, with the scale of RMB 15 billion, was established to support China's large passenger plane manufacturing project.

Chapter III: Problems, risks and policy barriers for life insurance funds to support the real economy in China

The challenges faced by life insurance funds in supporting the real economy include: Insufficient development of life insurance and inadequate transformation of development mode are not conducive to life insurance funds in supporting the real economy; irregularities weaken the effects of the support to the development of the real economy by life insurance funds; and the comparatively weak support by life insurance funds to private enterprises is not favorable to the transformation of the pattern of economic development. The risks existing in the support of life insurance funds to the real economy include asset-liability mismatches risks, credit risks, cross-market and cross-sector risks, and risks of increasing the implicit debts of local governments, etc. In addition, life insurance funds face new risks in participating in BRI development and participating in the emerging areas such as the disposal of non-performing assets. There are still some policy obstacles in the support of the life insurance funds to the real economy, including: the relevant management rules and regulations concerning infrastructure-based debt investment plans need to be improved; the scope for the insurance funds to invest in equity shall be further expanded; the policies on real estate mortgage registration needs to be improved; the policy environment on investing in the pension industry needs to be improved; tehrfe are constraints for life insurance funds to participate in PPP projects; the policy environment for life insurance funds to participate in disposal of non-performing assets need to be improved; and the liquidity hedging mechanism for alternative investments needs to be improved,

I. Challenges faced by life insurance funds in the support to the development of the real economy

(I) The underdevelopment of the life insurance industry is not conducive to life insurance funds in supporting the real economy

China's life insurance industry is still underdeveloped. By the end of 2017, the total assets of the insurance industry were RMB 16.75 trillion (including the total assets of life insurance companies of RMB 1.321 trillion, accounting for approximately 79% of the total assets of the insurance industry) (see Figure 1). Insurance assets accounted for approximately 6.6% of the assets of banking financial institutions (see Figure 2), which was a relatively low proportion in the financial assets, and was far lower than the proportion of insurance assets in the banking industry in 29 economies in 2016 (the average proportion stood at 21.3%) (see Figure 3). This means that the proportion of the insurance industry, especially the life insurance industry, in financial assets needs to be further improved.

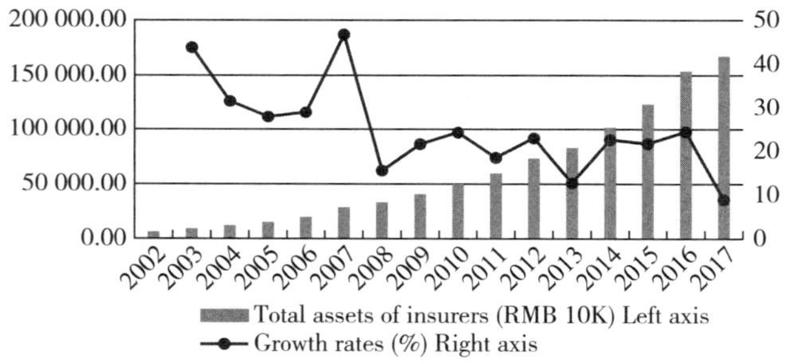

Figuer 1: The total assets of insurance companies in China and their growth trend

Source: Wind, CIRC

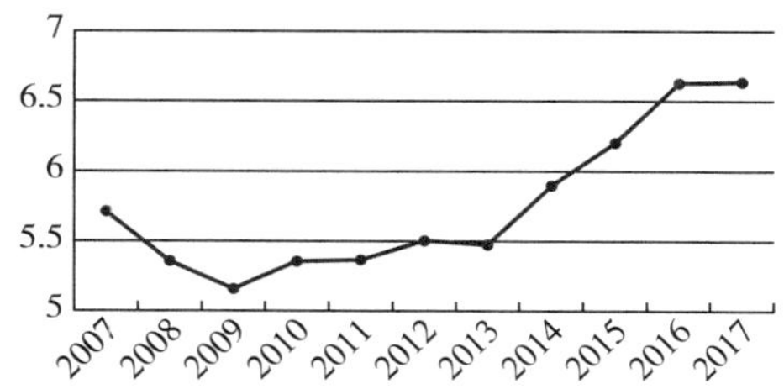

Figure 2: Insurance assets as a percentage of the assets of banking financial institutions in China in recent years   Unit: %

资料来源：Wind资讯、中国保监会、中国银监会。

Source: Wind, CIRC, CBRC

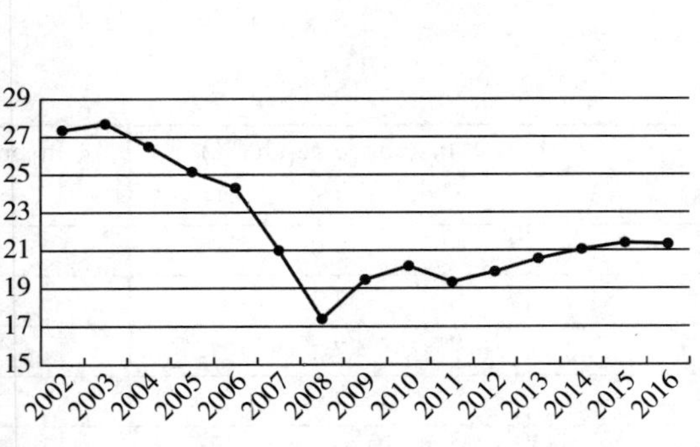

Figure 3: Insurance assets as a percentage of the assets of banking financial institutions in 29 economies in recent years   Unit: %

Note: 29 economies include Argentina, Australia, Belgium, Brazil, Canada, Cayman Islands, Chile, China, France, Germany, Hong Kong China, India, Indonesia, Ireland, Italy, Japan, South Korea, Luxembourg, Mexico, the Netherlands, Russia, Saudi Arabia, Singapore, South Africa, Spain, Switzerland, Turkey, the United Kingdom and the United States.

Source: National balance sheets and other data for relevant countries; FSB calculations.

At the same time, in 2017, China's insurance depth was 4.42%, and the insurance density was RMB 2,646 (see Figure 4). Compared with international levels, although the development level of China's insurance industry is higher than that of the emerging markets, it is still relatively low (see Table 1). The insurance depth and insurance density are not only lower than the global average, but also lower than the average level of major advanced economies.

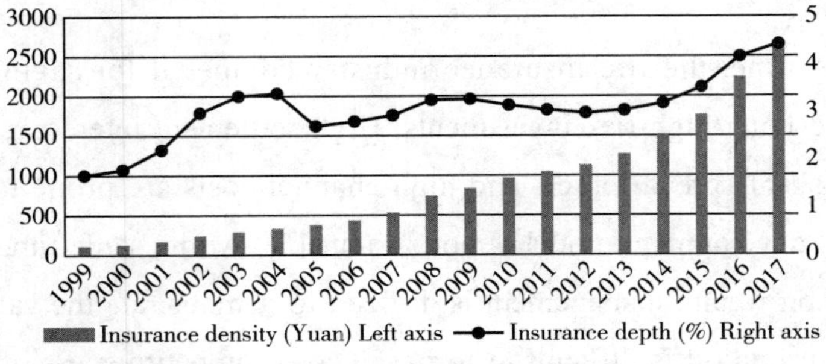

Insurance density (Yuan) Left axis   —●— Insurance depth (%) Right axis

Figure 4: Growth trend of China's insurance density and insurance depth (1999-2017)

Source: Wind, CIRC

Table 1: International comparison of insurance industry development level

	Insurance depth (%)	Insurance density (USD)
Global	6.3	638
Developed markets	8	3505
Emerging Markets	3.2	149
Emerging Markets (excl. China)	2.6	97

		Continuation
	Insurance depth (%)	Insurance density (USD)
OECD	7.5	2757
G7	7.9	3665
Eurozone	7.3	2528
EU	7.4	2383
EU-15	7.9	2911
NAFTA	7.1	3049
ASEAN	3.4	136
China (2017 data)	4.42	407

Note: Except for China, all available data for the economicies are from 2016.

Source: Swiss Re. World insurance in 2016: the China growth engine steams ahead. Sigma No.3,2017

Life insurance funds are the foundation for the life insurance industry to support the real economy development. The underdeveloped life insurance industry goes against the accumulation of funds with long maturities and high stability, and restricts the scope and depth of life insurance funds in supporting the real economy.

(II) The inadequate transformation of the development mode of life insurance industry goes against the support of life insurance funds to the real economy

For a long time, the life insurance industry competed for savings with high liability costs, driving high-risk investments. High settlement interest rates are prone to triggering risk of spread losses, and high channel costs are prone to the risks of fee losses. This development model is not sustainable. At the same time, the product structure based on wealth management is difficult to demonstrate the value of the life insurance industry and it is difficult to form the core competitiveness of the industry. As the life insurance investment activities are mainly based on debt activities, the inadequate transformation of the development mode of life insurance industry will result in irrational debt structure and be detrimental to life insurance funds' support to the real economy.

Since 2017, with the continued strengthening of supervision, products with medium and short duration represented by universal insurance products have been severely restricted. Affected by this, major life insurance companies adjusted the

premium structure mainly by increasing the proportion of original premium income of protection products, compressing such insurance types as universal insurance and investment-linked insurance, extending the duration of underwriting side, increasing the proportion of regular premium payment and transforming the business mode of lump-sum payment of premium to regular payment of premium. The specific demonstrations are as follows: Firstly, compared with the universal insurance and investment-linked insurance business, the growth of original insurance premium income of general life insurance business and participating life insurance business is faster. In 2017, the original premium income of general life insurance business of life insurance companies was RMB 1,293.648 billion, which was a year-on-year increase of 23.77%, accounting for 49.68% of all business income of life insurance companies, which had a year-on-year increase of 1.50 percentage points; and the original premium income of the participating life insurance business was RMB 840.320 billion, which was a year-on-year increase of 22.14%, accounting for 32.27% of all business income of life insurance companies, which had a year-on-year increase of 0.56 percentage point.

Secondly, the current-year new payment for the policyholders' investment funds and independent accounts dropped sharply this year. In 2017, the amount of current-year new payment for the policyholders' investment funds and independent accounts not included in the insurance contract calculation reached RMB 636.278 billion, a year-on-year decrease of 50.29%.

Thirdly, the new business premiums and regular premiums on new business increased significantly. In 2017, the original premium income on new business from life insurance business of life insurance companies was RMB 1,535.512 billion, a year-on-year increase of 10.66%, accounting for 58.97% of all business income of life insurance companies. Among them, the original regular premium income on new business[1] was RMB 577.217 billion, a year-on-year increase of 35.71%, accounting for 37.59% of original premium income on new business.

Fourthly, the structure of regular premiums on new business has been continuously optimized. In the original regular premium income on new business[2], the

---

① The original regular premium income on new business indicated here is financial data.
② The original premium income for different payment temrs indicated here are business data.

regular premium of less than three-year was RMB 15.413 billion, accounting for 2.60%, indicating a year-on-year increase of 1.70 percentage points; the regular premium of three- to five-year was RMB 177.695 billion, accounting for 29.93%, down by 2.22 percentage points year on year; the regular premium of five- to ten-year was RMB 91.890 billion, accounting for 15.48%, up by 0.49 percentage point year on year; and the regular premium of ten-year or longer was RMB 308.704 billion yuan, accounting for 52.00%, up by 0.03 percentage point year on year.

Finally, the channel structure has been further optimized. The business transformation has also brought about a change in the channel structure. The outstanding demonstration lies in the rapid growth of the personal agency business and the declining growth of the banking/postal agency business. In 2017, original premium income from the personal insurance agency business was RMB 1306.564 billion, a year-on-year increase of 30.43%, accounting for 50.18% of the total business income of life insurance companies, indicating a year-on-year increase of 4.00 percentage points; and the original premium income of the banking/postal agency business of insurance companies was RMB 1,058.402 billion, a year-on-year growth of 10.53%, accounting for 40.65% of the total business income of life insurance companies, which was a year-on-year decrease of 3.50 percentage points (see Table 2).

Table 2: Business developments of life insurance companies by channels in 2017
Unit: RMB 100 million, %

Business channels	Original premium income	YoY growth	Percentage	YoY growth of percentage (percentage points)
Banking/postal agency	10584.02	10.53	40.65	-3.50
Personal agency	13065.64	30.43	50.18	4.00
Direct sale by insurers	1751.89	8.43	6.73	-0.72
professional sale	179.65	48.64	0.69	0.13
Other sideline agency	274.11	15.09	1.05	-0.05
Insurance brokerage	184.24	47.22	0.71	0.13
Total	26039.55	20.04	100.00	—

Source: CIRC

Although the above achievements have been made in the transformation of the life insurance industry, the overall transformation has not been adequate. It is manifested in the following aspects:

Firstly, the percentage of single premiums is still relatively high. Although single premiums can increase the size of the premium income quickly in the short term, the sustainability of the premiums will be poor, and the insurance companies will continue to face bottlenecks after the premium income reaches a certain scale. In addition, some insurance companies receive premiums mainly through banking-insurance cooperation channel, which are greatly affected by the financial environment and policies, result in large fluctuations in the delivery of single premiums, and remain detrimental to the formation of stable life insurance funds.

Secondly, the product mix is still unbalanced. The development of long-term and protection products is still insufficient. In particular, life insurance which offers financial security against death risks, health insurance which offers financial security against illness and disability risks, and endowment and annuities insurance which offer financial security against longevity risks are all waiting to be developed.

Thirdly, the channel value needs to be improved. As for the banking-insurance cooperation channel, the cooperation level between banks and insurance companies is shallow, and it is difficult to transfer to the mode of regular premium and protection-focused insurance services. For the personal insurance agency channel, although there is a substantial increase in the number of agents, the per capita production capacity and sales efficiency need to be improved, and the sales practices need to be regulated.

The transformation of life insurance development methods is not in place, which is not conducive to the accumulation of long-term and stable life insurance funds and is not conducive to supporting the development of the real economy.

(III) irregularities weaken the effects of the support to the development of the real economy by life insurance funds.

Firstly, the problems of multi-layer nesting of products and regulatory arbitrage have weakened their support to the real economy. In recent years, with the continued innovations in the financial sector, financial products have become increasingly complex, and such phenomena as high leverage, multiple nesting, long investment chains, opaque transactions, and regulatory arbitrage have become serious and spread to the field of insurance funds application. Some insurance funds are engaged in illegal

multi-layer nesting and channel operations through such products as investment trusts and private equity funds, which blurred the true flows of funds and masked the true status of risks. For example, some insurance institutions invest funds in financial products such as trust plans and bank wealth management and trust companies and banks, etc. invest these funds in other financial products, which increases the leverage, reduces transparency and increases risks. Even private equity investment funds, equity investment plans and other insurance assets management products issued by some institutions by themselves suffer from multiple-layer nesting in varying degrees, which have large hidden risks, go against regulatory directions of deleveraging, de-nesting, and crowding out the foams, and weakens the effectiveness of life insurance funds in supporting the real economy.

The *Guiding Opinions of the People's Bank of China, the China Banking and Insurance Regulatory Commission, the China Securities Regulatory Commission, and the State Administration of Foreign Exchange on Regulating the Asset Management Business of Financial Institutions* (《关于规范金融机构资产管理业务的指导意见》) clearly proposes the requirements to abstain from guaranteed repayments, regulate the fund pool and eliminate multi-layered nesting, and explicitly prohibit maturity mismatches on non-standard assets, which is conducive to standardizing non-standard asset investment represented by various types of insurance asset management products, but the new regulations on asset management also bring certain challenges to non-standard assets and alternative investments. In the short term, the scale of insurance asset management products may shrink, and various types of non-standard assets will shrink significantly after the channel business and nesting are restricted. The growth rate of investment in non-standard assets by insurance funds may decline, and thus the negative impact on the return on investment may be greater.

Secondly, irrational acquisitions and radical operations are not conducive to life insurance in supporting the real economy. In recent years, due to such reasons as the alienation in the development of universal life insurance, the to-be-improved rules of the capital market and certain regulatory gaps resulting from cross-sector and coordinated financial development, such problems as irrational acquisitions, unfriendly investment with persons acting in concert, irrational cross-border or cross-sector large-

scale investment and M&As, radical operations and radical investments, etc., have occurred to life insurance funds in their support to the real economy, which have to a certain degree weakened their support to the real economy.

(IV) The structural problems of life insurance investments are not favorable to the transformation of the pattern of economic development.

By the end of 2017, the number of private enterprises in China had reached 27.263 million, the number of individual businesses reached 65.793 million, and the total registered capital had exceeded RMB 165 trillion. The contribution of the private economy to the national fiscal revenues exceeded more than 50%; the GDP, investment in fixed assets and outward direct investment of the private economy as percentage of the total all exceeded 60%; technological innovations and new products accounted for more than 70% of the total; and the private economy employed over 80% of the urban employees and contributed to over 90%of the newly added employment opportunities. Therefore, private enterprises are the main body in transforming the mode of economic development. However, the alternative investments by life insurance funds mainly flow to local governments and related state-owned enterprises and offers comparatively weak support to private enterprises, which is obviously unfavorable to supporting the financing of private enterprises, and not conducive to the transformation of China's economic development mode. In addition, life insurance funds are mainly invested debt investment plans with much less investments in equity investment plans. This structural problem is also not conducive to transforming the mode of economic development.

II. Major existing risks in the support to the development of the real economy by life insurance funds

(I) Asset-liability mismatch risks

The first risk is that the high liability-side costs have forced the investment-side

to increase the appetite for risk. In recent years, the liability-side costs of China's life insurance have been continuously rising. Although the liability-side financing costs has declined since 2017, it still remains at above 5%, which is still relatively high compared to the available fund supply channels for high-quality and safe assets, and the shortage of assets still exists. Under the influence of high liability-side costs of insurance policies and absence of high quality asset-side assets, the insurance companies increased investments with high returns, low liquidity and long durations, and the market risks and credit risks of the portfolios also increased.

The second risk is the mismatch of maturities. On the one hand, there are the phenomena of long-maturity funds matched to short-term assets. Due to the lack of long-term investment products on China's assets market, it is hard to allocate the long-term assets, and the long-maturity life insurance funds have to be passively matched to short-term assets, which not only reduced the returns on investment, but also increased the short-term volatility. On the other hand, there are also phenomena of short-maturity funds matched to long-term assets. For some time in the past, some small and medium-sized life insurance companies had large-scale short-term and medium-term insurance financial products, a single business structure, and relatively high liability costs. In order to obtain high returns, these short-maturity funds are invested in high-yield, low-liquidity and long-maturity immovable assets, infrastructure, trusts and other alternative assets, resulting in the highlighted phenomena of short-maturity funds matched to long-term assets.

The third risk is the liquidity risk. The structural adjustments of the liability-side business or repayment upon maturity might trigger such risks as liquidity shortage and insufficient solvency. Since 2016, the CIRC has stepped up efforts to supervise short and medium duration products. This is conducive to restraining the short-term behaviors of some market players and highlighting the protection function of insurance, but it also makes explicit some of the formerly hidden cash flow risks of life insurance companies. On the one hand, short and medium duration products are faced with the dual pressures of surrender and maturity payment. In 2017, life insurance companies suffered the surrender of RMB 611.793 billion, a year-on-year increase of 37.25%. The surrender rate was 6.52%, an increase of 0.92 percentage point from the same

period of last year. At the same time, the life insurance business paid RMB 457.489 billion upon maturity of products. The increase in surrender and maturity payments resulted in large cash outflows. On the other hand, business revenues have contracted rapidly, which makes it difficult to sustain the pattern of relying on new business cash inflows to make up for shortfalls, causing some companies to face more severe cash flow risks and pressures. In 2017, the net cash flows generated from operating activities in the insurance industry reached RMB 633.075 billion, a year-on-year decrease of 65.12%. Under this situation, the increase in the proportion of alternative investments further increases liquidity risk. While as the non-standard assets, the alternative investments have low liquidity, inactive trading and long cash conversion cycles, and have increased the risks of inadequate cash flow faced by some companies.

(II) Credit risks

The continuous exposure of credit risks has exposed the industry to greater risks. In the past two years, there have been frequent occurrences of defaults in the bond market. Against the backdrop of the transformation of the pattern of economic development, deleveraging, removal of stipulation on implicitly guaranteed repayment, the credit risks faced by the deployment of insurance funds have increased. In recent years, due to such impact as the downturn trend in the macro economy and the volatility of the bond market, there have been frequent cases of bond defaults, and the credit risks accumulated in certain industries have begun to appear. In 2016, a total of 79 bonds of 35 companies suffered payment crises, involving the funds of RMB 39.89 billion, which was a substantial increase from the RMB 11.71 billion in 2015. In 2017, a total of 40 bonds defaulted, involving a total of 17 issuers and the total amount of RMB 18.82 billion, which was about half size of the 2016 bond defaults. Judging from the number of defaulting parties, the number of bonds and the defaulted amount, the exposure frequency of the credit risks of the 2017 bond market was lower than that of 2016. In the increasingly tough financial regulatory environment, the monetary policy will remain stable and neutral, and the overall financing environment of the enterprises will continue to remain tight. Therefore, the credit risk of the bond market in 2018 may rise as a whole compared to 2017. At the same time, as more than 40% of the

credit bonds are local government debts, with the mounting debt burden of the local governments, the potential local credit risks might be released.

Against the above background, the credit risks of alternative investments have increased. Although there has been no payment crisis yet in the investment of life insurance funds in the real economy, credit risks have already shown up. There was a low possibility of massive defaults during the past period of credit expansion, and after the credit expansion slowed down in the future, the risk of massive defaults will increase due to the weak liquidity of non-standard products.

At the same time, as life insurance funds support the real economy mainly through debt investment plans, the increasingly complex structure of non-standard products and increased potential credit risks have also increased the overall potential credit risks in the insurance fund utilization industry.

Increased risk of credit default will reduce the credit ratings of credit products held, thereby increasing the minimum capital requirements and directly affecting the current profit and loss and the solvency of the insurance companies in the current period. At the same time, as credit products in the domestic market have poor liquidity, the means of disposal are very limited once credit risks arise. At present, apart from lawsuits, there is no other way to reduce losses. Therefore, once the credit risks break out, it will have a greater impact on the insurance industry.

(III) Cross-market and cross-sector risks

With the expansion of the scope and depth of life insurance funds in participating in the financial market and serving the real economy, fluctuations of such market as the stock market, bond market, foreign exchange market, and interest rates have increased the impact on insurance funds. The utilization of insurance funds has been deeply intertwined with economic and financial risks and the impact of various external market risks has increased significantly. In particular, as some non-standard products increase leverage in disguised forms by multiple-layer nesting, the purchase of these products by insurance funds may suffer from ambiguous underlying assets and violation of the regulatory ratios or the scope of fund utilization, and intensifies the transmission of risks across industries and markets.

At the same time, as financial products have become more complex, transaction process lack transparency and the investment chains have extended, the risks have become more covert. Some cross-sectoral investment behaviors are partially compliant and have the risks under control from the sectoral perspective, however, as a whole, the cross-product, cross-sector and cross-regulator infection and overlapping of risks has increased the difficulties in identifying and dealing with risks.

(IV) Risks of increasing the implicit debts of local governments

The guarantees offered by local government behind the investments of life insurance funds indirectly increase the implicit debt risks of local governments. For example, such irregularities as debt investments in fake equity in some equity investment plans have to a certain degree become the incremental debts of the local governments due to the fact that although debt investments in fake equity look like investors investing in the invested companies in the form of equity, the business actually contains a large number of clauses with debt attributes in practical operation. Compared with general equity investment, debt investments in fake equity can obtain pre-agreed fixed income, and the financiers generally promise that the principal will be withdrawn first. There are generally two types of commitments: the first type is to set a clear expectation of returns, and the investor is paid regular fixed investment returns every year; and the second type is the mandatory redemption of the investment principal by the invested company or an associated third party upon the expiry of the contract and. Debt investments in fake equity may distort the data, the macro-level distortions in risk management judgments and distorted focuses of measures. In the environment where micro-incentive and restraint mechanisms are not reasonable and even become softer, the above practices may exacerbate the excessive accumulation of debt opacity and harbor hidden dangers.

(V) Risks of overseas investment

Life insurance funds have certain overseas investment risks in the process of participating in the BRI infrastructure development. As far as the investments in and financing for infrastructure development are concerned, the projects worth the

investment come first before the financing and follow-up services. Identifying and fostering quality projects are key to promoting the participation of life insurance funds in the BRI development. Most life insurance policies demand the insurers to offer the minimum guarantees, which indicates that life insurance funds must be invested in quality projects which have good development prospects and can bring stable cash flows. In reality, the quality projects among the infrastructure projects along the BRI route are mainly centered in countries and regions with good foundations for development, while the countries and regions with an urgent need to tap the development potential through improving the infrastructure are short of quality projects, and are strictly restrained by the shortage of funds. Despite the various potential infrastructure investment projects in these countries and regions, the lack of quality projects is an inescapable fact and the largest obstacle for life insurance funds to participate in BRI development. Specifically, the following three aspects are included:

Firstly, the development environment of countries along the BRI route varies greatly. There are great differences among the countries and regions along the BRI route in terms of political institution, social and economic system and its stage of development, legal system and policy system, culture and religion, etc., and due to insufficient transparency and diversified languages adopted in these countries and regions, external capital usually has doubts when accessing the infrastructure development field of these countries and regions. It usually takes lots of energy and money to understand the investment environment of the host countries. Even with adequate preparations, external capital often fails to adjust to local markets after entry into these countries and regions. Moreover, due to the differences in various aspects, inter-country coordination has been notoriously difficult (certain cross-country infrastructure projects fail to obtain effective coordination after over 20 years), and it is very hard to offer effective coverage for the investments of external capital through inter-country cooperation. Overlapped by such inherent problems as large-size investment and long cycles for returns of these infrastructure projects, these problems have further increased the difficulties for attracting the entry of market capital. These problems are particularly remarkable in the countries with underdeveloped economy,

unstable political situations and a lack of sound legal system.

Secondly, lack of reliable and stable profit models. The profits from the infrastructure investments mainly come from three sources: firstly, the user charges; secondly, funds are arranged for payment from the fiscal revenues generated by the infrastructure improvements; and thirdly, the increase in commercial value of neighboring regions as a result of the infrastructure improvements. The third source of profits is also an important experience of China in the infrastructure development. All these three profit models have certain risks. As for the owners and operators of the infrastructure, the user charges model has the operating risk of the level of market development being lower than expected. There are higher possibilities that the level of market development is lower than expected in less developed regions. The fiscal fund charges model is subject to the overall fiscal capacity of the host country. Many countries along the BRI route suffer from serious fiscal deficits and there are higher risks of default on their debts. The risks of the model of commercial appreciation of neighboring regions lie in the land system of the host country. For countries adopting the private land ownership, the neighboring lands might not be provided to the infrastructure owners and operators for development and the benefits from the third-party development might not be shared with them. In practice, there is a higher probability of default on debts among the countries along the BRI route, and some international consulting companies even list some countries as higher-risk debtors.

Thirdly, higher geopolitical risks. With their unique energy resources and geographical locations, some countries and regions along the BRI route often find themselves in the central zone of great power rivalry for interests and extremely complicated political and economic situations, and international situations, especially those great powers, will certainly exert influences on the policies of these countries. Despite the common hopes of the countries along the BRI route to improve the infrastructure and achieve better development, the possibility of the existence of inseparable benefit appeals (in the political, military and economic fields) between these countries and other interest groups cannot be ruled out, which has resulted in uncertainties and increased investment risks to the infrastructure development of the region.

To solve the above problems, and turn the grand-scale infrastructure investment demands into concrete investments, the various subjects involved in BRI infrastructure development are expected to not only analyze, research and identify the quality project with great potential for development, but also make concerted efforts to improve the investment environment, and increase the attraction of infrastructure projects within the region to market funds, and form the virtuous cycle of "investment environment improved → the increased number of quality projects → broadened financing channels → rapid economic development → investment environment further improved".

(VI) the risks in expanding in the emerging fields

Life insurance funds also have certain risks in the emerging fields that support the real economy. Taking the disposal of non-performing assets as an example, the potential risks faced by the insurers include: (1) potential risks brought by the disposal methods of non-performing assets; (2) risks triggered by problems existing in non-performing assets disposal market; and (3) the risks resulting from insufficient risk prevention and control capabilities of the insurers.

Firstly, by the disposal methods of non-performing assets may bring potential risks. All non-performing assets disposal methods are intended to defuse financial risks. However, if they are used improperly, they may induce "unintentional consequences" that may even amplify financial risks. Taking the securitization of non-performing assets as an example, its purpose is to spread risks so as to avoid the outbreak of the crises. However, in reality, the securitization of non-performing assets converts and decentralizes the risk of individual banks into the risk of the entire financial market, and the corresponding debt instruments are transformed into derivatives tools, and their relevance to the real economy is reduced. As asset securitization products combine capital markets and monetary markets, creating a long business chain and involving multiple regulatory authorities, a lack of supervision or excessive securitization during the issuance of non-performing assets securitization may lead to bubbles and distortions in asset prices, which in turn triggers the outbreak

of more systematic risks.[①]

The same applies to debt-to-equity swaps. The intention is to reduce the leverage of enterprises and promote the better development of enterprises. However, debt-to-equity swaps may be alienated in the implementation process and bring many risks.[②] The first risk is the risk of distorting policy intentions. If companies take the debt-to-equity swaps as a policy "free lunch" and expect the governments to make up for every possible loss, there will be no incentive to improve operations, and the original irrational product and industrial structure may also be strengthened. The second risk is the risk of reducing the business benefits of debt restructuring. Debt-to-equity swaps have only adjusted the capital structure of the company, resulting in a reduction in the proportion of debts and an increase in the proportion of equity, while the company's asset structure and operational efficiency may not change qualitatively. If the reorganized enterprise cannot effectively operate assets and improve operating efficiency, not only the shareholders' rights and interests will be protected, but it will also lead to a series of economic risks. The third risk is corporate ethics or social credit risks. Inappropriate debt-to-equity swaps can easily become a way for companies to dodge debts, which will have an impact on the market belief of "debts must be paid".

Secondly, problems existing in non-performing assets disposal market may trigger risks. The market for disposing of non-performing assets in China is still not well established and various problems in the development process constitute the risks for insurance institutions participating in the disposal of non-performing assets. Taking the securitization of non-performing assets as an example, it is still in the initial stage of trials. There are problems such as inaccurate valuation, low liquidity, the need to raise the maturity of investor groups and markets, and imperfect legal mechanisms. For another example, due to the existence of information asymmetry and the imperfect exit mechanism of the capital market, debt-to-equity swaps also have problems and risks such as project screening, management and operation of the enterprises involved in the debt-to equity

---

①   GAO, B. & ZHANG, M. (2018). Disposition and Securitization of Non-performing Assets: International Practices and China's Prospects (不良资产处置与不良资产证券化：国际经验及中国前景). International Economic Review (《国际经济评论》), Issue 1

②   Yu, Y. & Liu, G. (2017, January 9). Debt-to-Equity to Drive Better Development of Enterprise (《用债转股促进企业更好发展》), People's Daily

swaps, and withdrawal from the enterprises which has undergone debt-to equity swaps. If these problems are not dealt with properly, they will also lead to risks.

Finally, insufficient risk prevention and control capabilities of the insurers may result in risks. The previous scope of insurance fund utilization by insurance institutions does not include participation in the disposal of non-performing assets. Therefore, insurance funds currently have relatively limited capability in identifying, controlling and managing risks of non-performing assets. For high-quality companies with good development prospects but experiencing temporary difficulties, banks can help these companies tide over difficulties through rollover loans and paying old loans with new loans. For companies running into heavy debts, the risk of investment may be higher. In addition, the information asymmetry of outstanding debts is more prominent than the new debts, and the legal relationship involved is also more complicated. Therefore, the investment, legal, and credit risks of disposal of non-performing assets are relatively high.[①] Specifically, the participation of insurance institutions in the disposal of non-performing assets has the following difficulties and risks: Firstly, the risk in the aspect of information acquisition. Such factors as blind spots of asset managers on the historical condition of assets, complicated debt collaterals and guarantee relationships which make it difficult to conduct due diligence, and banks having no motives to share information can lead to asymmetry in information acquisition. Secondly, the risk of valuation pricing. Unlike the general assets, non-performing assets even taken as collaterals may be affected by factors such as legal restrictions and repayment willingness, which in turn affects the valuation, pricing, and buying of assets, and may ultimately affect the profit margins. Thirdly, the risks of industry research. The value of collaterals is affected by the economy, interest rates, and the industry. Therefore, the overall judgment of economic trends, trends of non-performing loans, and real estate value requires a relatively high level of research. In practice, specific areas and specific industries may need to be studied. Fourthly, the risk in the aspect of legal application. The legal relationship of non-performing assets is generally more complicated, and the legal environment in various places

---

① Wei, X. (2016). Preliminary Analysis on Insurance Funds' Participation in Market-based Banking Debt-to-Equity (《关于保险资金参与市场化银行债转股的初步分析》). China Insurance Assets Management, Issue 6

differ greatly; and the use of legal means to deal with non-performing assets has a long process and involves many links. Therefore, investment in non-performing assets also has higher requirements for the application of laws.

In the face of the above difficulties and risks in the disposal of non-performing assets, if insurance institutions fail to effectively improve their risk prevention and control capabilities, they will bring risks to themselves. Taking debt-to-equity swaps as an example, the main appeals of companies that intend to implement debt-to-equity swaps are to increase equity capital and reduce interest-bearing liabilities, thereby reducing corporate leverage and interest burden, and laying the foundation for transformation and development of enterprises. However, enterprises undergoing debt-to-equity swaps often find themselves in a difficult position. If only funds were injected without effectively changing the existing operating mechanisms, the practices will lead to greater restructuring risks, pricing risks and exit risks for insurance institutions' equity investments, which is obviously in conflict with the attribute of lower appetite to risks of insurance funds.

III. Major existing policy barriers in the support to the development of the real economy by life insurance funds

(I) The relevant management rules and regulations concerning infrastructure-based debt investment plans need to be improved

The *Administrative Measures for the Indirect Investment of Insurance Funds in Infrastructure Projects* (《保险资金间接投资基础设施项目管理办法》) was formally implemented on August 1, 2016, but the revision of the supporting document titled the *Interim Provisions on the Administration of Infrastructure Debt Investment Plans* (《基础设施债权投资计划管理暂行规定》) has not been completed. Some management rules need to be improved in order to adapt to the actual needs of insurance funds to invest in the real economy. This is mainly reflected in the following two aspects:

In the first place, the conditions for the financing subjects to be exempted from credit enhancement need improvements. According to the Interim Provisions on the

Administration of Infrastructure Debt Investment Plans, the current credit enhancement requirements of debt investment plans set high standards and strict approaches. The product form of insurance debt investment plans is similar to that of such products as bank development loans, operating loans or project financing. In the operation of the projects, the insurance debt investment plans have a certain competitive relationship with the banks, especially in some high-quality projects, banks often directly provide loans to obtain interest rate spread, instead of providing financial guarantees for insurance debt investment plans to earn guarantees fees. It can be seen that against the backdrop of current bank-insurance relations and the strengthening of guarantee management in local government investment and financing platforms and large-scale enterprises, Type A and Type B credit enhancement (accounting for approximately 90%) have become more difficult and an important constraint on insurance funds in the investment on infrastructure. Although the Interim Provisions on the Administration of Infrastructure Debt Investment Plans also stipulates the conditions for exemption from credit enhancement, the requirements are too stringent, and in practice, the requirements for exemption from credit enhancement are rarely met.

In order to support the investment of insurance funds in major projects which are of great significance to the national economy and people's livelihood, and to further serve the real economy, the *Circular of China Insurance Regulatory Commission on Matters Relating to the Investment in Key Projects with Debt Investment Plans* (《中国保监会关于债权投资计划投资重大工程有关事项的通知》) (No.135 [2017] of the China Insurance Regulatory Commission) proposed that debt investment plans that invest in major projects that have been approved by the State Council or the investment authorities under the State Council and have the debt-paying subjects that have AAA long-term credit ratings may be exempted from credit enhancement. But in practice, few projects are exempt from credit enhancement in accordance with the principles of the *Circular*.

Therefore, in order to support investment in infrastructure by insurance funds, it is necessary to appropriately reduce the criteria for exemption from credit enhancement on the basis of risk control, and make clear provision on the matter.

In the second place, the scope for the fund utilization of investment plans

needs to be expanded. According to the *Interim Provisions on the Administration of Infrastructure Debt Investment Plans* (《基础设施债权投资计划管理暂行规定》) of 2012, funds for infrastructure debt investment plans can only be invested in one or the same type of infrastructure projects. With the gradual saturation of domestic infrastructure development market and the continuous deepening of state-owned enterprise reforms and structural reforms on the supply side, new financing needs for infrastructure projects have shown a downward trend, and corporate restructuring and financing needs for mergers and acquisitions have increased. Due to the restrictions on the utilization of funds for debt investment plans, insurance asset management institutions have to resort to other channels such as trusts to meet these new financing needs from reorganization and M&As, which not only limits the development of debt investment plan products, but also increases the financing costs of the financing subjects. Therefore, in addition to project financing, the utilization of funds for debt investment plans needs to be further broadened, for example, in such fields as mergers and acquisitions, restructuring, supplementing working capital or debt repayment of enterprises.

(II) The scope for the insurance funds to invest in equity shall be further expanded

In the first place, the scope for indirect investment on equity shall be expanded. According to the provisions of the Interim Measures for Equity Investment with Insurance Funds (《保险资金投资股权暂行办法》), the term "indirect equity investment" shall refer to an insurance company's investment in the equity investment funds and other relevant financial products launched and established by an equity investment management institution. In practice, in order to control risks, there are multiple investment modes for private equity funds, including both equity investments and debt investment in the form of entrusted loans. At present, the Asset Management Association of China adopts classified recordation of private equity funds, which stipulates that the investment institutions registered as equity fund managers can only initiate the establishment of equity-based private equity funds and the investment institutions registered as managers of other types of funds can initiate the establishment of debt-based private equity funds. However, at present, the scope of

indirect investment equity is limited to equity investment funds. If the scope is further liberalized, and insurance funds are allowed to invest in investment funds initiated by investment institutions registered as managers of other types of funds, insurance funds can be further invested in debt-based private equity funds.

In the second place, the scope for direct investment on equity shall be further expanded. The Interim Measures for Equity Investment with Insurance Funds (《保险资金投资股权暂行办法》) of 2010 stipulated that "direct investment of insurance funds in equity is limited to equity in insurance enterprises, non-insurance financial enterprises, and enterprises in such fields as pension, medical, and automotive services related to insurance business." The Circular on Certain Issues Concerning the Equity Investment and Real Estate Investment with Insurance Funds (《关于保险资金投资股权和不动产有关问题的通知》) of 2012 expanded the scope of the direct equity investment of insurance funds, and added the equity of energy enterprises, resource enterprises, and modern agricultural enterprises and new-type commercial circulation enterprises related to insurance business. As the direct equity investment of insurance funds is limited to the above-mentioned scope, industries and enterprises such as equipment and manufacturing, large-scale consumption, media information and communication services have not been included in the scope of direct investment in equity. These industries cover a large number of investment targets with good development prospects, healthy financial indicators, and high risk-return benefits, and include many important domestic leading enterprises that have undergone the transformation and upgrading of industries. Therefore, based on the principles of safety and value investment, it is necessary to moderately liberalize the scope of direct equity investment.

In the third place, the examination and approval system on the equity investments by insurance funds shall be relaxed. At present, the insurance equity investment plans and insurance private equity fund products still need the approval of the CIRC. Although it is conducive to preventing risks, it has reduced the efficiency of insurance equity investment to some extent. Therefore, with the strengthening of risk prevention awareness and capabilities of market entities, the regulatory authorities may consider relaxing the approval authority of equity investment products in a timely manner and

change to the system of recordation by Insurance Asset Management Association of China to increase efficiency.

(III) The registration policies on immovable property for mortgage need to be further improved

Due to the current policy restrictions, the life insurance funds fail to realize their creditor's rights through the mortgage or pledge of immovable property, which restricts the means and space for life insurance funds to serve the real economy.

According to the relevant provisions of the *Property Law of the People's Republic of China* (《中华人民共和国物权法》) and the *Guarantee Law of the People's Republic of China* (《中华人民共和国担保法》), the "right to use state-owned construction land" is a "mortgageable property" permitted by law, and as long as the debtor or the third party agrees to provide land use rights as mortgage guarantee, the "creditor" who has a legal claim on the debtor can apply for land mortgage registration as a "mortgagee". As legal creditors of real estate-related projects, insurance asset management companies can surely be used as mortgage rights holders of land use rights to apply for land mortgage registration. However, according to the relevant provisions of Article 5 of the *Opinions of the Ministry of Land and Resources on Regulating the Land Registration* (《国土资源部关于规范土地登记的意见》) (No. 134 [2012] of the Ministry of Land and Resources, hereinafter referred to as Document No.134 of the Ministry of Land and Resources) stipulates that "In accordance with relevant laws, rules and regulations, financial institutions that have obtained the *Financial Licenses* upon the approval of China Banking Regulatory Commission and microfinance companies established upon the approval of the administrative department of a provincial people's government may apply for the registration of land mortgage as the moneylenders." In this way, in practice, the Ministry of Land and Resources determines that only financial institutions (such as banks, trust companies, etc.), small loan companies or enterprises with "loans" in the business scope that hold the *Financial Licenses* issued by China Banking Regulatory Commission can act as a mortgagee of land use rights. Since the insurance asset management companies neither have a *Financial License* issued by the China Banking Regulatory Commission, nor

does it include "loans" in its scope of operation, they do not fall under the category of lenders who can apply for a land mortgage registration as specified in the Document No.134 of the Ministry of Land and Resources. Therefore, when insurance funds are directly or indirectly invested in real estate-related projects through debt or equity investment plans, land and resources authorities in many regions do not recognize insurance asset management companies as holders of land use rights to apply for land mortgage registration.

(IV) The policies on the investment of life insurance funds in the senior care/health care industry need to be further improved

In recent years, national policies have supported insurance funds to invest in the senior care/health care industry. The *Opinions of the State Council on Accelerating Old-age Services* (《国务院关于加快发展养老服务业的若干意见》) (No.35 [2013] of the State Council) proposed to "gradually relax the controls, and encourage and support the investment in old-age services with insurance funds." *Several Opinions of the State Council on Promoting the Development of the Health Service Industry* (《国务院关于促进健康服务业发展的若干意见》) (No.40 [2013] of the State Council) proposed that "efforts shall be made to encourage enterprises, charity institutions, foundations, and commercial insurance institutions, etc. to invest in the medical service industry by various means including contribution for new establishment, participation in the restructuring, trusteeship and private operation of public-funded institutions." The *Guiding Opinions of the National Development and Reform Commission and China Insurance Regulatory Commission on Matters concerning the Insurance Industry's Supporting the Major Engineering Construction* (《关于保险业支持重大工程建设有关事项的指导意见》) (No.2179 [2015] of the National Development and Reform Commission) proposed to "encourage the establishment of professional insurance assets management institutions covering real estate, infrastructure and senior care, etc., and support the insurance funds to invest in the equity and real estate in the relevant fields of senior care, medical services, and health care, etc."

There are no well-established and unified industry standards for the access standards, supporting facilities and professional services, etc. for the senior care

service industry; the relevant regulatory institutions are not complete; and there are no definite preferential policies concerning the type of acquired land and profitability. Investments in the senior care/health care industry has a significant role in stimulating the economy, and it caters to the the pension and healthcare insurance business. However, the specific implementing rules and preferential policies supporting the investment of insurance institutions in the senior care/health care industry are not yet perfect, and insurance institutions investing in the senior care/health care industry face barriers in such fields as market access, land and fiscal policies, etc. For example, there is no clear provision on the nature of the land for the senior care entities; China's senior care institutions are entitled to preferential policies such as business tax cuts and income tax cut, but it is usually limited to welfare and not-for-profit senior care service institutions, and for the profit-making senior care service industry, the preferential policies are not obvious; there are no well-established and unified industry standards for the access standards, supporting facilities and professional services, etc. for the senior care service industry, and there is also a lack of related regulatory systems, which brings many uncertainties that need further improvements to the practice of insurance companies investing in the senior care service industry.

(V) There are restrictive factors for life insurance funds to participate in public–private partnership (PPP) projects

On the one hand, the limited cash flow of PPP projects restricts the enthusiasm of life insurance funds to carry out equity investment. The typical feature of PPP financing is the limited recourse or non-recourse project financing and the focus of attention is on the future cash flow level of the projects. However, due to the unclear market capacity, charging mechanism, and exclusive mechanism of the future user reimbursement model of the franchise business model in China, government payments also have problems such as the leadership transition of government and government credit, which results in the loss of confidence in the the long-term cash flows of PPP projects for the next 10, 20, or even 30 years. This makes it difficult to attract investments in equity and leads to the evolution of PPP projects from an equity investment to an investment model that must give a reasonable level of return and that

must be taken over by the local government within a certain period of time. In turn, this makes the equity investment a form of debt financing with a certain return and a certain period. In the actual operation, equity investments have evolved into debt investments in fake equity in a variety of disguised forms, which become contingent debts of local governments and increase the debts of local governments, and thus become the targets of restriction and elimination, which has restricted the participation of insurance funds in PPP projects.

On the other hand, the equal contractual relationship and risk coverage mechanism etc. related to participation in PPP projects by life insuance funds calls for legal safeguards, which will influence the investment enthusiasm of the insurance institutions.

(VI) The policy environment for life insurance funds to participate in the disposal of non-performing assets should be further improved

Firstly, the policies on participation in the securitization of non-performing assets shall be further improved. Although relevant authorities have issued regulations to promote insurance funds to participate in asset securitization business, the regulatory authorities have not allowed insurance institutions to participate in the securitization of non-performing assets as investors. According to the Notice on Using Insurance Funds to Invest in the Relevant Financial Products (《关于保险资金投资有关金融产品的通知》) (No.91 [2012] of the China Insurance Regulatory Commission), the underlying assets for pooling of the credit asset-backed securities invested by insurance funds are limited to loans for normal and concerned categories. And in accordance with the principle of low credit ratings, the product credit ratings shall not be lower than the A rating or equivalent A credit ratings of the domestic credit rating institutions, which is difficult to achieve for non-performing assets.

The *Guiding Opinions of the China Insurance Regulatory Commission on the Support of the Insurance Industry for the Development of the Real Economy* (《关于保险业支持实体经济发展的指导意见》) (No.42 [2017] of the China Insurance Regulatory Commission) issued by China Insurance Regulatory Commission in May 2017 proposed that "efforts shall be made to support insurance assets management

institutions to conduct disposition of non-performing assets and other special situations investment business and incorporate special debt-to-equity funds by means of sponsorship", which has largely cleared certain policy barriers for the direct investment in non-performing asset securitization products in the future. However, specific policies involving operational aspects need to be further clarified.

Therefore, competent authorities are expected to open up the policies for insurers to participate in the securitization of non-performing assets, make specific provisions on the ratings and risk control, etc. of non-performing assets and improve relevant laws, rules and regulations in the future.

Secondly, there is a lack of supporting policies for insurers to participate in debt-to-equity swaps. In the first place, the rigid rules of floor trading for state-owned equity are not conducive to the implementation of debt-to-equity swaps. The major cooperative partners of current debt-to-equity swaps are large state-owned enterprises in cyclical industries. According to the relevant provisions of the Measures for the Supervision and Administration of the Transactions of State-Owned Assets of Enterprises (《企业国有资产交易监督管理办法》) promulgated by the SASAC in June 2016, floor trading is required for the capital increasement of the state-owned enterprises. Although it is stipulated in the Measures that capital increase can be achieved through agreements when "the corporate debts are swapped into equity", in the current practice, a considerable portion of the debt-to-equity swap pratices follow the route of purchase of shares before the swap of debts, which requires floor trading according to the strict regulations. Since the debt-to-equity swap is a comprehensive transaction arrangement, the major task is the plan design and clause arrangements and the final completion of the capital increase is only one of the results, the requirements on listed trading of all debt-to-equity swaps will not ensure that all institutions involved in the early preparatory work of the swaps can get listed, thereby blocking these institutions from participating in the debt-to-equity swaps.

In the second place, the rules for the evaluation of state-owned equity transactions need to be improved. The *Interim Measures for the Administration of Assessment of State-owned Assets of Enterprises* (《企业国有资产评估管理暂行办法》) promulgated by the SASAC in 2005 stipulates that the transfer of state-owned assets

and equity changes of state-owned shares of non-listed companies must be evaluated. The process of actual operation of assets assessment involves issues such as the complexity of the evaluation objects, the existence of valuation risks, the cumbersome procedures, and the uncertainty of the assessment time, which cause greater uncertainties to the investment institutions and affect the project process. In addition, the *Measures* also stipulates that the assessed value should not be lower than the net assets, but as most of the companies that perform debt-to-equity swaps are enterprises in difficult situations, their value might be lower than the net assets on the book, which do not meet the principle of market-based pricing.

In the third place, the taxation rules need to be improved. At present, as for corporate equity investment, investment institutions are entitled to the exemption from income tax only when they directly invest in the companies. If they invest in financial products, they face double taxation. In practice, taking into account factors such as spreading of investment risks and reduction of post-investment management pressures, insurance institutions more often than not engage in debt-to-equity swaps through investments in products, but the existence of double taxation has increased the comprehensive costs of enterprises involved in debt-to-equity swaps.

In the fourth place, there is certain tension between the market-oriented debt-to-equity swap of listed companies and the current rules and regulations. The insurance institutions that participate in the market-oriented debt-to-equity swaps of listed companies usually want to obtain shares in listed companies to achieve exit in the capital market, but this is in conflict with existing relevant regulations:

Firstly, the size and stock price of the offering are subject to the restrictions from the new rules on refinancing. In February 2017, China Securities Regulatory Commission issued a new regulation on refinancing, specifying that the maximum size of non-public issuance is 20% of the total share capital; the first day of the issuance period is the base day for pricing, and the issue price will fluctuate in line with market conditions. This has made it difficult for investors to perform internal decision-making processes and increased the uncertainty of investors' participation in market-oriented debt-to-equity swaps.

Secondly, there is strict supervision on repayment of loans by raised funds. At

present, the regulatory authorities require that when listed companies intend to repay the bank loans with all the funds raised through refinancing, they must meet two conditions: the investment should be locked for three years, and the maximum size of the repayment should be calculated through strict formulas. This imposes greater restrictions on investors' willingness to participate in debt-to-equity swaps. In addition, the review process of loan repayments with funds raised through refinancing is so slow to match the time requirements on the enterprises undergoing the debt-to-equity swaps.

Finally, creditors' rights cannot be included in the issue of shares to purchase target assets. According to the *Measures for the Administration of the Material Asset Restructurings of Listed Companies* (《上市公司重大资产重组管理办法》), the assets purchased through the issuance of shares must be operating assets. Therefore, even if it is conducive to improving continuous profitability, listed companies are not allowed to issue shares directly to purchase creditors' rights.

Chapter IV: International Experience, lessons and development trends in enabling life insurance funds to support the real economy

Although there is no universally applicable international experience due to different national conditions, some of the experience and lessons exhibited in the process of life insurance investment serving the real estate in some countries with a long history of life insurance development have common features which are worthy of China's reference, and some new development trends should arouse China's attention and reflection.

I. International experience

(I) The life insurance companies have played an important role in the field of real economy investment with their outstanding features of large sizes and long maturities, etc.

A developed financial system is a generic feature of developed countries. The insurance companies, life insurance companies in particular, have often grown to be an important driving force of economic growth in the developed countries and provided indispensable sources of funds for various financing activities. The indispensability is mainly reflected in two aspects of the large size and the long investment periods.

Firstly, the large size of funds. At the end of 2011, the total amount of assets owned by institutional investors in OECD countries exceeded USD70 trillion, among which insurance companies are the second largest institutional investors after various types of investment funds, with total assets of USD24.3 trillion, and showing an

upward trend (see Figure 1). In many countries, the total assets of the insurance industry have even exceeded the scale of GDP. For example, the total assets of Luxembourg's insurance industry are 2.6 times of GDP, Denmark 1.2 times, and the United Kingdom roughly flat (see Table 1). In the total assets of the insurance industry, the life insurance industry occupies the majority share. Take the Europe as an example. At the end of 2013, the total assets of the European life insurance industry were Euro 6.9 trillion, accounting for 53.1% of GDP; and non-life insurance assets were Euro 1.5 trillion, accounting for 11.6% of GDP.

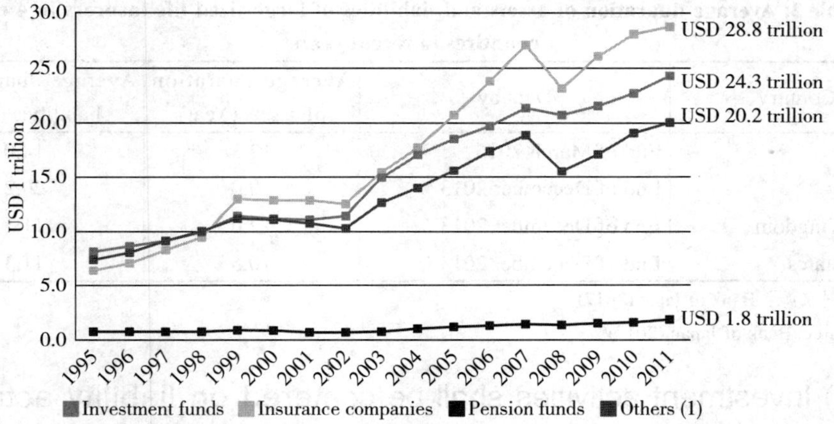

Figure 1: Changes of total assets of four types of institutional investors in OECD countries, 1995-2011

Source: qtd. in Della Croce, R. and J. Yermo (2013)

Table 1: Total assets of insurance industry as a percentage of GDP in selected OECD countries, end of 2011

Country	Total assets of insurance industry as a percentage of GDP (%)
Luxembourg	263.6
Denmark	124.8
Ireland	120.5
United Kingdom	103.2
France	91.7
Sweden	85.5
Japan	75.9
Canada	73.3
Switzerland	72.5
The Netherlands	68.9

Source: qtd. in Della Croce, R. and J. Yermo (2013)

Secondly, the long investment periods. Due to the generally long debt maturity of life insurance companies, the asset maturity is generally longer for asset-liability matching needs. Table 2 lists the asset and liability durations of major life insurance companies in Japan, Germany, the United Kingdom, and the United States in recent years. It can be found that the average asset duration is more than 10 years. Some studies have shown that in 2012, the total investments of all long-term investors in the world allocated to long-term assets amounted to Euro 2.43 trillion, and about 60% of them were held by pension funds and insurance companies[①].

Table 2: Average duaration of assets and liabilities of large-sized life insurers in 4 developed countires in recent years

Country	Data by	Average duaration of assets (Year)	Average duaration of liabilities (Year)
Japan	End of March 2016	12.3	14.0
Germany	End of December 2013	10.0	20.2
United Kingdom	End of December 2013	12.0	11.5
United States	End of December 2015	10.5	11.3

资料来源：Bank of Japan(2017)

Source: Bank of Japan (2017)

(II) Investment activities shall be centered on liability activities, and take the asset-liability matching as the fundamental guiding principle

Life insurance companies are engaged in classic liability-driven assets investment. To a large degree, the type of insurance portfolio determines the type of asset allocation portfolio. Ensuring the asset-liability matching is the overarching principle for the investment of life insurance funds.

In the United States, for example, before the 1940s, major products of the life insurance companies were the fixed-term life insurance, and accordingly, the investment portfolio was dominated by government bonds. Since then, as the type of insured risk has gradually shifted from the death risk to the survival risk and the longevity risk, providing a higher rate of return to customers has increasingly become

---

① Source: INREV RESEARCH & MARKET INFORMATION, "REAL ESTATE AS A LONG-TERM INVESTMENT: The impact of regulatory change on long-term investing strategies and on the real economy", 2013, http://www.europeanrealestateforum.eu/wp-content/uploads/2013/09/INREV_Real_Estate_as_a_Long-Term_Investment_20130408.pdf

one of the business demands. At the liability side, lifelong life insurance, annuity insurance, knvestment-linked insurance replaced term life insurance as the mainstream of insurance products; at the asset end, insurance companies also allocate their investment more in areas with higher risks and higher returns, including junk bonds, commercial real estate loans, and stocks. In addition, for insurers of different scales affected by factors such as marketing capability and market positioning, there are differences in product mix, the need for asset-liability matching, and the consideration of duration and liquidity risk are different. Therefore, the investment portfolio is also different. There is a big difference. In the United States, this difference is mainly reflected in small insurance companies holding more cash and short-term investments than large insurance companies (see Table 3).

Table 3: Portfolio Differences of Large and Small Insurance Companies in the United States in 2014

	small insurers	large insurers	Industry average
Bonds (%)	69	80	67
Common Stock (%)	10	9	12
Cash and Short-term Investments (%)	17	1	4

Note: small insurers—defined as those with less than $250 million book/adjusted carrying value (BACV) of total cash and invested assets; larger insurerss—defined as those with more than $10 billion in cash and invested assets.

Source: NAIC, http://www.naic.org/capital_markets_archive/151201.htm, 2015

In many cases, the principle of asset-liability matching has far more impacts on insurance investments than other financial institutions. For example, long-term Euro bond yields fell sharply in 2014 due to the implementation of quantitative easing policies. However, studies have shown that the demand for government bonds by German insurance companies rose rapidly in 2014. Obviously, this asset allocation adjustment has nothing to do with the pursuit of higher returns on investment but with the pursuit of the longer duration of the assets. On the contrary, there was no similar asset allocation adjustments found in German investment funds, banks, households and other sectors[1]. A similar situation has occurred in Japan. According to the statistics of the Bank of Japan, from 2004 to 2011, Japanese life insurance companies continued to increase their investments in Japanese government bonds, and in particular increased

---

[1]   Source: Dietrich Domanski, Hyun Song Shin and Vladyslav Sushko, "The hunt for duration: not waving but drowning?", BIS Working Papers No 519, 2015

the proportion of investments in ultra-long-term government bonds over 10 years. By the end of 2011, the share of investment in ultra-long-term government bonds had exceeded 40%, and the main driving force behind this adjustment is the duration matching of assets and liabilities, rather than the pursuit of yields.

(III) The investment of life insurance funds shall remain sensitive to the macro-economic trends and policies changes and make timely adjustments to the investment orientation and portfolio allocation.

Both the pursuit of returns on investment and the efforts to ensure that investment business effectively support the liability operations all require that insurance investment must follow the macroeconomic trends and actively respond to the various demands posed by the real economy. This means that even in countries with a highly developed market system such as the United States, the development of insurance investment activities is not the result of independent market decisions in an absolute sense, but is guided to varying degrees by government policies.

For example, in the 1940s and 1950s, with the economic prosperity of the United States and the advancement of industrialization, life insurance companies significantly reduced their holdings of government bonds and agricultural mortgages, and increased the holding of non-agricultural mortgages, especially private equity corporate bonds. This adjustment reflects the high sensitivity of the life insurance industry to the trend of the macro economy. Another example is that the US life insurance industry actively participated in the development of the housing finance system. The housing finance system in the United States has strong policy-oriented characteristics. In the primary and secondary markets, governments and financial institutions work closely together and play an irreplaceable role. In the primary market, the United States established the Federal Home Loan Bank System (FHLBs) in 1932. The FHLBs are government-supported agencies and consist of a head office and 12 branches, with each branch responsible for 4-5 states. FHLBs do not directly lend loans to individuals, but will provide financial institutions with low-cost financing after financial institutions apply to become FHLB members so that financial institutions can provide cheaper mortgage loans to individuals. Insurance companies are very active within the FHLB system and

are mainly involved in three ways: firstly, borrowing from FHLBs; secondly, investing in bonds issued by FHLBs; and thirdly, holding equity in local FHLBs branches. According to NAIC statistics, in general FHLBs branches, insurance companies account for 5% of the number of members and 10% of the loan amount (see Table 4). Outside the primary market, the U.S. housing finance system also has a well-developed secondary market, that is, a mortgage-backed securitization market. More than 80% of mortgage-backed securities in the secondary market are issued by Fannie Mae and Freddie Mac, two large government-supported enterprises. Life insurers are important investors in the housing mortgage securitization market. Figure 2 shows that almost throughout the 20th century, mortgage loans were a very important investment direction for asset allocation of life insurance companies in the United States. Through active participation in the primary and secondary markets of housing finance, life insurance companies have played a very important role in resolving housing problems for US residents and promoting the development of the US real estate market.

Table 4: FHLB members by the end of 2011

Type of members	Member Count	Regulatory Capital Stock Held ($million)	Member Borrowers	Total Advances ($million)	Average Advance ($million)
Commercial Banks	5424	22605	3605	208233	38.4
Savings Institutions/Thrift	1067	8281	779	95470	89.5
Credit Unions	1063	2519	401	22815	21.5
Insurance Companies	234	3387	100	46150	197.2
Community Development Financial Institutions	7	3	3	6	1
Total Membership	7795	36795	4888	372674	47.8

Source: http://www.naic.org/capital_markets_archive/121214.htm

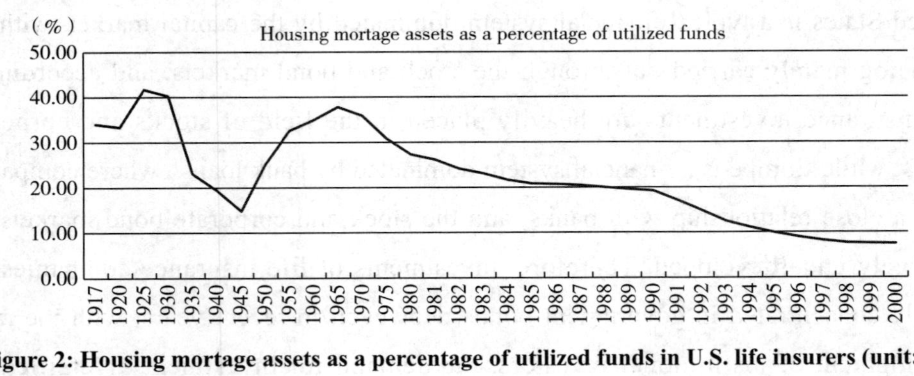

Figure 2: Housing mortage assets as a percentage of utilized funds in U.S. life insurers (unit: %)

(IV) The investment of life insurance funds shall keep close interaction with the capital market and make positive contribution of the deepening of the capital market

For different countries, the development of the life insurance industry might lead or lag behind the development of the capital market. In either case, there is symbiosis, co-incidence and mutual promotion between the capital market and the investment of life insurance funds, which indicates that the investment of life insurance funds is inseparable from a well-established capital market and varied line of financial products. Similarly, the deepening of the capital market has to rely on the drive of such long-term institutional investors as life insurance companies.

The international common feature is that the capital market is the main channel for the funds allocation by life insurance companies, but there are certain differences in the specific conditions of each country's investment portfolio, which are closely related to the characteristics of the capital market. For example, life insurance companies in the EU region invest heavily in government bonds, and the study by Domanski et al. (2015) shows that insurance companies are the largest holders of Eurozone government bonds. In 2014, 40% of the Eurozone government bonds were held by insurance companies. In contrast, life insurance companies in the United States invest more in corporate bonds and stocks. A study by Cummins and Weiss (2010) shows that at the end of 2009, life insurance investments accounted for approximately 16.7% of the total US corporate bond and foreign bond market investments, and 6.2% of the company's stock market value. The differences between Europe and the United States mainly reflect the difference between the two financial systems: the United States is a typical financial system dominated by the capital market, with the financing mainly carried out through the stock and bond markets, and accordingly, life insurance investments are heavily placed in the field of stocks and corporate bonds; while Europe is a financial system dominated by bank loans., where companies have a close relationship with banks, and the stock and corporate bond markets are relatively underdeveloped. Therefore, investments of life insurance companies are mainly concentrated in government bonds. However, in recent years, with the rapid development of institutional investors, the demand for investment diversification

has become increasingly strong, accelerating the development of the corporate bond market in Europe, and also promoting the asset allocation of life insurance companies in the corporate bond sector.

The role of institutional investors represented by life insurance companies in deepening capital markets in various countries is extremely crucial. Take the US corporate bond market as an example. In the past, the issue threshold of corporate bonds in the United States was high, and it was dominated by large investment banks and large companies. There was a lack of full competition from the issuance to pricing, and it was difficult for small businesses to issue bonds. In the 1970s, the situation changed due to the rise of institutional investors. As institutional investors pursued higher rates of return, new investment banks that focusd on transactions rather than securities issuance and underwriting arose and established close ties with institutional investors while encouraging companies to issue securities directly to institutional investors, which increased competition in the issuance process, and reduced distribution and transaction costs. Small businesses and low-credit-level companies have also been able to enter the bond market to issue bonds. As a result, the involvement of institutional investors such as insurance companies and pension funds has greatly promoted the expansion of the U.S. corporate bond market. A similar example occurred in the United Kingdom, where large, stable, long-term capital inflows including the insurance companies and pension funds promoted its stock market to become one of the world's largest and most liquid markets. It can be said that the contributions of institutional investors represented by insurance companies and pension funds to the most developed capital market systems of the world in the United States and the United Kingdom cannot go unnoticed.

II. International Lessons

(I) Insurance asset and liability business shall maintain stable operations and avoid overaggressive moves

Due to the special features of insurance business (e.g. based on the law of large numbers and involving huge public interests), stable operations are very important

for both the individual insurers and the whole sector. Stable operations include both the liability business and asset business. If the whole business model deviates from the stability principle and remains excessively radical, even the good asset-liability matching will drag the companies into dangerous situations and even create impacts on the stability of the whole industry and even the financial system.

There are many bankruptcy cases of international life insurance companies (see Table 5). Although there are differences in the specific background and details of these cases, most of them can be attributed to the common cause of the violation of the principle of prudent operation. When a life insurance company adopts radical measures to engage in competition, launches aggressive insurance products, such as giving customers excessively generous guaranteed returns, too low refund penalty, or allowing policy holders to easily withdraw funds before the contract expiration date, etc., they often need to adopt radical investment strategies to cooperate with such measures at the same time, such as excessive investment in high-risk assets such as mortgages, real estate etc. Under the aggressive business model, changes in internal and external factors can easily lead to a chain reaction, which results in pressures on both the solvency and liquidity of life insurance companies and ultimately leads to failure of the business.

Table 5: Several well-known life insurance bankruptcy cases

Entities going bankrupt	Time of bankruptcy	Causes of bankruptcy
Executive Life Insurance Company (ELIC), USA	1991	Liabilities business: operating a large number of non-traditional annuity businesses, providing clients with significantly higher guaranteed returns than their peers in the market; many products can be surrendered, only with a very low surrender fee charged. Investment business: The concentration of asset allocation is high, and the proportion of investment in junk bonds is significantly higher than that of peers; the guaranteed return rate of debt business is highly dependent on the performance of junk bonds. As the U.S. economy went into recession in the 1990s, the value of junk bonds fell
Mutual Benefit Life Insurance Company (MBL), USA	1991	Liabilities Business: invested in a large number of commercial real estate mortgages and other real estate investments in the 1980s, and the investment ratio was much higher than that of peers. With the national commercial real estate market turning sluggish in the 1980s, the mortgage default rate increased, and the value of assets fell sharply, and affected solvency

Continuation

Entities going bankrupt	Time of bankruptcy	Causes of bankruptcy
Confederation Life Insurance Company (Confed), Canada	1994	Liabilities Business: In most of its history, it had been a conservative and traditional mutual insurance company. In the early 1980s, the company's new management began to develop more aggressive insurance business in order to seek more rapid growth, hoping to transform the company into a comprehensive financial group Asset Business: Commercial mortgage loans and other real estate investments jointly accounted for more than 70% of the portfolio. With the Canadian real estate market plunged into a severe recession, default rates for non-performing assets and commercial mortgages rose sharply in 1993 and early 1994.
8 Japanese life insurers	Late 1990s and 2000s	Liabilities Business: In order to attract policy holders, life insurance companies sold contracts at a high guaranteed interest rate, and the minimum guaranteed interest rate offered to policyholders is completely decoupled from the insurers' returns on assets. Asset business: Life insurance companies significantly increased the allocation proportion of high-risk assets such as stocks and real estate. With the bursting of the bubble economy in the early 1990s and the reduction of interest rates by the Bank of Japan, the high guaranteed interest rate policies sold in the bubble era formed a large number of interest rate losses, directly leading to the bankruptcy of several major life insurance companies.

(II) The investment of life insurance funds is not independent from effective supervision, the lack of which would easily result in serious problems

The life insurance industry needs strict regulation and is highly dependent on market innovations. How to maintain the equilibrium between risk control and encouraging innovation has remained a difficult issue for all regulatory authorities. However, past cases have shown that although there is still much room for discussion on how to tackle the strengths and methods of supervision, the so-called "least supervision is the best supervision" is not entirely applicable to the life insurance industry. Without the effective supervision and against the backdrop of large regulatory gaps and regulatory arbitrage, the market competition would easily deviate from the normal tracks, generate various problems and even trigger the outbreak of

systematic risks. The two examples of the USA are sufficient testimonial of the serious consequences caused by the lack of effective supervision.

The first example occurred in the early development of the life insurance industry. At the end of the 19th century and the beginning of the 20th century, most states in the United States had already begun to implement insurance supervision, but a perfect supervision system had not yet been established. At that time, life insurance companies in the United States developed rapidly, accumulated substantial funds, and engaged in a lot of investments, including buying the control of banks and other companies. The increase in the strength of the insurance industry was accompanied by many problems, including frequent management errors, frauds, and corruption cases, which led to the Armstrong Investigation in New York in 1905. The survey revealed many problems in the insurance industry, and eventually the introduction of new insurance supervision rules, including the prohibition of insurance companies investing and holding ordinary shares, underwriting bonds and so on.

The second example occurred during the 2008 international financial crisis. As the largest insurance group in the world at the time, AIG was considered to be one of the important contributors to this crisis. The issue of AIG was the result of the combined effects of multiple factors. One of the key factors was the failure of the US financial regulatory system. That is, despite the existence of different financial regulatory authorities in the United States, there was a lack of a regulatory authority to exercise overall supervision on large-scale, complex, global financial groups. The issue of AIG reveals the necessity of macroprudential supervision.

III. International Development Trends

(I) Life insurance companies are making more positive moves into the long-term investments in infrastructure and new ventures and the share of alternative investments has witnessed a remarkable increase

For life insurance companies, alternative investments refer to new types of investment channels, including infrastructure, PE/VC, hedge funds and real estate funds, other

than traditional investments such as stocks and bonds[①]. Due to the long-term low-rate environment and the growing uncertainty of investment in the open stock and bond markets since the global financial crisis of 2008, a remarkable move of the global investment of life insurance funds is the significant increase of allocation ratio of investment in alternative assets in pursuit of higher returns on investment and the improvement of diversification of investment to flatten the short-term fluctuations and reduce the risks. According to a survey conducted by Insurance Europe in 2017 covering 11 countries in the European Union, the interest of European insurance companies in infrastructure investment continued to grow, and several major European insurance companies had publicly promised to improve their infrastructure investments and the total investments in the future years will total about Euro 50 billion. In the U.S. statutory reporting system, non-traditional investments are classified in Schedule BA assets. Statistics show (see Figure 3) that although the ratio of investment allocation of US insurance companies in bonds has remained relatively stable since 2008 at about 72%, the ratio of investment allocation in cash and short-term bonds dropped from 6.5% in 2008 to 4.1% in 2013. At the same time, the ratio of investment allocation in Schedule BA assets increased from 3.8% in 2008 to 5.4% in 2013, while the ratio of investment allocation of life insurance companies in Schedule BA assets increased from 3.5% to 4.3% during the same period.

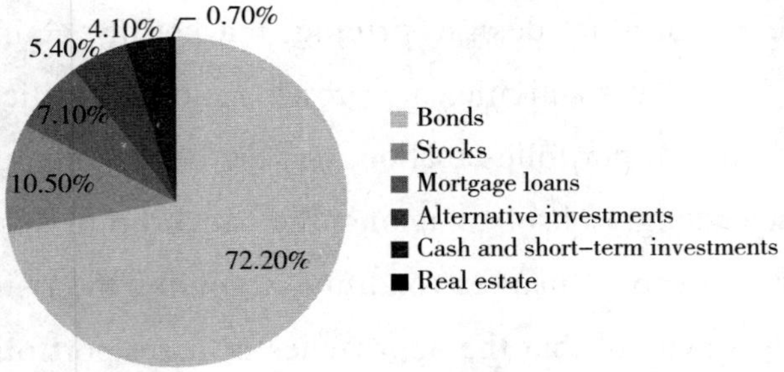

Figure 3: Asset allocation of general account of US insurance industry, 2013

资料来源：Sneed（2015）

Source: Sneed(2015)

---

① In the USA, another definition for the alterantive investments is as follows: "Alternative investments are assets that are not listed on any national exchanges or over-the-counter markets, or for which quoted market prices are not available from sources such as financial publications, the exchanges, or the National Association of Securities Dealers Automated Quotations System [NASDAQ]. These investments generally do not fall under any federal or state regulator and have greater flexibility in investment strategies than registered investment companies." Source: AICPA, "Alternative Investments in Employee Benefit Plans", Jan.2009

(II) More and more life insurance companies are investing in insurance technologies in the hope of improving the risk management and increase the returns on investment from portfolios

In recent years, emerging technologies such as blockchain, artificial intelligence, big data, and cloud computing have been developing by leaps and bounds, and have been rapidly applied to the insurance industry. This has caused disruptive effects on the development of the entire industry, and even the term "insurance technology" has emerged. The so-called insurance technology (InsurTech) refers to the practice of applying different scientific and technological means to all aspects of insurance operations to improve operational efficiency. In 2014-2016, the global investments in insurance technology, whether it is the number of transactions or transaction amount, doubled, and the total investment in 2016 reached USD1.7 billion. Most of the current insurance technology investors come from outside the insurance industry, but investment activities carried out by insurance companies through their internal venture capital departments are increasing year by year. For example, in all insurance technology trading activities in 2014, the investment from insurance companies accounted for only 3%, which increased to 12% in 2015, and further increased to 14% in 2016[1].

Insurance technologies have bright prospects in investing activities apart from such modules as product design, pricing, marketing, claims, etc., mainly because insurance investment activities are growing more complicated. Firstly, the conventional approaches of portfolio creation, e.g. the debt/equity allocation ratio of 6:4, has become increasingly obsolete against the backdrop of sustained low rates and continuously rising capital market volatility. Secondly, the rising proportion of alternative assets is a symbol that the approaches of asset portfolio creation have become more complicated. Thirdly, new regulatory rules including the Solvency II Directive have raised new requirements on the development of information infrastructure in insurance companies. For example, the new regulatory rules adopt the penetrating principle, which requires that insurance companies provide the basic data of the underlying investors, even they are included in the funds or fund of funds. In

---

[1]   Source: http://www.ftchinese.com/story/001072018

response to the above new changes, insurance companies need to take more dynamic and complicated approaches than before to arrange asset-liability matching, and need more timely and accurate data and rapid and highly efficient capabilities in asset portfolio creation to support such matching. The development insurance technologies will help to place insurance companies in a better position to conduct investment management and adapt to the requirements of the new trends and developments.

(III) The correlation between the insurance industry and the systematic risks is on the rise and how to prevent and control risks of the asset and liability business and maintain the stability of the industry has become a huge challenge

In the past, the general consensus was that the insurance industry was not a source of systemic risks, but rather an important force for maintaining the stability of the economy and financial system. Bobtcheff, Chaney and Gollier (2016) calculated the volatility of various industries in the United States from 1960 to 2008 and found that the volatility of the insurance industry was only 20% of the GDP volatility, while the volatility of the investment banks is almost twice of the GDP volatility. Commercial banks are between the insurance industry and the investment banking industry (see Figure 4). It can be seen that the insurance industry is an important stabilizing force for the U.S. economy.

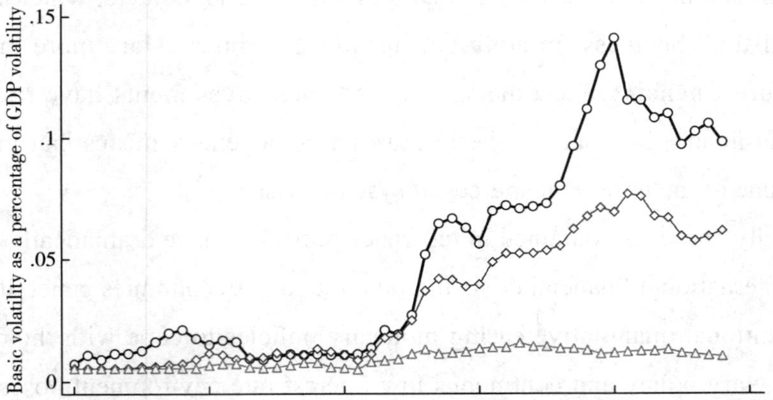

Figure 4: Volatility of three financial sectors as a percentage of GDP volatility in the USA, 1960-2008

Source: Bobtcheff, Chaney and Gollier (2016)

However, after the international financial crisis, more and more people began to agree with a new idea, that is: when compared to the past, the insurance industry have become more and more instable with the correlation with the systematic risks remarkably increased.

First of all, the homogeneity between the insurance industry and the financial sectors of banking and securities, etc. have increased. The wave of financial liberalization that began in the 1980s and 1990s led to the proliferation of integrated operations. The business boundary between the insurance industry and other financial sectors has gradually become blurred, and business models have become more and more similar. Traditional insurance companies have begun to engage in many non-traditional businesses. The most typical example is AIG, which involved a large number of banking activities such as CDs and securities lending, resulting in a significant increase in the volatility of the entire industry. After the international financial crisis in 2008, the trend of increasing homogeneity did not stop, but there was an increasing trend. In particular, low interest rates after the crisis posed a great challenge to the operations of life insurance companies. As a result, life insurance companies have to constantly adapt to the new business environment by changing the product mix and asset allocation. For example, in the face of shrinking investment income, life insurance companies in Europe have had to sell more investment-linked insurance in order to transfer market risks to policyholders, which in essence is a mutual fund business. In addition, insurance companies are more involved in infrastructure financing and other areas, and such investments have traditionally been mainly financed by banks. The increase in homogeneity means that insurers are inevitably one of the important sources of systemic risks.

Secondly, the risks contained in insurance portfolios have dramatically increased. After the international financial crisis in 2008, the major economies generally adopted ultra-conventional quantitative easing monetary policies to cope with the crisis. The easing monetary policy and continuous low interest rate environment poses a serious challenge to life insurance companies. In order to pursue higher rates of return, life insurance companies in the US and Europe have deviated from their original investment habits and have invested more in low-rated bonds. From 2008 to 2016, the

proportion of U.S. and European life insurers investing in A-rated and above bonds dropped by 8 and 18 percentage points respectively; and the proportion of investment in BBB-rated bonds increased by 6 and 19 percentage points, respectively (see Table 6). Insurance companies responded to low interest rates by adjusting their portfolios to higher-yield bonds and lower liquidity assets. This also means that they will assume more credit risks, market risks, and liquidity risks.

Table 6: Bond asset allocation of European and U.S. life insurance companies

	U.S.A.		Europe	
	2008	2016	2008	2016
AAA /AA/A	75	67	83	65
BBB	18	24	4	23
Noninvestment grade	3	3	2	4
No grading and others	4	5	11	8

Source: IMF 2017

IV. Conclusion

1. Investment is an important way for the life insurance industry to serve the development of the real economy. It can generate positive effects such as providing long-term financing sources and deepening the development of the capital market. However, life insurance investment activities are not necessarily positive. If there is a lack of policy guidance and effective supervision, the positive effects of life insurance investment will not only be insufficient, but may also have many negative effects.

2. Government guidance and policy support are crucial to bring into play the role of insurance investment

The role of the governments is to provide a clear direction for insurance investment in the real economy and provide appropriate empowerment, including allowing insurance companies to provide funds for infrastructure, industrialization, etc.; and encourage more investment in the real economy. Through preferential taxation and other means.

3. Effective supervision ensures that insurance investment achieves balance between innovation and stability

Through more engaging in alternative investment channels including

infrastructure, insurance investment will play a more direct and important role in serving the real economy. At the same time, the correlation between the insurance industry and systemic risks is clearly rising. How to balance the risks and benefits, innovation and stability poses a great challenge to insurance supervision. The role of the insurance industry in the economy and finance must be viewed in a more systematic way, and the issue of risk prevention and control should be taken seriously in a both macro-prudential and micro-prudential approach.

Chapter V: Policy Recommendations to Facilitate the Real Economy through Life Insurance Funds in China

The premise of life insurance funds supporting the real economy is to promote the transformation and high quality development of the life insurance industry. Only when the life insurance industry achieves high-quality development through transformation can it accumulate long-term and large-scale life insurance funds to meet the financing needs of the real economy. In order to promote life insurance funds to support the development of the real economy, it is necessary to adhere to the market-oriented operation and uphold the basic principles for the utilization of life insurance funds. promote the integration of liability-side insurance business and asset-side investment business, strengthen the application of science and technology in the field of asset management. In order to prevent life insurance funds from supporting the risks in the real economy, it is necessary to further guide the life insurance industry in adjusting the asset-liability structure, strengthen the risk management capabilities of the insurance institutions with asset and liability management as the core, and improve the life insurance capital utilization supervision system centered on risk prevention to strengthen the monitoring and prevention of the risks in the key fields, strengthen the coordination and cooperation among financial regulatory authorities, and improve the investment environment through cooperation. Enhance the spirit of the contract among local gooernments, and strengthen industry risk management. At the same time, it is necessary to improve the policy environment for life insurance funds to support the real economy, including deepening the market-based reform of the utilization of insurance funds, clarifying real estate mortgage registration policies, eliminating policy barriers to investing in the pension industry, improving related supporting policies

in the PPP sector, and optimizing the policy environment for life insurance funds to participate in the BRI development and disposal of non-performing assets. Explore life insurance funds to carry out loan business, and actively cultivate the insurance asset management market.

I. Efforts shall be made to promote the transformation and high quality development of the life insurance industry

The premise of life insurance funds supporting the real economy is to promote the transformation and high quality development of the life insurance industry. Only when the life insurance industry achieves high-quality development through transformation can it accumulate long-term and large-scale life insurance funds to meet the financing needs of the real economy.

(I) Efforts shall be made to promote the transformation of the life insurance industry

Life insurance investment activities are mainly based on liability activities And the basic guiding principle is the assets and liabilities matching. Therefore, in order to promote life insurance funds to support the development of the real economy, it is necessary to promote the transformation of the life insurance industry, with the risk protection function as the core and the liability business as the foundation. Therefore, the life insurance industry must make a transition to the protection function-based business plus wealth management. That is, we must take the health insurance and pension insurance and other protection-related businesses as the lead, develop under the support of tax deferrals and pretax deduction policies, establish a sustainable asset-liability management model, create value for customers and society, and become an important part of the pension and health insurance system.

1. Efforts shall be made to achieve the transformation of the mode of premium increase from lump-sum payment–driven to renewal-driven

The biggest difference between premium income growth models of lump-

sum payment and regular payment is the sustainability and the stability of business development. It is difficult for the regular premium payment to quickly increase the scale of premium income in the short term, but the rate of premium growth will accelerate after a certain period of time of accumulation. In addition, the stability of the business operations of the companies with a larger proportion of regular premium payment was also higher. Therefore, the transformation of the industry needs to gradually transform the growth model of premium income from the lump-sum payment–driven growth model to the renewal-driven growth model, so as to increase the sustainability of growth in premium income and the stability of business development.

2. Adjustments of product structures.

The insurance industry and insurance companies need to innovate the product system. Firstly, efforts are needed to concentrate on providing life insurance which offers financial security against death risks. According to a previous study by Swiss Re, the death protection gap in China in 2015, 2016, and 2017 was USD 37 trillion, USD 43 trillion, and USD 50 trillion, and the gap is still increasing. The development of life insurance, especially term life insurance, can provide financial protection for the death risk and narrow the death protection gap. The development of life insurance represented by term life insurance is also a lesson of developed countries in the insurance industry. In the United States, for example, the US life insurance market sold nearly 10 million life insurance policies in 2016 through personal business channels, of which about 4 million were term life insurance policies, which accounted for 40% of the total policies and only 20% of total life insurance premium income, but the term life insurance policies provided 70% of the death risk protection in the United States, with the average insured amount for each term life insurance policy standing at USD 430 thousand (equal to about RMB 2.80 million), and the average premium per term life insurance policy standing at USD 948 (equal to about RMB 6,000). has 87 million. Nearly 70% of families in the United States, equal to nearly 87 million families, have life insurance protection.

Secondly, efforts shall be made to develop the health insurance which offers

financial security against illness and disability risks. With the further ageing of China's population, the demand for health insurance such as medical insurance, critical illness insurance, disability income insurance and long-term care insurance is increasing. To this end, it is necessary to take into consideration the existing problems in the pilot projects of health insurance business involving individual tax preferences to lay a firm institutional foundation forthethe development of commercial health insurance. In the first place, we should relax the control of products and promote competition. At present, health insurance business involving individual tax preferences has raised a lot of requirements for product design, which is conducive to protecting the interests of consumers and improving the value of health insurance business involving individual tax preferences to the insured. However, it also brings problems such as adverse selection and uncontrollable moral hazards and high transaction costs. To some extent, it weakens the economic incentives to market players. Therefore, it is necessary to relax product controls at a proper time, maintain the free choice of market actors, protect the interests of consumers through competition, and achieve "consumer sovereignty" in the process of market entities chasing and competing with profits.

In the second place, efforts are needed to raise tax exemptions to increase demand. At present, the health insurance business involving individual tax preferences is deducted before the individual income tax in accordance with the limit of RMB 2400/year. Due to the limited amount of pre-tax deductions, the effect of tax savings is not obvious, and it is difficult to substantially increase the demand for health insurance. International experience shows that the development of commercial health insurance is closely related to the strength of pretax deductions. In order to give fuller play to the role of the market mechanism in China's medical security system, the amount of pre-tax deductions for individual purchases of commercial health insurance must be greatly increased, and tax incentive levers should be used to stimulate demand to promote the development of commercial health insurance. At the same time, the procedures for tax deduction should be simplified to facilitate the operation in practice.

In the third place, efforts are needed to promote competition in the field of medical services. The development of commercial health insurance requires a competitive medical service market. A relatively competitive market for medical

services will help commercial health insurance control the costs of medical expenses and the intervention of medical services. An important obstacle to the development of China's commercial health insurance is that due to administrative regulations and the monopolization of public hospitals, imbalances in supply and demand in the medical service market make it difficult for insurance institutions to control medical expenses, and it is even more difficult to intervene in the medical service process, and It is difficult to promote managed care and payment system reform. Administrative system control and monopoly make market access strictly restricted. A large number of market resources, private resources and international resources face difficulties in enterring the medical service market, and a diversified and competitive medical service supply pattern cannot be formed, resulting in a de facto monopoly of public hospitals. Therefore, it is necessary to break the monopoly in the field of medical services and lay a good institutional foundation for the development of commercial health insurance. To achieve this goal, it is necessary to realize the two-way opening up of the medical service sector internally and externally, and at the same time promote the reform of the public hospitals system and promote the marketization of medical services and drug prices. The government should treat public hospitals and private hospitals equally, and create a fair environment for competition among various types of hospitals.

Finally, efforts are needed to promote competition among social health insurance agencies. To achieve the transformation of social medical insurance agencies from the government agencies to the market- and social-based multi-sector agencies, to establish a multi-center governance structure, so as to provide the institutional basis for commercial health insurance participation in competition, improve and optimize the operation efficiency of social medical insurance.

Thirdly, efforts are needed to develop the endowment and annuities insurance which offers financial security against longevity risks. Since May 1, 2018, Shanghai, Fujian Province (including Xiamen City) and Suzhou Industrial Park have implemented the pilot scheme of personal tax-deferred commercial pension insurance. We must promote the pilot scheme of tax-deferred commercial pension insurance from such aspects as development orientation, improving tax preferential policies, and increasing industry supply efficiency, and promote

the development of pension insurance.

In the first place, we must clarify the development orientation of commercial pension insurance. We must give full play to the role of market mechanisms in the pension system, and truly regard commercial pension insurance as the "third pillar" of China's pension system to correct structural imbalances in the pension system. In the pension system reform and policy adjustment, we must fully consider the interaction between commercial pension insurance as the third pillar and basic pension insurance. It is necessary to effectively reduce the payment proportion of basic pension insurance, reduce the payment burdens of enterprises and residents, and provide space for the development of commercial pension insurance.

In the second place, efforts are needed to improve tax incentives and increase the demand for commercial pension insurance. At present, the pilot scheme implements the EET tax incentive model, that is, the original investment and returns or income or accumulation on the investment are exempt from tax but any maturity amount or withdrawals are subject to tax, which can play an incentive role for tax deferral. Due to the small scale of taxpayers receiving income from wages and salaries in China, the actual population entitled tax benefits is very limited. The number of people employed in the informal sector in China is large. In the future, we can consider implementing the TEE tax incentive model at the same time, that is, the original investment is taxed but the returns or income or accumulation on the investment and any maturity amount or withdrawals are exempt from tax. This will help increase the choices of pension account holders, expand their coverage, expand the coverage of tax incentives, and increase the demand for commercial pension insurance.

Finally, efforts are needed to improve the supply efficiency of commercial pension insurance. The life insurance industry must change its development concept, take the protection function as the basis, combine risk management with wealth management, and promote the transformation and upgrading of the industry. The life insurance industry should take the pension insurance as the leading business, develop the pension insurance under the support of tax incentives, create value for customers and society, and become an important part of the pension system. Life insurance companies should strengthen product innovation and meet and adapt to diversified

senior care security needs. At the same time, guided by marketization, Life insurance companies should broaden the utilization of insurance assets, increase the capacity and efficiency of asset management, and increase the competitiveness of commercial pension insurance.

3. Efforts shall be made to increase the values of channels

For the bank-insurance company channels, efforts shall be made to take advantage of the regulatory integration to promote the in-depth integration of banks and insurance companies in the business field, facilitate the deepening of the bank-insurance cooperation and the upgrading of bank-insurance mode, turn to the protection-based business based on regular premium payment, increase the value of new business and enhance the value of bank-insurance company channels.

For the personal insurance agency channel, we need to increase the per capita capacity and marketing efficiency of the insurance agents, regulate the marketing practices, protect the consumers' interests, focus on fostering highly efficient and high-quality personnel and realize the leap forward transition from quantitative expansion to quality enhancement. Accompanied with the transformation of product values, the development mode shall gradually transfer from pure pursuit of premium income scale to the pursuit of high quality premium income.

4. Efforts shall be made to forestall and defuse liquidity risks in the transformation of the life insurance industry

Since 2017, due to changes in the regulatory orientation and the transformation of the industry, the originally hidden liquidity risks of the life insurance industry has gradually become obvious, and some of the life insurance companies have a relatively high risk of cash flow risks. The first problem is the pressure on premium inflows. In face of the increasingly tightened supervision, the scale of some companies' lump-sum premium income has rapidly declined, while the increase in the turnover of regular premium income has not been able to compensate for the contraction in the volume of lump-sum premium income, resulting in a significant reduction in the inflow of new business premium income. At the same time, the stability of renewal premium income of some companies is relatively poor. When the external environment

changes, their renewal premium inflows may be lower than expected, and the premium inflow pressure will be greater. The second problem is the increase in cash outflows. Companies with large stocks of short- and long-duration products face pressures from surrender and maturity payment, and the liquidity is under pressure in the short-term. The third problem is that the management of liquidity has become more difficult. With rising interest rates and prolonged debt durations, personal insurance companies have previously allocated more long-term assets. When a liquidity crisis occurs, the long-term asset realisation cycle will be longer, which will increase the difficulty of liquidity management.

Therefore, in order to advance the transformation of the life insurance industry in a stable way, it is necessary to avoid the sharp decrease of premium income within a short period of time and try best to match the increment of the renewal premium income with the decrease of lump-sum premium, make a huge but not sharp turn and avoid triggering new risks. Therefore, attention shall be paid to maintain balance between the regulation and the transformation of the insurance industry and leave the time and space for the companies to advance structural adjustment.

It is worth pointing out that from January to March in 2018, the amount of current-year new payment for the policyholders' investment funds and independent accounts not included in the insurance contract calculation in life insurance companies reached RMB 338.701 billion, a year-on-year increase of 40.51%, which is much faster than the growth rate of original insurance premium income of life insurance companies. This will help ease the cash flow gaps of some companies and provide more room for transformation and development. Of course, in this process, life insurance companies should pay attention to the matching of assets and liabilities, and avoid high debt costs that may cause spread losses and radical investments on the assets side.

5. High attention should be paid to the risks of new interest spread loss and fee loss during the transformation process.

Under the dual pressures of competition and transformation, some small and medium-sized life insurance companies may passively increase channel fees, lower product pricing, switch from low-value products with lump-sum premium payment to

low-value products with regular premium payment, or use long-term annuity products with high guaranteed interest rates to obtain premium income, which may result in risks of spread loss and fee loss. At the same time, the complexity and long-term nature of long-term protection and pension and annuity products, high guaranteed interest rates and high-cost rates have become less visible, further concealing the risks of spread loss and fee loss. therefore, efforts shall be made to forestall and defuse the risks of interest spread loss and fee loss caused by the middle- and short-term practices during the transformation process.

(II) Efforts shall be made to promote the high quality development of the life insurance industry

Promoting the high-quality development of the life insurance industry is the basis for life insurance funds to support the real economy. In order to promote the high quality development of the life insurance industry, enhance the proportion of insurance assets in the total assets of the financial industry and the development of the life insurance industry, it is needed to deepen the commitment to the supply-side structural reform of the industry, continuously deepen the market-based reform of the allocation of insurance factors, increase the supply quality, enhance technological innovation and promote the optimized upgrading of the industry. To this end, efforts shall be made to promote the life insurance industry to realize the reform of quality, efficiency and driving forces, and continuously improve the total factor productivity of the insurance industry.

The promotion of the high quality development of the life insurance industry necessitates bringing into full play the role of insurance mechanism in the economic transformation, promoting the life insurance industry to play the roles of long-term stable risk management and security, and reshaping the institutional foundation for the well-ordered operation of the life insurance market.

1. Bringing into full play the role of insurance mechanism in the economic transformation

Firstly, the potential risks in the process of economic transformation require that

the role of the life insurance industry be better played. China's economy has shifted from a high-speed growth stage to a high-quality development stage. During this process, the international and domestic development environment and conditions have undergone profound changes; the time and space constraints of transformation and reform have been continuously strengthened; the competition on such fields as the markets, resources, talents, technology, standards, etc. have become more intense; global issues such as climate change and energy and resource security have become more pronounced, and there are still some uncertainties and potential risks. When solving the risks that may arise in the transition process through the commercial insurance market-based approach, we can not only adhere to market-oriented reforms, which will give better play to the decisive role of market allocation of resources, but also effectively promote social harmony and stability.

Secondly, changes in the major social contradictions in the process of transformation need to give better play to the role of life insurance. At present, the main social contradictions in China have been transformed into "the contradiction between the people's growing needs for good living and unbalanced insufficient development." After 40 years of reform and opening up, China's social productivity has improved significantly, and social needs have been escalating. Insurance services in various fields such as birth and illness, food, clothing, housing, sports, culture and entertainment have become the necessities for ensuring a better life for the people. The huge gaps in the areas of senior care, medical care and other fields provide a vast space for development for the insurance industry.

Thirdly, the implementation of major development strategies in the transition process needs to give fuller play to the role of life insurance. In order to promote China's economy from a high-speed growth stage to a high-quality development stage, the 19th National Congress of the Communist Party of China proposed a series of major strategies such as accelerating the development of an innovative country, rural revitalization, and coordinated regional development etc., which provided new opportunities for the development of the insurance industry. As a market-based mechanism of risk management, social management, and disaster relief, insurance can realize the enhancement of the industry value by serving the country's major strategies.

2. Promoting the life insurance industry to play the roles of long-term stable risk management and security

High-quality development requires the promotion of the long-term robust risk management and protection function of the life insurance industry, and the expansion of the risk protection function of the insurance market. The key to high-quality development of the life insurance industry lies in giving full play to the core functions of insurance in delivery of economic benefits, risk management, and financing, diversification and transfer of various personal risks, and participation in risk management to use professional risk management techniques to effectively manage disease risks and longevity risks. At the same time, we must give full play to the long-term advantages of life insurance funds, promote capital financing, rectify the imbalance between indirect financing and direct financing, and optimize the financial structure.

The first is to increase the insurance penetration rate and give play to the function of economic benefits delivery. The primary function of life insurance is economic benefits delivery, that is, the pooling and dispersion of various personal risks so that individuals and families can receive timely and adequate benefits in the event of personal risks. At present, the economic benefits delivery function of the life insurance industry still needs to be further developed. At present, the insurance coverage rate of long-term life insurance policies is not high. In 2016, only 40 million people purchased long-term life insurance policies in China, and the insurance coverage rate was less than 3%, indicating a big gap with the countries and regions where the insurance industry is developed. For example, in 2015, the number of valid individual life insurance policies in Japan was 160.11 million; the number of valid individual annuity insurance policies was 20.75 million; the group life insurance covered 38.75 million people; and the cumulative number of valid insurance policies was 21.961 billion. The registered population in household registration in Japan was 127.11 million in 2015 and the insurance coverage rate is 172.77%, which is equivalent to 1.73 life insurance and annuity insurance policies per person. For another example, in 2015, the number of valid individual life insurance policies was 47.934628 million; the number of valid individual annuity insurance policies was 1.150546 million; the

group life insurance covered 5.923496 million people; and the accumulated effective number of valid insurance policies was 55.0087 million. The registered population in household registration in China Taiwan was 23.492 million in 2015 and the insurance rate is 234.16%, equivalent to 2.34 life insurance and annuity insurance policies per person.

Therefore, the life insurance industry must continue to base itself on the fundamental attributes of protection, increase product penetration through the innovation of insurance products and business models, and increase the proportion of compensation for economic losses caused by various personal risk accidents, so as to better realize the function of economic benefits delivery, and disperse and transfer risks.

The second is to strengthen risk management functions. The risk management function of insurance is derived from the economic benefits delivery function. The insurance mechanism is the unification of loss compensation and risk control. In addition to guarantees, insurance should also fully utilize the functions of risk management and provide professional risk management services to families and the society.

The life insurance industry should give full play to its advantages of pooling and dispersing various personal risks and specializing in risk management to improve the level of risk management. Taking health insurance as an example, China's health care costs have shown a rapid growth in recent years, and the operating pressure of social health insurance systems has increased. In more and more places, the basic health insurance fund is experiencing a deficit. Compared with social insurance institutions, a prominent advantage of commercial insurance institutions is that they have a full-process medical risk management and control technology that includes "pre-illness health management, monitoring during medical treatment, and verification after treatment", thus playing a certain constraint role on the rising medical costs and the waste of medical resources. Therefore, through the participation of commercial insurance organizations in basic medical insurance agencies, the risk management and control technology of commercial insurance is applied to the examination of the costs of basic medical insurance to reduce the expenditure on unreasonable medical expenses, improve the efficiency of the use of funds, reduce the burdens of medical expenses for the insured people, help suppress the continued rise in

medical expenses and maintain the balance of payments of social security funds. For example, the insurance companies deployed the intelligent monitoring system to the hospital terminals to carry out pre-warning, in-process monitoring, and post-event supervision of the entire process of risk control and establish a quality medical insurance management service platform. In addition, commercial health insurance agencies have the drive and interest dving mechanism to conduct in-depth cooperation with medical service providers, and promote the integration of medical services and medical insurance in market competition, thereby effectively improving the health of the population.

The third is to give play to the financing function and optimize the financial structure. Life insurance has the function of financing, and support the development of the real economy through the use of funds and investments. The life insurance industry can use its financial resources to optimize financial structure and promote economic development.

Firstly, the development of the life insurance industry helps to correct the imbalance between indirect financing and direct financing. The development of the life insurance industry can promote the development of bonds and the stock market through investment, and directly enter the real economy through equity investment, thus helping to correct the structural imbalance between direct financing and indirect financing in China's financial sector.

Secondly, the development of the life insurance industry can promote the optimization of the capital market structure. At present, the development of China's capital market is lagging behind the developed countries. There is an urgent need for effective institutional investment funds in the capital market. The development of the life insurance industry is an important way to promote the optimization of the capital market structure. As institutional investors, life insurance companies have the characteristics of high professionalism, strong investment planning, emphasis on long-term investment, and diversified investment channels. Thy also pay attention to long-term investment and focus on long-term income and they can enhance the stability of the capital market and promote the sound and healthy development of the capital market. It can be seen that the development of the life insurance market and the capital

market is mutually promoting and is prerequisite for each other. Life insurance funds can become an important force for promoting the development of the capital market.

3. Reshaping the institutional foundation for the well-ordered operation of the life insurance market

At present, the factors influencing the high-quality development of the life insurance industry include deviations in regulatory positioning, inadequate differentiation of regulatory policies, "excessive pursuit of large scale and quick returns" among shareholders, and inherited experience and inertia of the management. Fundamentally speaking, these problems stem from the relatively weak institutional basis for a well-run life insurance market. In order to promote the high-quality development of the life insurance industry, it is necessary to reshape the institutional basis for the operation of the life insurance market, that is, to promote the reform of property rights, promote the deepening of the market division of labor, and highlight entrepreneurial spirit.

The first is to promote property rights reform. The most important institutional foundation for the development of the life insurance market is a reasonable property rights system. Only if the property rights system is reasonable can insurance companies learn to "grow up and grow stronger," instead of "become bigger and stronger." The current market is full of logic that is called "becoming bigger and stronger," rather than the logic of "growing up and growing stronger " that respects the law of life. The root of the problem lies in the system of property rights. Therefore, we must attach great importance to the reform of the property rights system in the insurance market. Only by establishing a reasonable system of property rights can the life insurance market truly have a market-based institutional basis, and can the pursuit of short-term benefits be fundamentally curbed. The second is to deepen the division of labor in the market. The important reason that restricts market participants from deepening the division of labor and improving professional management is that the marketization mechanism of insurance has not received sufficient attention. The role of life insurance, pension insurance, and health insurance in the social security system should be further expanded in order to expand the scope of the market, strengthen the rule of law, eliminate and limit the powers of the governments, and create a division of labor that

conforms to the logic of the market, and lay a firm foundation for the emergence of various forms of "professional management." The third is to demonstrate entrepreneurship. The fundamental driving force for the development of the life insurance market is to fully demonstrate entrepreneurial spirit. In order to release entrepreneurial innovation, we must adhere to market-oriented reforms, reduce government control and intervention, protect property rights, and realize the rule of law. Only in this way can reforms that demonstrate entrepreneurial spirit as the basic orientation become the institutional dividend for the high-quality development of the life insurance industry.

II. Ideas on promoting the life insurance fund to support the development of the real economy

(I) We should follow the market-oriented principles

The requirements on the profitability and security of the life insurance funds make it necessary for the funds to adhere to the market-oriented principles and the funds shall be invested in quality projects of the real economy with promising development expectations to achieve sustainable development. On the contrary, real economy projects with low investment returns and large investment security challenges are not suitable for investment of life insurance funds. Based on the market operation, life insurance funds can take advantage of large scale, long duration, and high stability to support the development of the real economy.

Apart from market-based approaches to support the major national strategic development, to adhere to the market-based operation requires that we explore how to use life insurance funds to support the development of private sectors, enable the market to play a decisive role in the utilization of life insurance funds and promote the transformation of the pattern of economic development.

(II) We should uphold basic principles for the utilization of life insurance funds.

Firstly, the principle of stability and prudence. Life insurance products often

have requirement on the minimum return on investment, which makes life insurance funds focus on safety. Establishing a stable and prudent investment philosophy is the foundation for the utilization of life insurance funds;

Secondly, serving the core business. At present, the life insurance industry is shifting to the protection function-based business plus wealth management, and the use of life insurance funds should serve the development of the principal business of the life insurance. It is worth pointing out that we cannot confront the the protection function and the principle that "the insurance industry should focus on the insurance business" with the function of wealth management. Faced with a huge gap in insurance coverage, it is necessary to increase the long-term security and risk management functions of insurance. "The insurance industry should focus on the insurance business" does not mean that insurance cannot be involved in wealth management. Although the current principle that "the insurance industry should focus on the insurance business" emphasizes that returning to the protection and risk management functions is both necessary and urgent, it must be clear in the direction of development. That the insurance industry, on the basis of effectively improving the operating capacity of insurance funds, combines risk protection advantages and participates in wealth management, especially providing guarantee for the longevity risks, is the proper meaning of principle that "the insurance industry should focus on the insurance business" and return to the protection function. To this end, the life insurance industry must be based on the protection function, combining risk management with wealth management to promote the transformation and upgrading of the industry. At the same time, in order to lay a firm foundation for participating in the foundation of wealth management, the insurance industry needs to effectively improve the capability to utilize insurance funds to achieve the matching of asset and liability management.

Thirdly, long-term investment, value investing, and diversified investments. Life insurance funds are long-term funds and debt funds. Their pursuit of safety and stability has determined that the use of insurance funds must adhere to long-term investment, value investing, and diversified and distributed investments. Therefore, life insurance funds need to be long-term funding providers, market value discoverers, well-intentioned investors, and risk managers with diversified, multi-tiered asset allocations.

Fourthly, the asset-liability matching management. The asset-liability matching management is an important foundation for the stable and robust operation of the life insurance companies, and the core content of risk management. The asset liability management of ife insurance companies needs to consider various factors such as interest rate risks, liquidity risks, market risks, credit risks, reputation risks and so on.

Fifthly, compliance with laws and regulations. On the one hand, we must strictly abide by the rules governing the use of insurance funds. On the other hand, it is necessary to continuously strengthen the institution's own system and rules, and effectively prevent and resolve risks.

(III) Efforts are needed to support the utilization of life insurance funds to serve the development of the real economy

On the basis of following the market-oriented principles and adhering to the basic rules for the utilization of life insurance funds, we should support the life insurance funds to serve the development of the real economy and

The essence of finance is to serve the real economy. Internationally, especially in advanced economies such as the United States, Japan, and Europe, the life insurance funds display natural advantages in such aspects as serving the development of the real economy, promoting the industrial transformation and upgrading, and improving the efficiencies of the economic and financial systems., and has palyed very positive and crucial roles, including: firstly, they can become a substantial provider of funds for the infrastructure and urbanization development; secondly, they are an important booster for economic transformation and upgrading and the development of the new economy. Insurance funds have become the key to supporting the development of emerging industries, mergers and acquisitions, and elimination of outdated production capacity; and thirdly, they are a key player in serving the micro- and small-sized enterprises and innovating financial products. Insurance funds play a distinctly different role from the traditional banking system which has heavy assets, short duration, and low risk preferences. They can better serve small-, medium- and micro-sized enterprises, industrial innovation, and economic transformation and upgrading.

Combining China's national conditions, insurance funds have obvious advantages

in serving the real economy. Firstly, insurance funds are long-term and stable sources of funds and have rich and varied forms of investments which can better adapt to the financing needs for the development of the real economy under different economic development cycles. Secondly, insurance funds can be an effective supplement to bank funds, form differentiated advantages, and better compensate and promote the financing needs of economic transformation and upgrading. Thirdly, insurance funds can make full use of a sound capital market and a wealth of financial product media and bridges to achieve the development of real estate insurance funds to serve the real economy. Fourthly, insurance institutions are not merely providers of funds. Special agencies can also be set up to initiate the establishment of financial instruments, such as mergers and acquisitions funds, leveraged funds, and mezzanine funds, to make up for shortcomings and deficiencies in capital markets and financial instruments, and to improve the efficiency of the financial market.

(IV) Promoting the integration of liability-side insurance business and asset-side investment business

The matching of assets and liabilities is not only reflected in maturity matching, yield matching, but also in the matching of asset and liability attributes. With the deepening of the transformation, life insurers are increasingly committed to the mining and expansion of health insurance and pension insurance. As the proportion of health insurance and pension insurance in the liability-side business continues to increase, in order to achieve effective allocation of assets and liabilities, the asset allocation field should include the investment in pension and health industries, and realize the coordinated development of liability business and pension and health industries.

The investment by life insurers in the pension and health industries has good industrial synergies by connecting upward to the pension insurance, health insurance, nursing insurance and other products and connecting downward to the elderly medical care, aged care and other industries, which enables the insurance products design, research and development, sales to achieve synergistic development, integrate relevant industries, build a whole life industry chain, and realize mutual promotion of the main insurance business and the pension and health industries. The insurance industry has a

large customer base and a strong service network. By introducing health management and old-age security into insurance, and providing customers with a full range of services, we can achieve win-win results for insurance institutions, policyholders, and related industries.

Life insurance funds have large-scale and long-term attributes, which are highly compatible with the development needs of the pension and health industries. The investment of life insurance funds in pension and health industries can alleviate the mismatch pressure of insurance funds, avoid economic cyclical risks, weaken the impact of capital market instability on the investment yields of insurers, and bring stable cash flow yields to life insurers, so that the match between assets and liabilities can tend to be reasonable, thus improving the insurers' ability to resist risks and maintain sustainable development.

Therefore, it is necessary to further tap into the advantages of life insurance funds and promote the development of health and old-age industries. Efforts shall be made to support insurance funds to participate in the investment in the medical, pension and health industries, and support insurance funds to invest in building old-age communities through such means as new projects, shareholding, mergers and acquisitions, etc. to increase the supply of social pension resources, and promote the common development of the insurance industry and the pension industry.

(V) Strengthening the application of science and technology in the field of asset management

In the process of supporting the real economy, the proportion of alternative investment in life insurance funds has been increasing, which makes the building of insurance portfolios more complicated, and it is urgent to strengthen the application of technology in asset management. At the same time, in order to prevent financial risks, the regulatory authorities implement the "penetration" supervision of the underlying assets, which requires the insurers to provide the basic information of the most underlying level of investment. This also requires insurers to adopt a more dynamic approach to asset-liability matching management, which in turn requires more timely and accurate data and rapid and efficient asset portfolio building capabilities. The

application of technology can help insurers to better manage their investments and adapt to the needs of supervision and developments of the new situation.

In recent years, the insurance asset management industry has actively explored the application of new technologies. From the early application of Internet technologies, various analytical models and information technology systems, the industry has gradually shifted to the application of new technologies such as big data, cloud computing and artificial intelligence. At present, the application of financial technology in the insurance asset management industry mainly includes the following aspects:[①] First, the application of artificial intelligence technology to smart investment research, smart investment, smart investment consulting and so on. For example, through the comprehensive use of artificial intelligence, we can carry out deep mining of historical data, real-time tracking of market conditions, assisting professionals in value judgment and risk judgment, and keenly capturing market opportunities.[②] Second, the application of big data analysis to credit rating and risk control, public opinion analysis, and precision marketing, etc.. For example, in the aspect of risk control, all kinds of useful information of investment companies and their counterparties are collected through big data, so as to realize credit risk monitoring of investment objects or trading objects.[③] Third, the application of blockchain technology in order to drive financial innovation. The application of blockchain in the asset management industry is mainly reflected in mid- and back-office operations, payment transfer, and financial

---

[①]   Insurance Asset Management Association of China (IAMAC): China Insurance Asset Management Development Report (《中国保险资产管理业发展报告2018》), China Financial & Economic Publishing, 2018

[②]   China Life Asset Management Co., Ltd. and Taikang Asset Management Co., Ltd. have successively launched their own artificial intelligence investment consulting platforms, marking a new stage of the application of insurance asset management technology.

[③]   In January 2018, PICC Asset Management Co., Ltd. launched the "Artificial Intelligence Development and Application Group" in order to achieve breakthroughs in the field of "intelligent risk control". The team started with the big data such as the change of credit qualifications of the debt issuers, and started to develop the "machine learning algorithm" with the characteristics of PICC assets: through precise program setting, they allow the computer to "study" and "learn" the general law of qualification changes, and conduct independent intelligent credit rating according to the financial indicators disclosed by the enterprises in the market. At the same time, by relying on big data and artificial intelligence technology, PICC Asset Management Co., Ltd. has developed a "credit and public opinions intelligent analysis system" that uses machine learning and natural language processing to quickly filter reports, news, and stories that are widely spread in the market. The computer can judge the tendency of the texts, so as to warn in advance the clues of the changes of the subjects of the debt issue, and use them as one of the basis for dynamically adjusting its credit rating, and making early arrangements for the investment operation.

intelligence contracts. [1]

The combination of technology and asset management will effectively enhance the internal vitality and creativity of the asset management market. The application of financial technology in the insurance investment and investment research business can gradually realize such functions as automatic report generation, financial search engine, intelligent auxiliary investment decision-making and quantitative investment; in the sales and customer service parts, such functions as customer segmentation, customer retention and investment portfolio expansion, sales promotion, sales team maintenance, and business optimization can be gradually realized; in the risk management process, such functions as credit risk warning, market risk warning, and operational risk warning can be gradually realized; and in daily management, the operational capacity of insurance asset management institutions can be gradually enhanced in such aspects as scientific and technical office operations, human resources management, knowledge management and enterprise service support .

In order to further promote the application of science and technology in the field of asset management, firstly, insurers have increased their exploration and investment in the field of science and technology. In order to improve the efficiency of the insurance asset management industry, insurers should increase their integration with science and technology, and explore investment and financing information, platform integration, electronic trading, big data interaction and other systems based on cutting-edge technologies such as machine deep learning, knowledge mapping, big data, cloud computing, and blockchain.

Secondly, insurers should improve the regulatory system to adapt to the development of insurance technology. The regulatory authorities should treat the development of insurance technology with an open and inclusive attitude and provide innovative space for market players. At the same time, we must actively explore the

---

[1]   Shanghai Insurance Exchange has already made some useful attempts in utilizing the blockchain to serve the asset management business. In view of the opacity of the duration of the insurance asset management business, the fraud of the contract information and the information asymmetry of the relevant parties of the business, Shanghai Insurance Exchange increases the efficiency of data flow by monitoring the underlying information of the product, and monitors the real situation of the assets in real time, provide transparent and real asset information to managers, investors and regulators, and increase the trust of the parties in the transaction chain to the underlying assets.

"insurance technology sandbox" mechanism to carry out technological innovation business within a limited scope in a risk-controlled manner. In addition, it is necessary to develop regulatory technology and comprehensively improve the level of risk management.

Thirdly, insurers should promote the development and sharing of insurance industry data infrastructure. It is necessary to promote the establishment of a unified base business data rules for insurance business asset management products, improve the standardization of data; on the basis of the integration of the product registration system and the china insurance registration and trading system of China Insurance Asset Registration and Trading System Co., Ltd., gradually promote the systematic connectivity between more market players including insurance asset management institutions, industry investors, custodian banks, and etc, strengthen the linkages with external institutional systems, and form an industry-wide, on- and off-exchange trading ecosystem.

III. Efforts shall be made to prevent the risks in the support to the development of the real economy by life insurance funds

(I) Efforts are needed to further adjust the asset-liability structure of the life insurance sector

The mismatch of insurance assets and liabilities is to solve the problem of high cost of liabilities. Controlling the cost of liabilities within a reasonable range will help reduce the pressure of misalignment and gradually realize the long-term goal of matching assets and liabilities. Therefore, it is necessary to start from the liability side and solve the problem of high liability-side costs forcing the investment-side to raise the appetite to risks. The insurance industry needs to have a good grasp of the primary and secondary relationship between the risk protection function and the financial management function in the liability side, and form a differentiated competitiveness with other financial institutions. The life insurance sector shall

establish the sustainable asset-liability management modes with the protection function as the basis and pension and healthcare insurance as the top priorities and combining the risk management and wealth management, establish the sustainable mode of asset-liabilty management and become an important component of the national senior care/health care system.

(II) Efforts are needed to strengthen the risk management capabilities of the insurance institutions with the asset-liability management as the core

Insurance companies shall take advantage of the issuance of the *Rules of Supervision on the Assets and Liabilities of Insurance Companies (1-5)* (《保险资产负债管理监管规则 1–5 号》), improve the risk management capability with asset-liability management as the core, achieve the sound interaction between the asset side and liability side, and establish the sustainable mode of asset-liability management. To this end, we must include asset and liability management in the strategic plan, raise the importance of the entire asset liability management to the most prominent position of insurance companies, and promote the coordinated and centralized work of insurance companies to a unified platform. Firstly, insurance institutions shall continue to improve the awareness and capability of asset-liability management, strengthen the development of the organizational system and mechanism, establish the decision-making system for the asset-liability management, set up the horizontal communication and coordination mechanism between the various intra-company departments, especially the liabilities management office and assets management office, and enhance the information communication and feedback between various intra-company departments. Secondly, the team building of insurance companies shall be optimized. Assets and liabilities management and major insurance assets allocation are the core and most basic capabilities of insurance companies in the long run and require sufficient talent pools. Insurance companies must establish a professional team of asset and liability management and capital allocation to promote the comprehensive development of insurance investment. Thirdly, we should change the ideas of the executives of the insurance industry. The management should fully understand the

balance sheet and establish the overall asset allocation concept. Fourthly, we should fully improve the liquidity of the invested assets and liabilities. The investment team needs to understand in-depth the characteristics of the liabilities and the logic behind them to the liability side. On this basis, it guides the liability side business and forms a good interaction mechanism between the investment side and the debt side. Fifthly, efforts shall be made to optimize the evaluation system and promote the effective implementation of the asset-liability management.

For emerging businesses, such as participating in the disposal of non-performing assets, insurance institutions should adopt market-oriented methods to select professional intermediary service agencies, investment consultants, or investment managers to use external resources to improve risk prevention and management capabilities and cope with various investment, legal, and credit risks in the disposal of non-performing assets.

(III) Efforts are needed to improve the life insurance capital utilization supervision system centered on risk prevention

Firstly, efforts shall be made to make a quick move to promote the supervision on asset-liability management, and realize the positive interaction between the asset side and the liability side, for which efforts are needed to establish such rules as quantitative evaluation, qualitative evaluation and pressure test, etc., comprehensively evaluate the asset-liability matching situations and assts allocation capability of the insurers, implement the differentiated solvency policies and fund utilization policies, further classify and adjust the type and proportion of major classes of assets, correct the risk factors of the China Risk Oriented Solvency System (C-ROSS) and optimize the capital constraints on different types of assets and investing behaviors. Secondly, efforts shall be made to comprehensively and strictly enhance the supervision on the utilization of insurance funds by various means including promoting external auditing, capital supervision, information disclosure, classified regulation, internal control and public supervision, etc. Thirdly, efforts shall be made to promote the development of the insurance statistical information system and insurance asset management supervision information system, and further enhance the docking of insurance fund

custodian bank system with the regulatory information system. Fourthly, efforts shall be made to study and explore the ways for insurance funds to invest in gold and relevant financial products, and use stock index futures, treasury bond futures, interest rate swaps and more financial derivatives to hedge and manage the risks. Fifthly, efforts shall be made to strengthen the coordinated and interconnected supervision on insurance services, fund utilization and solvency, and form the supervision synergy.

(IV) Efforts are needed to strengthen the monitoring and prevention of the risks in key fields

Firstly, efforts shall be made to strengthen the front-end and back-end management and risk prevention and control for debt investment plans of insurance funds, and prevent credit risks. Secondly, efforts shall be made to evaluate the impact of asset allocation plans on cash flows by conducting asset allocation pressure tests, and make the contingency plans for the cash flow risks for protection against asset-liability mismatch risks and liquidity risks. Thirdly, efforts shall be made to regulate the equity investment plans to avoid increasing the implicit debts of the local governments. Therefore, we should return to the basics of equity investment, and stamp out debt investments in fake equity in some equity investment plans, and strengthen the proactive management, passageway business and multi-layer nesting of products in an effort to prevent financial risks.

(V) Efforts are needed to enhance the coordination and cooperation between the financial regulatory authorities

The insurance, securities and banking regulatory authorities shall enhance the coordination and cooperation with each other to guard against regulatory arbitrage, and eliminate the regulatory gaps from cross-sector financial activities; keep a close eye on the possible impacts to the insurance sector by the changes of macro factors including currency, finance and taxation, foreign trade, foreign exchange, interest rate, real estate, stocks, and social security, etc., analyze and evaluate the risk transmission mechanism and transfer channels, and effectively prevent cross-market and cross-

sector risks.

(VI) Efforts are needed to improve the investment environment through cooperation

As for the participation in the BRI development by life insurance funds, identifying and fostering quality investment targets in the field of infrastructure development within the region is key to improving the attraction to life insurance funds. Therefore, efforts shall be made to strengthen cooperation and strongly support infrastructure investment environment within the region. There are four focuses of cooperation: firstly, efforts shall be made to strengthen the bilateral and multilateral communication and negotiation between and among the countries along the BRI route and create the cooperation and dialogue mechanism dedicated to improving the infrastructure investment environment of the whole region. Secondly, efforts shall be made to create a platform for information, risk and benefit sharing between the life insurance funds and infrastructure projects, and take the lead to form the institutionalized cooperation mechanism in the fields with mature conditions. The creation of an open and shared project financing information platform can relieve the asymmetry of information of various project participants, help to guide life insurance funds to strengthen communication and coordination with multilateral international organizations including the World Bank, AIIB, New Development Bank BRICS and Silk Road Fund, etc. to form the synergy of capital support, dock with the BRI investment and financing demands in a timely manner, and increase the operating efficiency for life insurance funds to support the BRI development. Thirdly, cooperation shall be strengthened to identify, prevent and deal with the infrastructure investment risks within the region. Any sign of disturbance, including the change of government, sharp rise or drop of the interest rates, intervention of foreign countries, civil protests or religious movements, etc., during the infrastructure development may result in the halt or even termination of the projects, and the exposure to such risks will bring serious losses to the interests of the enterprises, financial institutions and the countries involved. To this end, the countries along the BRI route shall conduct active cooperation in terms of the design of risk evaluation indicators, risk factor monitoring

and significant risk prevention and control, etc. Fourthly, efforts shall be made to accelerate the projects with good investment and financing conditions, make them part of the early harvest program, and give play to their demonstration and guiding role to enhance the confidence of the investors within and without the BRI region in BRI projects.

(VII) Enhancing the spirit of the contract among local governments

At present, a large part of the alternative investment in insurance funds is invested in local governments and their affiliated enterprises in the forms of insurance asset management products such as infrastructure investment plans. Therefore, the spirit of the contract of local governments directly affects the risks and yields of investment. The general return rates of the debt investment plans are not very high, and the risk is required to be relatively stable. However, in the implementation of the projects, if the government does not comply with the contract, the risk will increase significantly. At present, some investment plans of insurance funds have encountered the situations where some local governments failed to use funds according to the original plan or unilaterally requested to modify the rate of return clauses, etc., reflecting to varying degrees the lack of the spirit of the contract among governments. In addition, as the infrastructure investment plans have long investment periods and often have to go through two or more governments, the lack of the spirit of the contract among the governments will inevitably lead to the default risks brought by the government change, which will bring losses to insurance investment.

In the cooperation between the government and enterprises, the government is in a strong position because it has mastered the right to formulate policies and rules, and the enterprises are in a relatively weak position. In a market economy, only when the status is equal can a fair transaction be made. Since there are natural inequalities between the government and enterprises, it is necessary to use contracts to stipulate the rights and obligations of both parties to ensure that the two parties can conduct fair trade on an equal footing. Therefore, in order to promote life insurance funds to support the real economy, we must improve the cooperation contracts and enhance the

spirit of the contract of local governments. The insurers and the government must enter into contracts on an equal footing to establish a mechanism for sharing benefits and risks. At the same time, both parties must respect and abide by the contracts, and the government shall refrain from abusing their powers. In the short run, it is necessary to formulate a strict contract text to form substantive constraints on the government that is difficult to break. In the long run, it is necessary to raise the level of rule of law, and use a sound system to regulate and constrain the behaviors of the governments.

(VIII) Strengthening industry risk management

It is necessary to strengthen the coordination of relevant authorities and strengthen industry risk management.[1] Relevant industry organizations in the insurance industry should give full play to the role of the platform, strengthen the monitoring of local debt risks involved in the use of insurance funds and strictly check investment compliance in the work related to the enrollment and registration of insurance asset management products such as infrastructure investment plans. At the same time, they should accelerate the exploration and establishment of an industry-wide regional credit risk assessment framework, gradually improve the industry-based risk early warning mechanism, and promptly indicate risks to insurance institutions. The offices of the government debt management leading groups of all provinces (autonomous regions, municipalities directly under the central government, and municipalities separately listed in the state plan) should speed up the establishment of cross-sector joint monitoring and prevention and control mechanisms, and statistically monitor the medium and long-term expenditures of insurance institutions on governments and the debt investment provided to financing platform companies, strengthen information sharing and data verification, regularly report monitoring results, and support insurance institutions to improve their risk management systems.

---

① The Guiding Opinions on Strengthening the Management and Use of Insurance Funds and Supporting the Prevention and Mitigation of Local Government Debt Risks (《关于加强保险资金运用管理 支持防范化解地方债务风险的指导意见》) (No.6 [2018] of CIRC) jointly printed and distributed by the former CIRC and the Ministry of Finance

IV. Efforts shall be made to improve the policy environment for life insurance funds to support the real economy

(I) Efforts are needed to deepen our commitment to the reform of market-oriented utilization of life insurance funds

Efforts shall be made to expand the investment fields, turn to the market subjects more choices and rights to choose under the precondition of compliance with the laws, and take the support to the development of the real economy as the starting point and foothold for innovating the ways to utilize the insurance funds.

(I) we need to deepen our commitment to the reform of market-oriented capital utilization.

Firstly, we should expand the investment scope of insurance funds. At present, there are three main ways of alternative investment by insurance funds: the first way is to directly carry out major equity investment and real estate investment; the second way is to invest in insurance investment products such as debt investment plans, equity investment plans, and asset-backed plans; and the third way is to invest in collective trust plans. Major equity investment and real estate investment have high requirements for insurance institutions' funds, resources and professional capabilities. With the restraints from risk prevention and the ability of insurance institutions, these plans are still mainly available to a few leading enterprises, and it is difficult to become a general investment mode in the insurance industry in the short term. The debt investment plans are mainly limited to real estate and infrastructure investment. These investment fields have large capital demand, long cycles, and high maturity matching of insurance funds. However, under the current economic restructuring and regulatory situations, the direction of capital investment and trading counterparties are greatly affected by policies, results in the relatively scarce medium and long-term assets available for the investment by insurance funds. In this context, the strict restrictions on the investment fields will make it difficult to meet the demand of

insurance funds for non-standardized investment. Therefore, in order to better serve the needs of the real economy, it is necessary to gradually liberalize investment areas that can effectively match the demand for insurance funds. To this end, the regulatory authorities should promote the promulgation of such policies as the participation of insurance funds in the long-term rental market and other policies as soon as possible, and expand the scope of investment in a timely manner, increase the supply of high-quality debt investment plans and equity investment plans, expand the asset-backed plans business, and gradually allow insurance funds to invests in assets with good liquidity and long-term value-added potential, such as asset-backed securities (ABS), real estate trust investment trust funds (REITs), private placement notes (PPN), gold, commodities, etc., thus giving the market greater asset allocation options space. [1]

Secondly, the detailed business rules for insurance asset management products shall be introduced. The introduction of detailed rules can further clarify regulatory requirements and business norms, so that market subjects can better implement these rules at the actual operational level. [2] The rules should focus on the long-term goals and take into account the characteristics of insurance asset management products, which will help support the innovation of asset management products, maintain a smooth transition of business, promote fair competition in the market, and play the role of insurance funds in supporting the real economy. In the detailed rules of insurance asset management product, it is necessary to actively promote the development of the multi-level insurance asset management product system based on providing services to the main insurance business and increasing the strength in supporting the real economy, and more fully and effectively meet the diversified demand of insurance capital asset allocation. [3] To this end, the first way is to increase appropriate flexibility to grant more options to both investors and financing persons or organizations in the

---

[1]   Cao Deyun, Detailed Business Rules for Services for Insurance Asset Management Products Called for ASAP, http://www.cs.com.cn/xwzx/hg/201807/t20180728_5849197.html

[2]   Cao Deyun, Detailed Business Rules for Services for Insurance Asset Management Products Called for ASAP, http://www.cs.com.cn/xwzx/hg/201807/t20180728_5849197.html

[3]   Han Xiangrong, Hu Xuewen: Retrospection and Expectation of Non-Standardized Asset Investment of Insurance Asset Management (《保险资管非标投资反思与展望》), Insurance Asset Management of China, Issue 3 of 2018

process of promoting the conversion of existing debt investment plans and asset-backed plans into standardized products. Because once it is included in the scope of standardized products, although the liquidity and openness of the products have improved, the liquidity risk and the market risk premium will be diluted accordingly, and the yield will show a downward trend, which will increase the difficulty of raising the rate of return on insurance. Therefore, it is necessary to increase the flexibility of switching to standardized products according to the needs of market trading entities. If the trading entity pays more attention to liquidity and information transparency, it can choose open listing and transfer and meet the corresponding standardized product regulatory requirements; if the financing party, investors or managers pay more attention to the non-liquidity premium, there is no need for public listing, and the products shall be allowed to choose to complete the corresponding registration or filing process in the form of private offering products. The second way is to gradually add standardized non-standardized product sequence on the basis of existing product systems such as debt investment plans and asset-backed plans. It is necessary to allow the insurance asset management enterprises to develop non-standardized products that are compatible with the insurance fund investment styles and risk appetite according to the characteristics of the funds and with the risks under control, and bring into full play the professional advantages of insurance funds to meet the demand for insurance funds and better meet the financing needs of the real economy.

Thirdly, relevant regulatory requirements shall be improved. First, according to the actual situation and market needs, the provisions of the current laws and regulations that are not operational and applicable shall be adjusted to appropriately expand the space for investment operation. For example, the issuance of current insurance asset management products is mainly subject to strict regulations on financing entities, direction of capital investment, credit enhancement measures, credit ratings, and risk management, etc. [1] Among them, the provisions on credit enhancement measures adopt an enumerated method, and the requirements for various

---

[1]   Han Xiangrong, Hu Xuewen: Retrospection and Expectation of Non-Standardized Asset Investment of Insurance Asset Management (《保险资管非标投资反思与展望》), Insurance Asset Management of China, Issue 3 of 2018

types of credit enhancement are more stringent. The above provisions help to improve the safety of the utilization of insurance funds, but also lead to a relatively simple transaction structure of existing insurance asset management products, making it difficult for insurance asset management products to adapt to the individual needs of financing parties, and difficult to improve professional investment capability and product design capability of the insurance asset management enterprises, resulting in their passive position in the asset-side competition. Therefore, we must adhere to the regulatory concept of "opening up the front end and managing well the back end" and optimize the relevant provisions for product issuance. Efforts can be made to appropriately relax and optimize the product issuance conditions and credit enhancement measures, focus the regulatory priorities on information disclosure, and return product design capabilities and risk control methods to market entities, thereby enhancing the professional capabilities of in utilizing insurance funds. The second way is to improve the management rules related to the infrastructure debt investment plans. It is necessary to improve the conditions for financing entities to avoid credit enhancement, and expand the purposes of funds of these investment plans in a timely manner. The third way is to release the scope for insurance funds to invest in equity in a timely manner, including the timely liberalization of the scope of indirect investment on equity, the timely liberalization of the scope of direct investment on equity; and the timely change of the approval system of the equity investment of insurance funds to the recordation system. The fourth way is adopt the differentiated supervision by hierarchical classification of the levels of investment capacity of insurance institutions and better guide the safe operation of insurance funds. The fifth way is to guide the insurance institutions to lengthen the assessment period, optimize the performance appraisal system, and advocate long-term investment concepts.

(II) Efforts are needed to clarify the real estate mortgage registration policies

It is recommended to define the equal status of insurance institutions and banks and other financial institutions as subjects in terms of fund provision, and promote the state land administration authorities to issue the policies to regulate the mortgage and

pledge registration of land, and allow insurance institutions to handle the procedures of mortgage and pledge registration of land according to the laws.

According to the relevant provisions of the *Property Law of the People's Republic of China* (《中华人民共和国物权法》) and the *Guarantee Law of the People's Republic of China* (《中华人民共和国担保法》), the "right to use construction land/right to use state-owned land" is a "mortgageable property" permitted by law, and as long as the debtor or the third party agrees to provide land use rights as mortgage guarantee, the "creditor" who has a legal claim on the debtor can apply for land mortgage registration as a "mortgagee". The above two laws do not impose any other restrictive provision on the creditor as the mortgagee of the land use rights. The insurance asset management company, as the legal creditor of the real estate investment plans it initiated to establish, can of course act as a land use rights mortgagee. As a mortgage holder of land use rights, an insurance asset management company must, together with the mortgagor, apply for land mortgage registration with the relevant authorities of land and resources, otherwise the land use right mortgage cannot be established according to law.

It is precisely because China's property law and guarantee law as a higher law stipulates that "the creditor is the mortgagee" and does not impose any other restrictive provisions on the land use rights mortgagee, Article 5 of the Document No.134 of the Ministry of Land and Resources issued by the Ministry of Land and Resources on September 6, 2012 only stipulates that lenders can apply for land mortgage registration (it is not stipulated that only lenders can apply for land mortgage registration), and enumerates that only the banking financial institutions and microfinance companies that operate microfinance businesses who hold the Financial Permits issued by China Banking Regulatory Commission can act as lenders. This is because the "creditors" referred to in China's property law and guarantee law do not only include "lenders", but also include other companies or natural persons that generate legal creditor'srights due to borrowing, buying, selling, and other civil activities.

Therefore, the original intention of the Document No.134 of the Ministry of Land and Resources is not to make a restriction that only the banking financial institutions and microfinance companies that operate microfinance businesses and hold the

Financial Permits issued by China Banking Regulatory Commission can act as land use mortgageholders and insurance asset management companies and other companies or natural persons cannot apply for land mortgage registration as a land-use right mortgagee. However, many local land and resources authorities have made "reduced interpretation" of the relevant provisions of the Document No.134 of the Ministry of Land and Resources, leading to the practice that insurance asset management companies as the legal creditors of the "Real Estate Investment Plan of the Insurance Asset Management Companies" cannot apply for land mortgage registration as a land use right mortgagee.

In order to solve the problems in practice, it is recommended that relevand departments jointly issue a document clarifying that insurance asset management companies can apply for land mortgage registration. China Banking Regulatory Commission and the Ministry of Land and Resources jointly issued the *Notice on Matters concerning Real Estate Mortgage Registration in the Business and Operation of Financial Assets Management Companies and Other Institutions* (《关于金融资产管理公司等机构业务经营中不动产抵押权登记若干问题的通知》) in June 2017 clarified that financial asset management companies and their affiliates, when operating within the scope of their legal scope of business,, need to secure their creditors' rights by real estate mortgage guarantees, they may apply for registration of real estate mortgage rights in accordance with the law.

It is suggested that relevand departments should jointly publish documents on the basis of a similar approach, clarifying that insurance institutions are entitled to the same dominant status as financial institutions such as banks in terms of capital provision, and urge the authorities including the land and resources authorities to promulgate policies to standardize the mortgage and pledge registration of land and allow the insurance institutions to go through the formalities for mortgage and pledge registration of land. That is, as long as the debtor or the third party agrees to provide the land use rights mortgage guarantee, the insurance asset management companies as the legal creditors of the real estate related projects can apply for the land mortgage registration as the land use right mortgagee, and the relevant local land and land authorities should handle the mortgage registration formalities for land use rights for

the insurance assets management comapnies.

(III) Efforts are needed to eliminate the barriers when investing in the senior care/health care industry

Efforts are needed to eliminate the barriers faced by the insurance institutions in such fields as market access, land and taxation& fiscal policies when investing in the senior care/health care industry. Therefore, it is necessary to specify the industry standards for the access standards, supporting facilities and professional services, etc. for the senior care/health care industry, and specify the type of acquired land for the senior care/health care industry and preferential taxation policies for the for-profit senior care/health care industry.

(IV) We need improve the relevant supporting policies in the PPP field

Firstly, it is necessary to further improve the legislation in the fields of cooperation between the government and private capital, and enhance the support to the insurance institutions in terms of land and taxation and fiscal policies, etc. in their investment.

Secondly, it is necessary to explicitly define the enterprise income tax-free policy on the proceeds from the investment of insurance funds in equity financial products. As for dividend income, Article 26 of the *Enterprise Income Tax Law* (《企业所得税法》) defines " Dividends, bonuses and other equity investment proceeds" as "tax-free incomes" of enterprises i.e. these proceeds are exempt from enterprise income tax. The income derived from the transfer of equity investment of enterprises shall be incorporated into the taxable income of the enterprises, the enterprise income tax on which shall be paid in accordance with the law. However, the *Enterprise Income Tax Law* does not specify the tax treatment for the dividends of equity financial products issued by asset management institutions. This means that, in practice, insurance funds are subject to the double taxation when investing in equity financial products, including the equity investment plans, issued by insurance asset management institutions, that is, the source of the income that the invested company pays in the

form of dividends to the equity plan is its after-tax profit, and the enterprise has paid the enterprise income tax, which is the first taxation; and the dividends received by the equity investment plans and distributed to insurance fund investors is included in pre-tax profits of insurance companies and is subject to corporate income tax again. This is the second taxation. The current corporate income tax law does not clearly stipulate the related tax treatment of the equity investment plan projects. In the implementation, there are also different understadning and recognition among the parties concerned, resulting in operational difficulties. Therefore, it is recommended that the proceeds from the investment of insurance funds in equity financial products be explicitly exempted from corporate income tax.

Thirdly, it is necessary to strengthen the protection of investor rights and interests. Some major projects invested by insurance funds are faced with the situation where investors' rights and interests cannot be guaranteed. Therefore, it is necessary to speed up the market-oriented reform of centrally-administered State-owned enterprises, increase the transparency of centrally-administered State-owned enterprises, and protect the legitimate rights and interests of insurance institutional investors.

Fourthly, it is necessary to improve the performance evaluation mechanism for the investment projects of the state-owned insurance companies and define the cooperation policies with private enterprises. Due to the imperfect system and mechanism, state-owned insurance companies have relatively conservative investment risk preferences, and it is hard for them to accept investment losses and risks. They have concerns about cooperation with private enterprises and have little investment in small, medium and micro enterprises and emerging industries. Therefore, it is necessary to perfect the performance appraisal mechanism for state-owned insurance company project investment, and create a favorable policy environment for its investment and cooperation with private enterprises.

(V) Efforts are needed to optimize the policy environment for life insurance funds to participate in the BRI development

The responsibility of the government lies in providing a sound institutional

environment and strong support for life insurance funds to participate in the BRI development through optimizing the policy environment. Relevant supporting policies shall be improved when they involve the overseas investment of life insurance funds in the BRI development and their direct docking with the real economy projects. As the premium income of life insurers in the majority of the countries are largely denominated in their local currencies, the excessively high proportion of overseas investment might result in the risk of currency mismatch. Moreover, due to the uncertainties of the overseas investment market and considering the security of the investment funds, the insurance regulatory authorities of various countries cannot be too prudential in reviewing the overseas investment and the foreign exchange administrative authorities shall be prudential on the outflows of the insurance funds. Overseas investment will be encouraged by vesting more rights to judge the risks and to choose the investment projects to the investing compang, which will certainly give rise to more sources and types of risks; however, by strengthening the in-process and ex post supervision and creating the modern regulatory system, we can effectively deal with the above risks and hazards. Therefore, it is recommended that the insurance regulatory and foreign exchange administrative authorities of various countries shall support the life insurance funds to conduct prudential overseas investments on the basis of effective regulation. To this end, more countries along the BRI route shall be included in the list of countries or regions worth the investment by life insurance funds in due time. At the same time, we should encourage and support the life insurance fund management institutions to develop BRI-related investment products. The life insurance fund management institutions may develop various investment products centered on quality assets in the countries along the BRI route according to the demands of the clients, and help their clients to share the benefits from the investment in BRI quality assets.

(VI) Efforts are needed to improve the policy environment for life insurance funds to participate in the disposal of non-performing assets

Firstly, efforts shall be made to open up the policies for insurers to participate in the securitization of non-performing assets at appropriate time. Asset securitization

is the main tool to rely on market forces to dispose of non-performing assets and has great potential for development. In order to support the investment of insurance funds in the securitization of non-performing assets, competent authorities shall make specific provisions on the ratings and risk control, etc. of non-performing assets and improve relevant laws, rules and regulations.

Secondly, efforts shall be made to improve the supporting policies on debt-to-equity swaps. In the first place, efforts need to be made to combine the debt-to-equity swaps and mixed ownership reform of SOEs, promote the such reforms as the restructuring of state-owned enterprises, employee-held stocks, and equity incentives of debt-to-equity swap companies, focus on transforming the operational mechanism of enterprises and stimulate the enthusiasm of corporate and social investors in participating in debt-to-equity swaps.

In the second place, it is necessary to establish a sound equity exit mechanism. Only with a smooth exit channel can institutional investors actively participate in debt-to-equity swaps, thus avoiding the real debts in fake equity. It is possible to support the exit mechanism of market-oriented debt-to-equity swaps by improving the supporting policies on IPOs, asset injections of listed companies, and private placements.

In the third place, it is necessary to improve the policies on the floor trading and appraisal of state-owned equity transactions, and to promote the implementation of debt-to-equity swaps in accordance with the principles of marketization and the rule of law.

In the fourth place, it is necessary to perfect the tax policies concerning ebt-to-equity swaps, implement debt-to-equity swaps on the financial institutions through financial products, and and discuss the possibility of canceling the double taxation on income taxes

In the fifth place, it is necessary to promote the implementation of the market-oriented debt-to-equity swaps of listed companies by improving the relevant policies concerning the non-public offering at locked prices, the size of non-public offerings, the use of funds raised, and the scope of assets purchased through the issuance of shares.

(VII) Exploring life insurance funds to carry out loan business

The Measures for the Administration of the Utilization of Insurance Funds (《保险资金运用管理办法》) (No. 1 [2018] Order of the China Insurance Regulatory Commission) stipulates that investment assets formed by the utilization of insurance funds shall not be used to provide guarantees or loans to others, except for personal policy pledge loans. This means that current life insurance funds cannot be directly used to issue loans.

It is very necessary to explore how life insurance funds can engage in loan business. First, it is conducive to alleviating the problem of long-maturity funds matched to short-term assets, and better achieving asset-liability matching. Life insurance funds have a longer period of time of more than seven years for most part. With the transformation of China's life insurance industry, the proportion of life insurance funds with the maturities of over 10 years will continue to increase. However, due to the short period of fixed-income products such as treasury bonds and financial bonds in China, it is difficult to find high-quality long-term fixed-income products when the insurance funds are deployed. Some long-term, fixed-rate loan businesses can meet the allocation needs of such assets. Second, the loan business can supplement the shortcomings of bank loans and meet the demand for long-term loans. As the deposit periods are usually short (with relatively small proportions of deposits with over five-year maturity), the problems of short-maturity loans matched to long-term assets may emerge when banks engage in long-term loans. Compared with banks, life insurance funds have longer maturities and are more conducive to long-term loan business. Therefore, compared with banks, the maturities structure of life insurance funds is more closely matched with the long-term loan business, which can better meet the long-term loans demand. Third, the direct engagement in loan business by life insurance funds will help break through the shortcomings of the debt investment plans. At present, debt investment products have placed too much emphasis on credit enhancement measures. In essence, they are more focused on credit risk prevention of the counterparties rather than the risks of products and underlying assets, resulting in a higher degree of homogenization of such businesses with bank credit

lines, but such business by insurance funds lacks advantages in the corresponding financing costs and product issuance efficiency, etc.[①] It can be seen that insurance asset management products such as debt investment plans have insufficient flexibility in terms of basic assets, transaction structure and credit enhancement measures, and their competitiveness has declined compared with bank loans. At the same time, when monetary policy is loose or the scale of bank lending is relaxed, due to the competitive relationship between insurance funds and bank loans, it is difficult for insurance funds to obtain project resources and credit enhancement support from bank channels. Therefore, life insurance funds directly carrying out the loan business will help break through the deficiencies of the debt investment plans and enhance their competitiveness relative to bank loans. Fourth, the life insurance funds engaging in loan business is the experience of the utilization of life insurance funds in many countries and regions. Insurance funds carrying out loan business has always been one of the important investment channels of developed countries and regions such as Europe and the United States.[②] In the early 20th century, the United States began to allow insurance funds to invest in mortgage loans. Japan allowed life insurers to lend to SMEs in the late 1960s to promote the development of SMEs. South Korea and Taiwan Province allowed insurance funds to be used as mortgaged loans in the 1970s and 1980s. In addition, the United States, Taiwan Province and other countries and regions allow insurance funds to indirectly flow to the credit market by subscribing to securitized products such as mortgage-backed securities (MBS). Allowing life insurance funds to carry out loan business not only supports the real economy's demand for long-term funds, but also obtains better returns, thus supporting the development of underwriting business.

The current exploration of life insurance funds carrying out loan business also has a strong realistic foundation. First, life insurance funds are connected to real economic projects through alternative investments such as debt investment plans, which are largely attributed to loans. Insurers and insurance asset management companies have

---

① Han Xiangrong, Hu Xuewen: Retrospection and Expectation of Non-Standardized Asset Investment of Insurance Asset Management (《保险资管非标投资反思与展望》), Insurance Asset Management of China, Issue 3 of 2018

② Wu Jie: Path Selection and Risk Prevention in Loan Business by Insurance Funds (《保险资金开展贷款业务的路径选择与风险防范》), Shanghai Insurance Monthly, Issue 10 of 2016

accumulated experience in investing in real economy projects through alternative investments, laying a good foundation for the development of loan business. Second, some loan businesses can provide life insurance funds with relatively low risk investment areas. For example, China's personal housing mortgage loans are currently reviewed more rigorously. In addition to requiring higher down payment ratios and purchasing mortgage guarantee insurance, lenders are also required to maintain stable income sources, therefore, the business risks are relatively low. These low-risk areas can be a good entry point for life insurance funds to carry out loan business.

In order to actively and steadily promote life insurance funds to carry out loan business, it is necessary to relax policy restrictions at an appropriate time, select appropriate ways to carry out loan business, and strengthen organizational management and risk control.

Firstly, the restrictions on the direct issuance of loans for life insurance funds shall be relaxed at an appropriate time. It is necessary to strengthen communication and coordination between the China Banking and Insurance Regulatory Commission and the People's Bank of China and other authorities, and allow life insurance funds to directly issue loans to specific targets within a certain scope. In addition, the prohibition of direct issuance of loans by life insurance funds is fundamentally subject to the current financial system of separate operations. Therefore, to remove the restrictions on direct lending of life insurance funds, it is necessary to gradually revise and improve the current financial laws and regulations and reform the current financial system.

Secondly, different types of insurers should choose different ways of conducting loan business according to the difference in resource endowments. Among them, large insurance group companies with large assets and full coverage of financial licenses can choose to independently carry out loan business. The advantage lies in that it saves the intermediate business expenses required by the entrusted banks. However, the insufficiency is that the insurers or the insurance asset management companies need to set up an independent department that is engaged in the loan business and hire the corresponding business personnel. Small- and medium-sized insurers and banking insurers with smaller scales can choose the "banking-insurance cooperation" to carry

out the loan business, that is, the insurers cooperate with the banks and entrust the bank with the task of approving and issuing loans. The advantage of this approach is that insurers do not need to set up new business units or institutions to avoid the operational risks of professionals and lack of experience. But the shortcoming is that the bank's intermediate expenses have to be paid and the profits are diluted. Insurers can also indirectly conduct loan business by holding securitized products such as mortgage-backed securities (MBS). Since MBS products have been classified as fixed-income bond products after risk isolation and credit enhancement, the risk is lower and the income is relatively higher, which is more suitable for the investment by life insurance funds which do not have too much direct experience in loan issuance.

Thirdly, the authority management and audit of branches shall be strengthened and the operation of loan business shall be regulated. Once the insurance funds are liberalized to carry out the loan business, the insurance institutions that independently carry out the mortgage business need branches to operate related businesses. In order to prevent financial risks, the approval authority for lending funds can be managed by the headquarters, and branches and outlets are responsible for business operations, for the purpose of avoiding the chaotic situations where loans were granted at grassroots branches for personal connections or out of favors, etc. during the loosening period of the utilization of insurance funds in the 1980s and 1990s. At the same time, we should pay attention to the inspection of branches and ensure the good operation and healthy development of the loan business.

Fourthly, risk management and control should be strengthened. It is necessary to strengthen the credit risk assessment of the borrowers, and the post-loan issuance dynamic assessment of the value of the collaterals, and adjust the mortgage ratio in time to achieve risk management and control.

(VIII) Actively cultivating the insurance asset management market

An important way for life insurance funds to support the development of the real economy is alternative investment. An important feature of alternative investments is non-standardized investments, which enjoy higher liquidity risks and market risk premiums due to longer lock-up periods and lower liquidity. At the same time, life

insurers are one of the most important long-term institutional investors in the financial market, and are more likely to withstand higher liquidity risks and market volatility risks to obtain higher risk premiums. Therefore, insufficient liquidity is an important endogenous attribute of alternative investments. The insurance industry can promote the building of trading platforms for non-standardized insurance assets, establish a tradable mechanism for non-standardized assets, provide support for insurers to manage liquidity, and improve the utilization efficiency of insurance funds. At the same time, increasing the liquidity can also increase the attractiveness of insurance asset management products and expand the scale of products, thereby further enhancing the capability of insurance funds to serve the real economy. In addition, through the product transaction, a scientific and reasonable rate of return curve can be formed to play a benchmark role in the pricing of the medium and long-term capital market.

For a long time, the insurance industry lacked the trading platform for non-standardized insurance assets, which led to the lack of liquidity hedging mechanism of insurance asset management companies. The lack of liquidity of non-standardized assets inhibited the advantages of insurance funds to a certain extent. Therefore, relevant policies have always encouraged the insurance asset management industry to strengthen platform building and improve product liquidity. In the Several Opinions of the State Council on Accelerating the Development of the Modern Insurance Service Industry (《国务院关于加快发展现代保险服务业的若干意见》) issued in 2012, it is proposed to actively cultivate alternative investment markets, strengthen market infrastructure construction, and set up asset management centers and insurance asset trading platforms for the whole industry; in the government work report of 2016, the establishment of the insurance asset trading mechanism was again proposed. In the same year, the Outline of the Thirteenth Five-Year Plan for National Economic and Social Development of the People's Republic of China (《中华人民共和国国民经济和社会发展第十三个五年规划纲要》) further proposed to establish an insurance asset trading mechanism. The Measures for the Administration of the Utilization of Insurance Funds (《保险资金运用管理办法》) which was officially implemented on April 1, 2018, stipulates that "the insurance asset management institutions shall carry

out the issuance, registration, custody, transaction, settlement, information disclosure and related credit enhancement and pledge financing and other services on the asset registration and trading platforms approved by the CIRC when they carry out business on insurance asset management products." In 2017, Shanghai Insurance Exchange Co., Ltd. established a professional subsidiary, namely China Insurance Asset Registration and Trading System Co., Ltd., which is responsible for the construction and operation of the China Insurance Assets Registration and Trading System launched in 2018. When insurance asset management products are listed and traded, they can revitalize the liquidity of existing assets through an open market trading mechanism. [1]

In order to cultivate the insurance asset management market, we will continue to strengthen platform construction and improve product liquidity in the future.

The first is to strengthen the platform construction. For standardized products, we can rely on the Shanghai Insurance Exchange to connect with other on-exchange markets to achieve interconnection and provide more adequate liquidity support and fair pricing. To this end, we must continue to strengthen the construction of the Shanghai Insurance Exchange and the insurance asset trading platform, and continuously improve the construction of the insurance asset centralized registration system and the insurance asset trading system during the operation; further upgrade the insurance asset management product registration system of the Insurance Asset Management Association of China, strengthen data and statistics analysis and processing functions, and develop product valuation models to provide basic support for the insurance asset trading platform. [2] For trust-like products, the transaction structure depends on the risk expectations of both parties, and as they are more individualized, they are more suitable for the transaction information filing and listing transfer in the OTC market. [3] The Insurance Asset Management Association

---

[1]   Zeng Yujin: Lay a Firm Foundation and Build High Quality Insurance Asset Registration and Trading Platform (《夯基实础，高质量建设保险资产登记交易平台》), Modern Bankers, Issue 5 of 2018

[2]   Cao Deuyun: Practical Difficulties and Countermeasures for Innovation of Insurance Asset Management Products (《保险资产管理产品创新的现实困难与应对措施》), Tsinghua Financial Review, Issue 6 of 2016

[3]   Han Xiangrong, Hu Xuewen: Retrospection and Expectation of Non-Standardized Asset Investment of Insurance Asset Management (《保险资管非标投资反思与展望》), Insurance Asset Management of China, Issue 3 of 2018

of China or the Shanghai Insurance Exchange can take the lead in setting up the over-the-counter market, distinguishing it from the market in terms of listing conditions, information disclosure, transaction settlement, product design, investor constraints, etc., and classifying trust-like products into the record for further management, which will make it easier to conduct market monitoring and risk control, provide a place for listing and transfer of such products and offer appropriate liquidity options to investors.

The second is to promote the standardization of insurance asset management products. Insurance asset management products are more complicated in terms of product governance, transaction structure, and operational processes. From the perspective of facilitating the listing and trading, we must gradually promote product standardization, including standardization of contract texts, standardization of factor meanings, and standardization of transaction structures.[1]

The third is to promote the standardization of non-standardized assets. On the basis of centralized registration, through the construction of an active on-market trading market, a scientific and fair product valuation system will be formed, and non-standardized insurance assets will be converted into standard assets, further stimulating the market vitality of insurance asset management products.[2]

---

① Cao Deuyun: Practical Difficulties and Countermeasures for Innovation of Insurance Asset Management Products (《保险资产管理产品创新的现实困难与应对措施》), Tsinghua Financial Review, Issue 6 of 2016

② Zeng Yujin: Lay a Firm Foundation and Build High Quality Insurance Asset Registration and Trading Platform (《夯基实础，高质量建设保险资产登记交易平台》), Modern Bankers, Issue 5 of 2018

Postscript

In order to better promote the financial industry to serve the development of the real economy, the Research Institute of Finance of the Development Research Center of the State Council and the relevant departments of the Prudential Plc of the United Kingdom formed a joint research team to carry out the research of life insurance funds in support of the real economy. In the nearly one-year long research, the research team has extensively investigated the insurance regulatory authorities and relevant market subjects, and has in-depth understanding of the status quo, outstanding problems, major policy obstacles and risks of China's life insurance funds in supporting the real economy development. The research team also visited Singapore and Indonesia and conducted in-depth exchanges with foreign experts on issues such as the development of the life insurance industry, the investment of life insurance funds in infrastructure development and the support to the real economy. On the basis of in-depth research, the research team completed the research report draft in mid-2018, and held the research results release and expert seminar in September 2018. On the basis of fully absorbing the feedback and suggestions from domestic and foreign experts, the research team further revised and improved the report, and finally formed the book.

In the research of the subject and the publication of this book, the research team has received strong support from all parties concerned. Wang Yiming, Vice President of the Development Research Center of the State Council, has always attached great importance to and guided the research of the topic. The International Cooperation Department of the Development Research Center of the State Council

has provided extensive support for the development of the project. Michael A. Wells, CEO of Prudential Plc, Paul Lynch, Regional Director, Government Relations of Prudential Corporation Asia, and Prudential Life Assurance Company Limited Beijing Representative Office provided important support for the research. Our thanks also go to leaders from a number of regulatory authorities, and experts from research institutions and insurance companies who have contributed to the research of the research team and holding of the seminars.

In the research of the topic, we abide by the principles of professional research, objectively analyze the problems, risks and policy obstacles of life insurance funds supporting the real economy, and put forward corresponding policy recommendations. However, due to factors such as theoretical depth, accumulation of experience and insufficient research, the discussions on some issues may not be deep enough and some opinions and judgments may be inappropriate. I urge experts, scholars and readers to offer their criticism and suggestions.

Research Team on Life Insurance Funds in Support of the Real Economy

October 2018